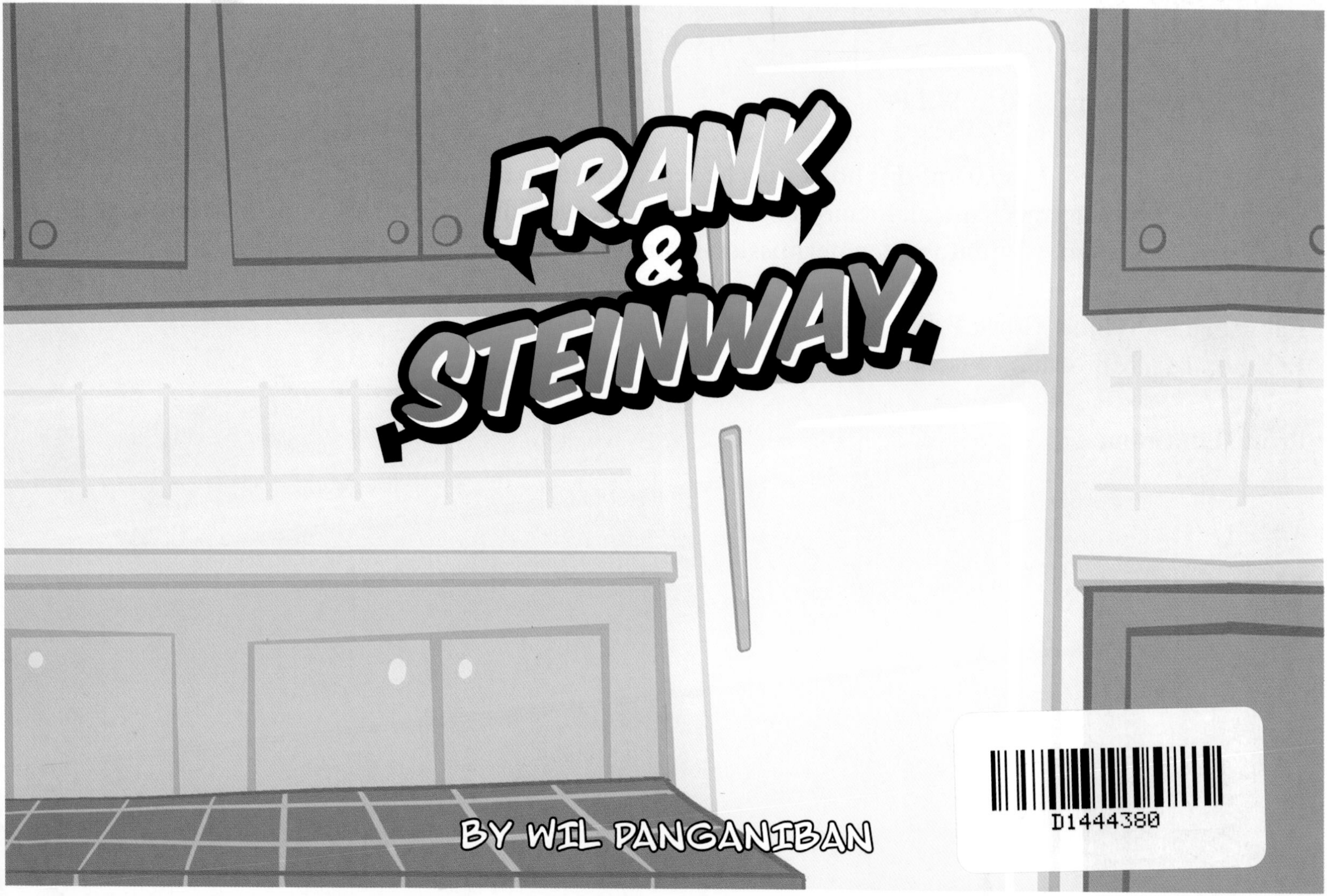

FRANK & STEINWAY

BY WIL PANGANIBAN

Published by Willow Creek Press, Inc.
P.O. Box 147, Minocqua, Wisconsin 54548

Printed in China

"Frank and Steinway" is a funny strip. If it's your first time reading it, you'll find the characters likable, and, as you work your way through the book, more and more personable...alive even.

Which is interesting, since they're both dead.

My favorite ingredient in this first collection is the banter between the two main characters, I see two characters developing a repartee and I find Wil's writing and humor is at its strongest. You may disagree, but that's the beauty of a comic strip, readers don't have to agree on what makes a strip relatable and likable, because the best quality of a comic strip is its reflectiveness to the reader.

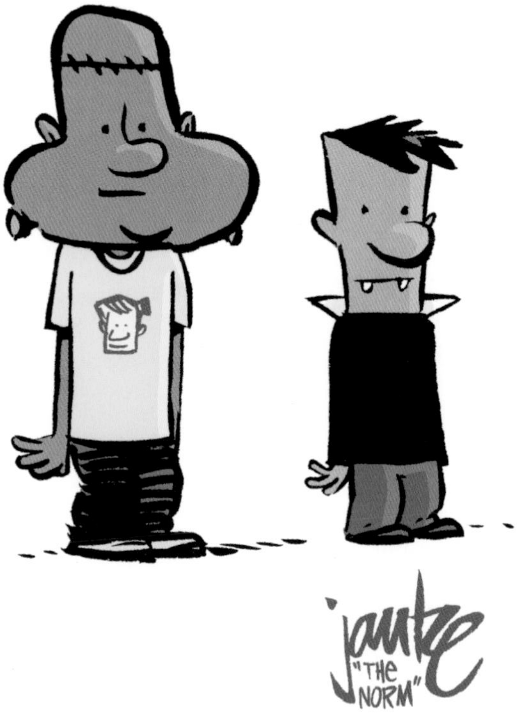
"THE NORM"

So get a cup of coffee or a pint of fresh blood, and get to know "Frank and Steinway" your own way, I'm sure you'll see someone in this strip you know...it may even be you.

TO FRED, JEAN, SARAH, ARIEL,
NATHAN, NOLAN, NORAH, NIKO

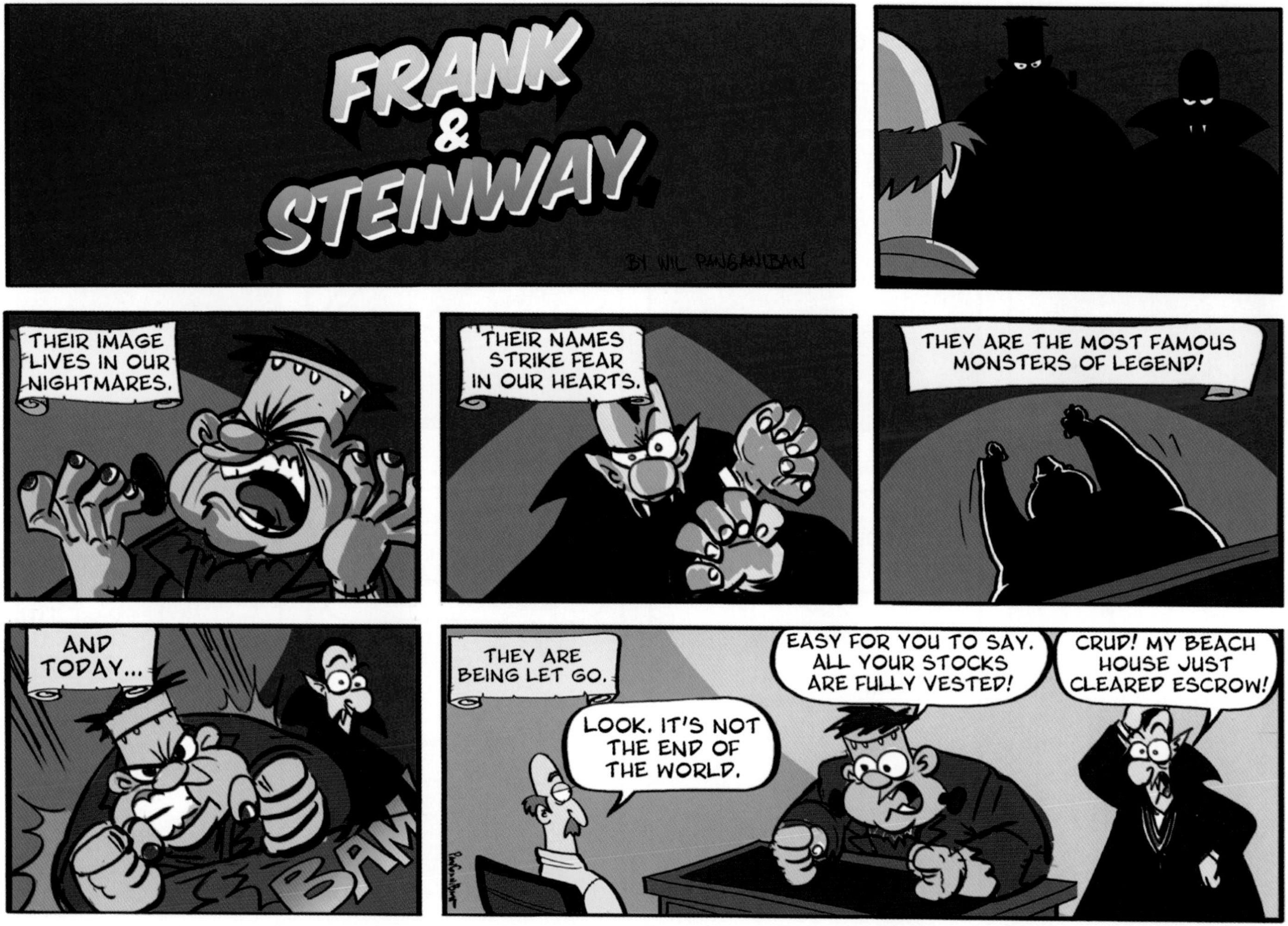
FRANK & STEINWAY
BY WIL PANGANIBAN
THEIR IMAGE LIVES IN OUR NIGHTMARES.
THEIR NAMES STRIKE FEAR IN OUR HEARTS.
THEY ARE THE MOST FAMOUS MONSTERS OF LEGEND!
AND TODAY...
BAM
THEY ARE BEING LET GO.
LOOK. IT'S NOT THE END OF THE WORLD.
EASY FOR YOU TO SAY. ALL YOUR STOCKS ARE FULLY VESTED!
CRUD! MY BEACH HOUSE JUST CLEARED ESCROW!

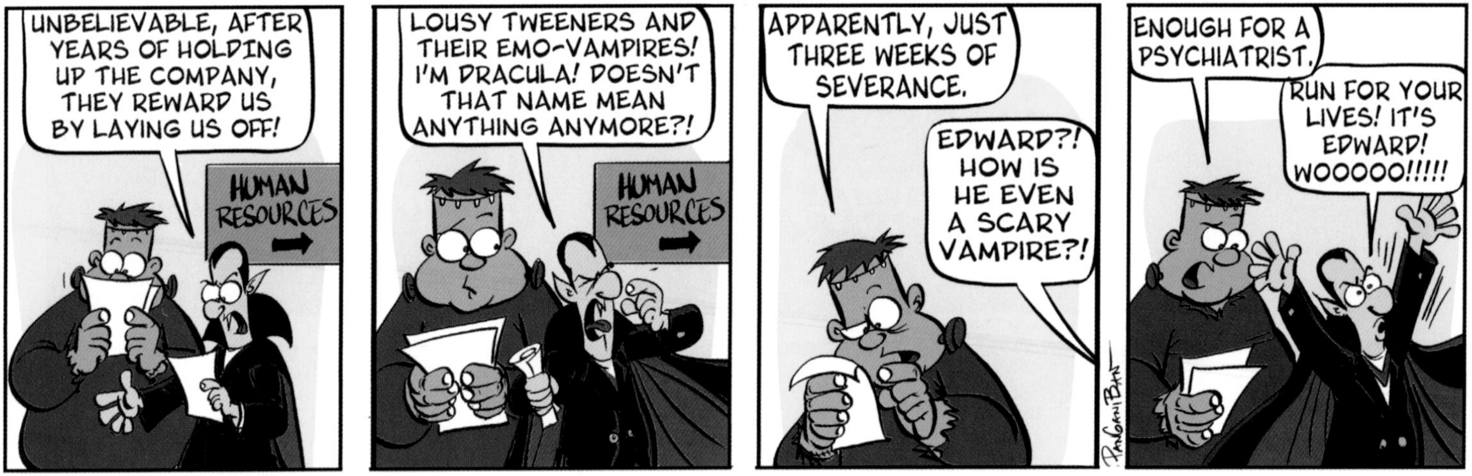
UNBELIEVABLE, AFTER YEARS OF HOLDING UP THE COMPANY, THEY REWARD US BY LAYING US OFF!
HUMAN RESOURCES
LOUSY TWEENERS AND THEIR EMO-VAMPIRES! I'M DRACULA! DOESN'T THAT NAME MEAN ANYTHING ANYMORE?!
HUMAN RESOURCES
APPARENTLY, JUST THREE WEEKS OF SEVERANCE.
EDWARD?! HOW IS HE EVEN A SCARY VAMPIRE?!
ENOUGH FOR A PSYCHIATRIST.
RUN FOR YOUR LIVES! IT'S EDWARD! WOOOOO!!!!!

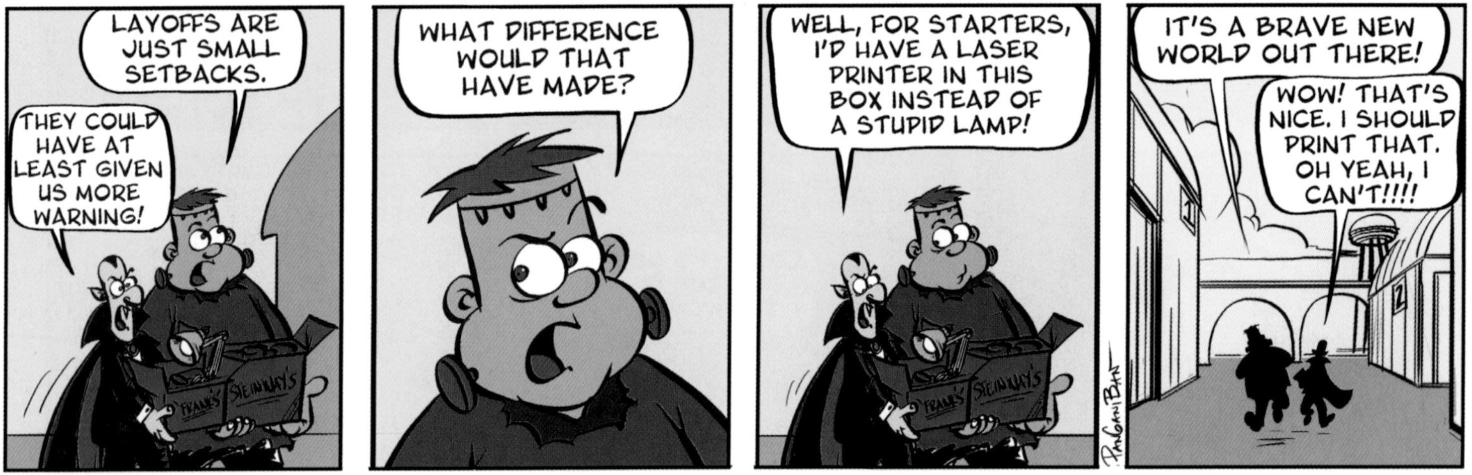
THEY COULD HAVE AT LEAST GIVEN US MORE WARNING!
LAYOFFS ARE JUST SMALL SETBACKS.
WHAT DIFFERENCE WOULD THAT HAVE MADE?
WELL, FOR STARTERS, I'D HAVE A LASER PRINTER IN THIS BOX INSTEAD OF A STUPID LAMP!
IT'S A BRAVE NEW WORLD OUT THERE!
WOW! THAT'S NICE. I SHOULD PRINT THAT. OH YEAH, I CAN'T!!!!

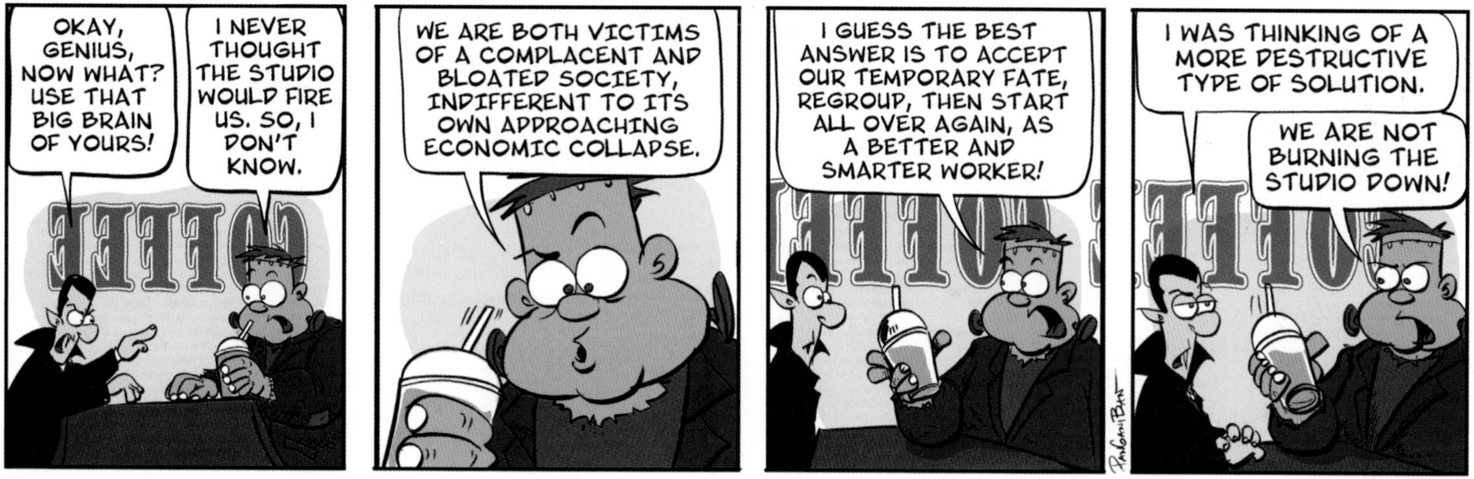
OKAY, GENIUS, NOW WHAT? USE THAT BIG BRAIN OF YOURS!
I NEVER THOUGHT THE STUDIO WOULD FIRE US. SO, I DON'T KNOW.
WE ARE BOTH VICTIMS OF A COMPLACENT AND BLOATED SOCIETY, INDIFFERENT TO ITS OWN APPROACHING ECONOMIC COLLAPSE.
I GUESS THE BEST ANSWER IS TO ACCEPT OUR TEMPORARY FATE, REGROUP, THEN START ALL OVER AGAIN, AS A BETTER AND SMARTER WORKER!
I WAS THINKING OF A MORE DESTRUCTIVE TYPE OF SOLUTION.
WE ARE NOT BURNING THE STUDIO DOWN!

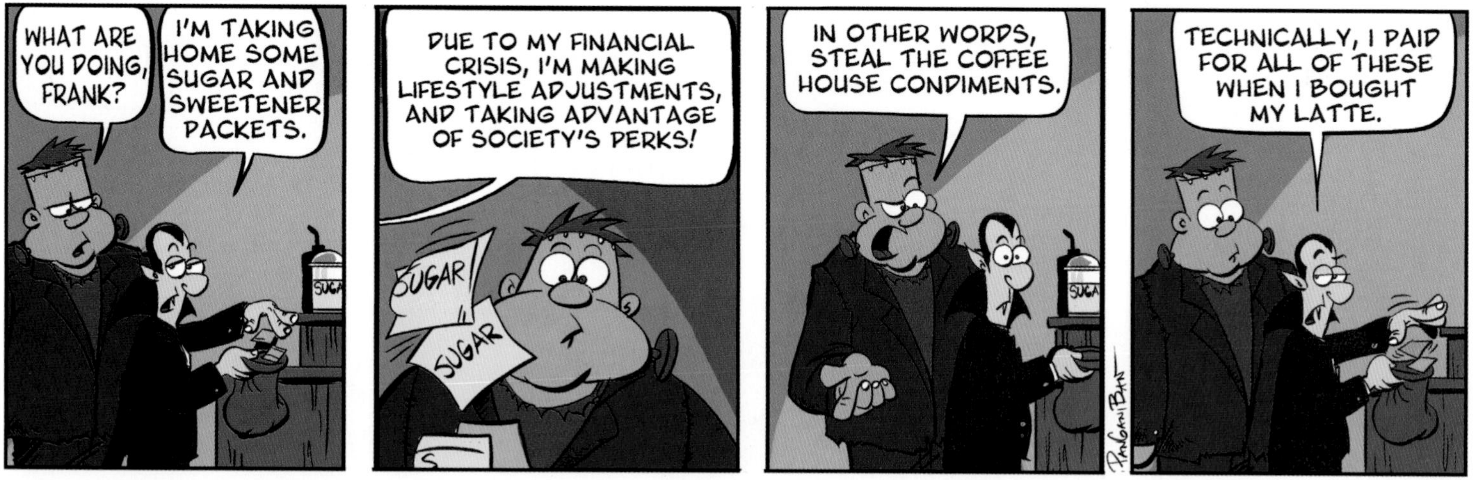
WHAT ARE YOU DOING, FRANK?
I'M TAKING HOME SOME SUGAR AND SWEETENER PACKETS.
DUE TO MY FINANCIAL CRISIS, I'M MAKING LIFESTYLE ADJUSTMENTS, AND TAKING ADVANTAGE OF SOCIETY'S PERKS!
SUGAR
SUGAR
IN OTHER WORDS, STEAL THE COFFEE HOUSE CONDIMENTS.
TECHNICALLY, I PAID FOR ALL OF THESE WHEN I BOUGHT MY LATTE.

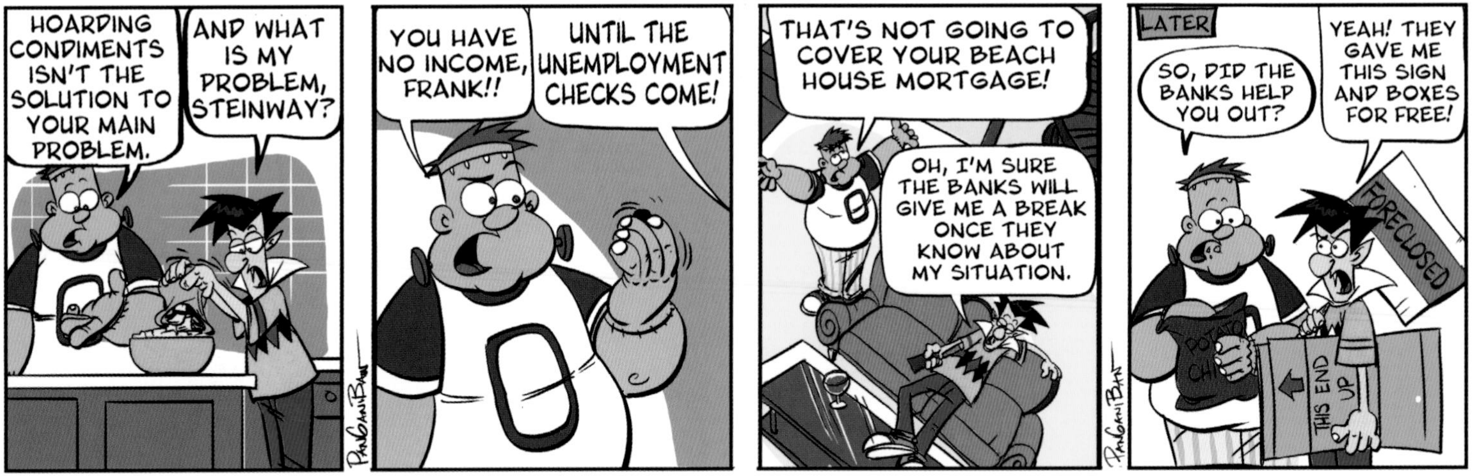
HOARDING CONDIMENTS ISN'T THE SOLUTION TO YOUR MAIN PROBLEM.
AND WHAT IS MY PROBLEM, STEINWAY?
YOU HAVE NO INCOME, FRANK!!
UNTIL THE UNEMPLOYMENT CHECKS COME!
THAT'S NOT GOING TO COVER YOUR BEACH HOUSE MORTGAGE!
OH, I'M SURE THE BANKS WILL GIVE ME A BREAK ONCE THEY KNOW ABOUT MY SITUATION.
LATER
SO, DID THE BANKS HELP YOU OUT?
YEAH! THEY GAVE ME THIS SIGN AND BOXES FOR FREE!
FORECLOSED
THIS END UP

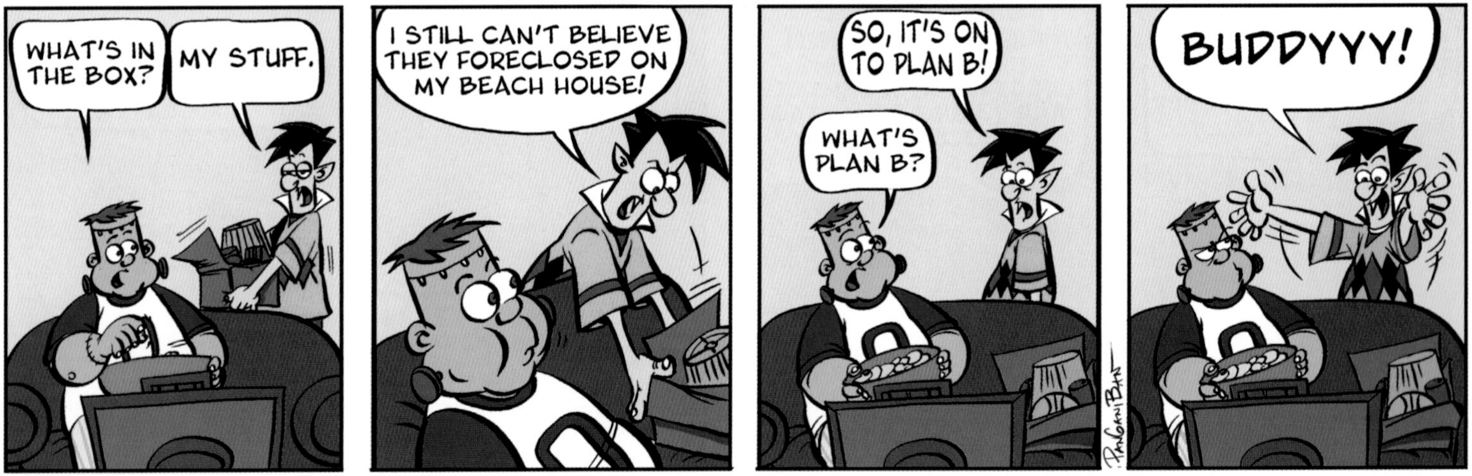
WHAT'S IN THE BOX?
MY STUFF.
I STILL CAN'T BELIEVE THEY FORECLOSED ON MY BEACH HOUSE!
SO, IT'S ON TO PLAN B!
WHAT'S PLAN B?
BUDDYYY!

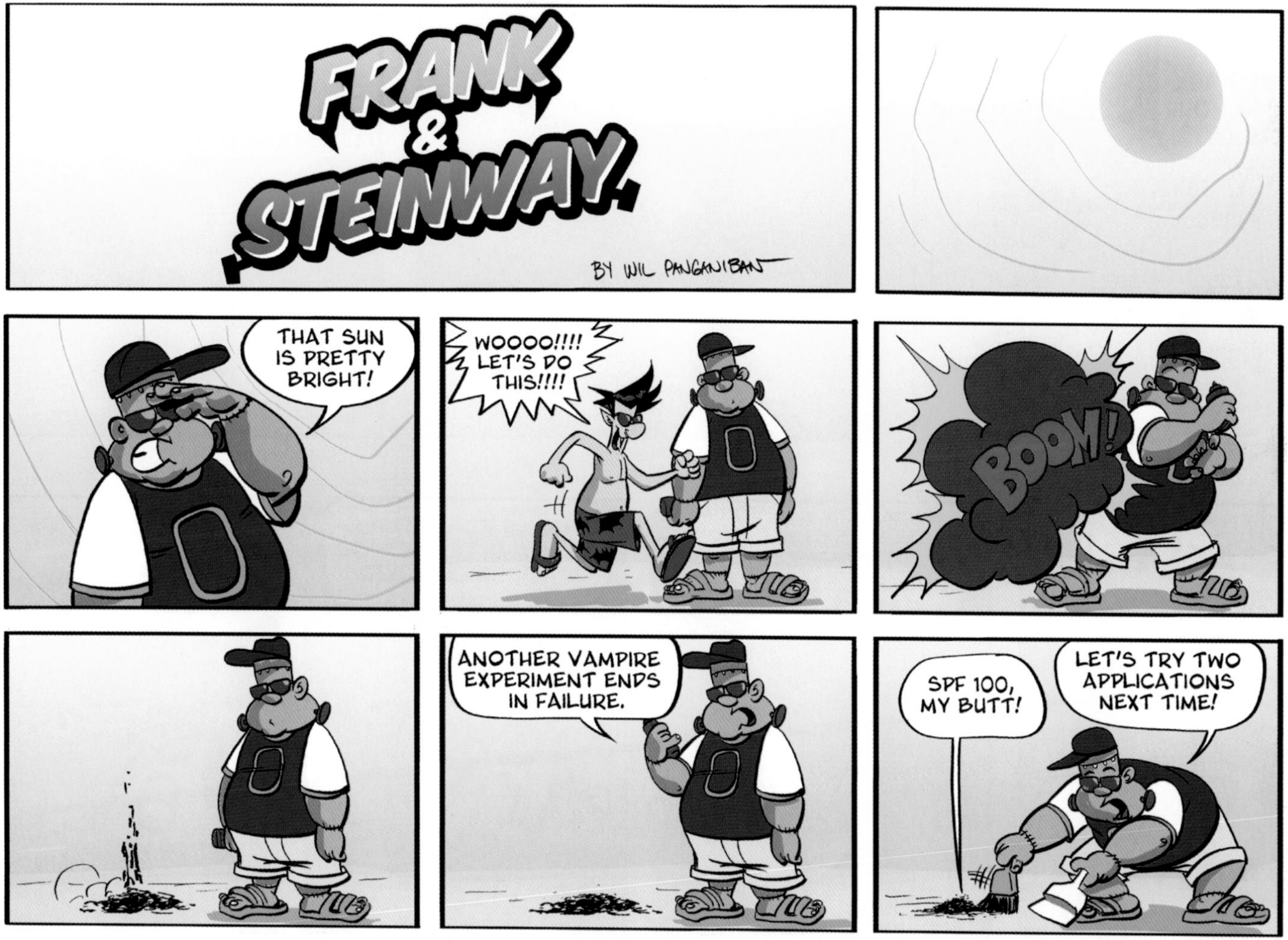
FRANK & STEINWAY
BY WIL PANGANIBAN
THAT SUN IS PRETTY BRIGHT!
WOOOO!!!! LET'S DO THIS!!!!
BOOM!
ANOTHER VAMPIRE EXPERIMENT ENDS IN FAILURE.
SPF 100, MY BUTT!
LET'S TRY TWO APPLICATIONS NEXT TIME!

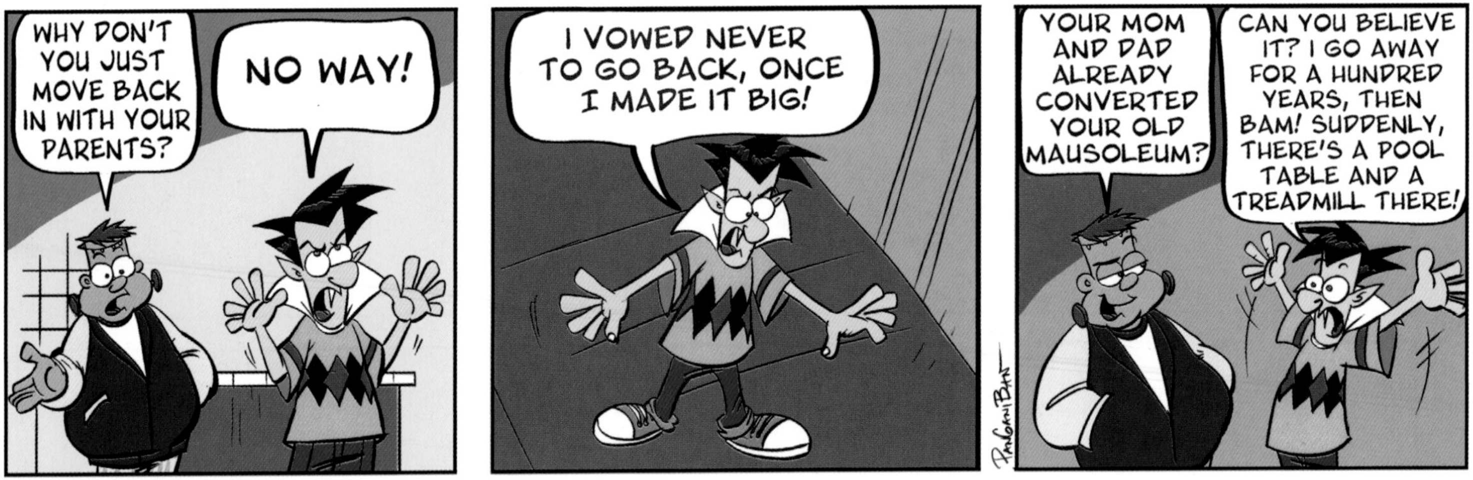
WHY DON'T YOU JUST MOVE BACK IN WITH YOUR PARENTS?
NO WAY!
I VOWED NEVER TO GO BACK, ONCE I MADE IT BIG!
YOUR MOM AND DAD ALREADY CONVERTED YOUR OLD MAUSOLEUM?
CAN YOU BELIEVE IT? I GO AWAY FOR A HUNDRED YEARS, THEN BAM! SUDDENLY, THERE'S A POOL TABLE AND A TREADMILL THERE!

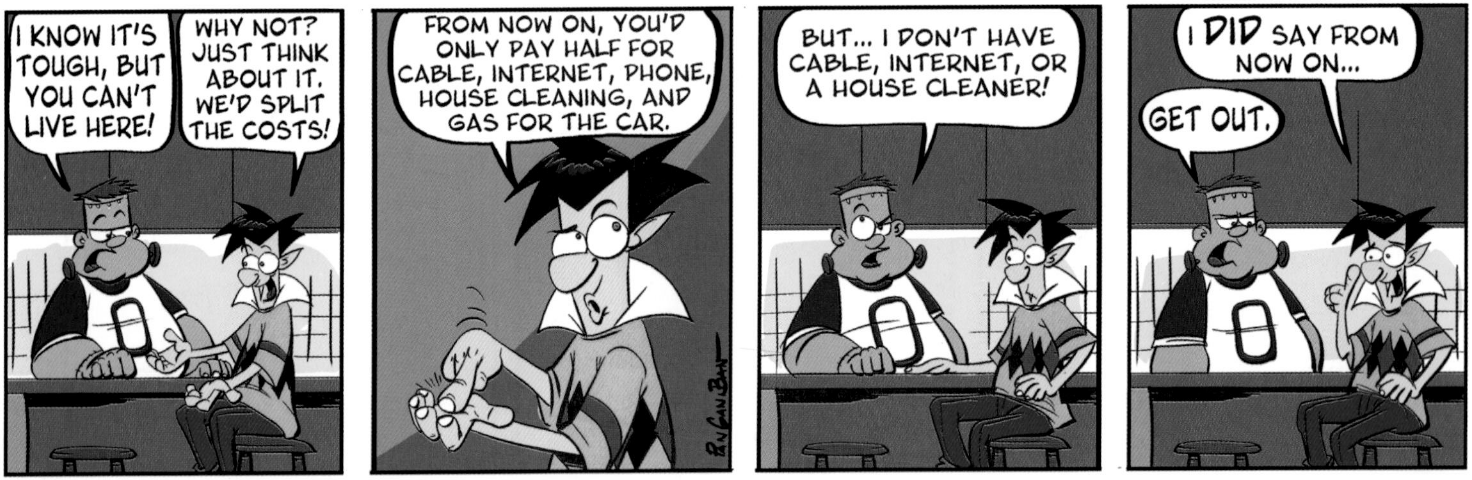
I KNOW IT'S TOUGH, BUT YOU CAN'T LIVE HERE!
WHY NOT? JUST THINK ABOUT IT. WE'D SPLIT THE COSTS!
FROM NOW ON, YOU'D ONLY PAY HALF FOR CABLE, INTERNET, PHONE, HOUSE CLEANING, AND GAS FOR THE CAR.
BUT... I DON'T HAVE CABLE, INTERNET, OR A HOUSE CLEANER!
I DID SAY FROM NOW ON...
GET OUT.

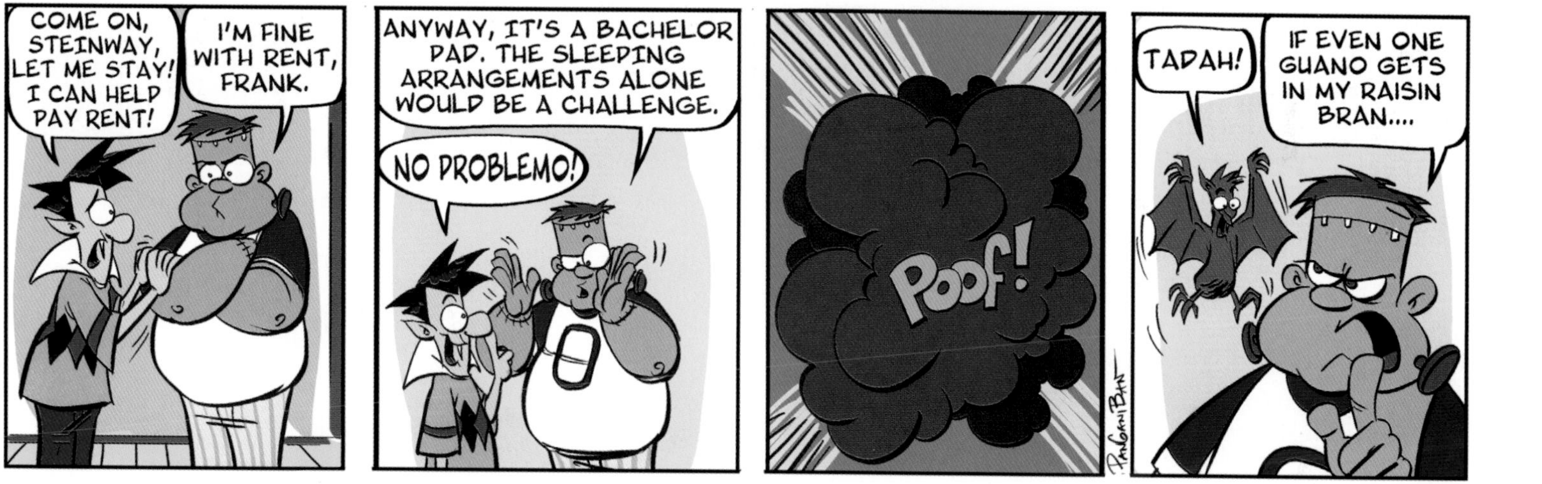
COME ON, STEINWAY, LET ME STAY! I CAN HELP PAY RENT!
I'M FINE WITH RENT, FRANK.
ANYWAY, IT'S A BACHELOR PAD. THE SLEEPING ARRANGEMENTS ALONE WOULD BE A CHALLENGE.
NO PROBLEMO!
POOF!
TADAH!
IF EVEN ONE GUANO GETS IN MY RAISIN BRAN....

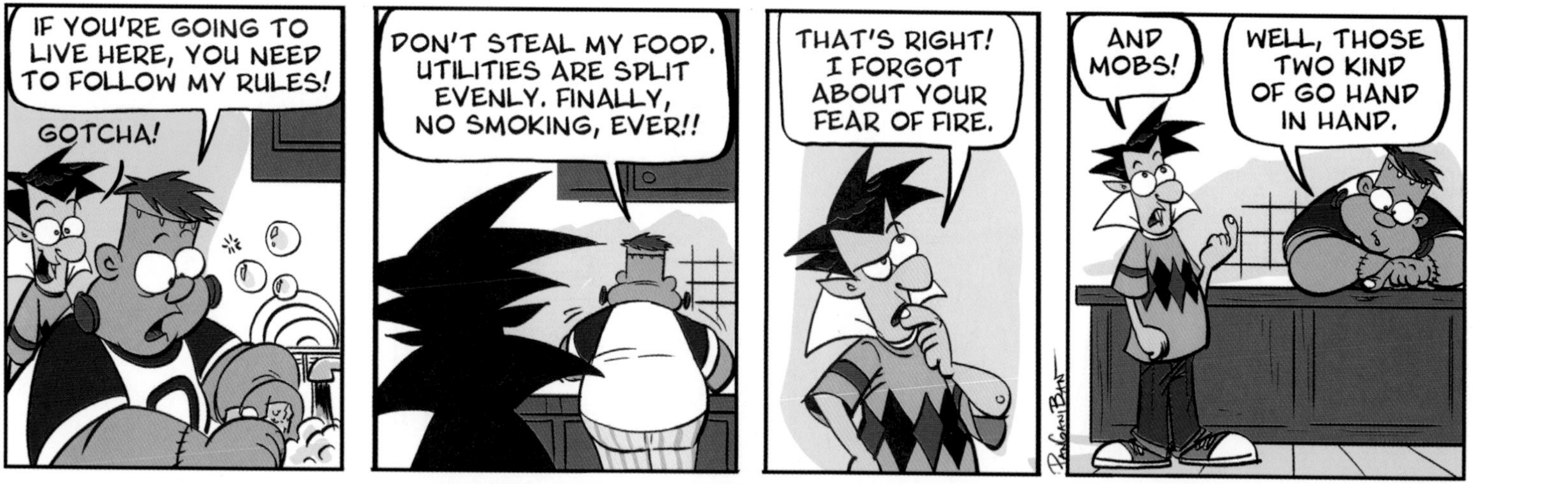
IF YOU'RE GOING TO LIVE HERE, YOU NEED TO FOLLOW MY RULES!
GOTCHA!
DON'T STEAL MY FOOD. UTILITIES ARE SPLIT EVENLY. FINALLY, NO SMOKING, EVER!!
THAT'S RIGHT! I FORGOT ABOUT YOUR FEAR OF FIRE.
AND MOBS!
WELL, THOSE TWO KIND OF GO HAND IN HAND.

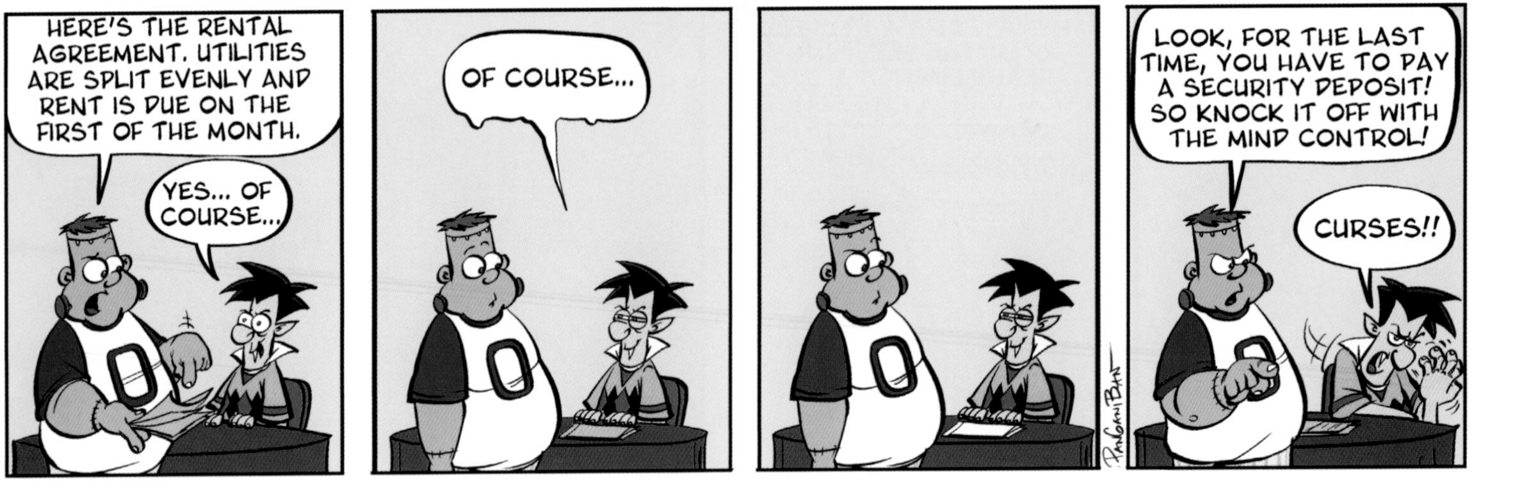
HERE'S THE RENTAL AGREEMENT. UTILITIES ARE SPLIT EVENLY AND RENT IS DUE ON THE FIRST OF THE MONTH.
YES... OF COURSE...
OF COURSE...
LOOK, FOR THE LAST TIME, YOU HAVE TO PAY A SECURITY DEPOSIT! SO KNOCK IT OFF WITH THE MIND CONTROL!
CURSES!!

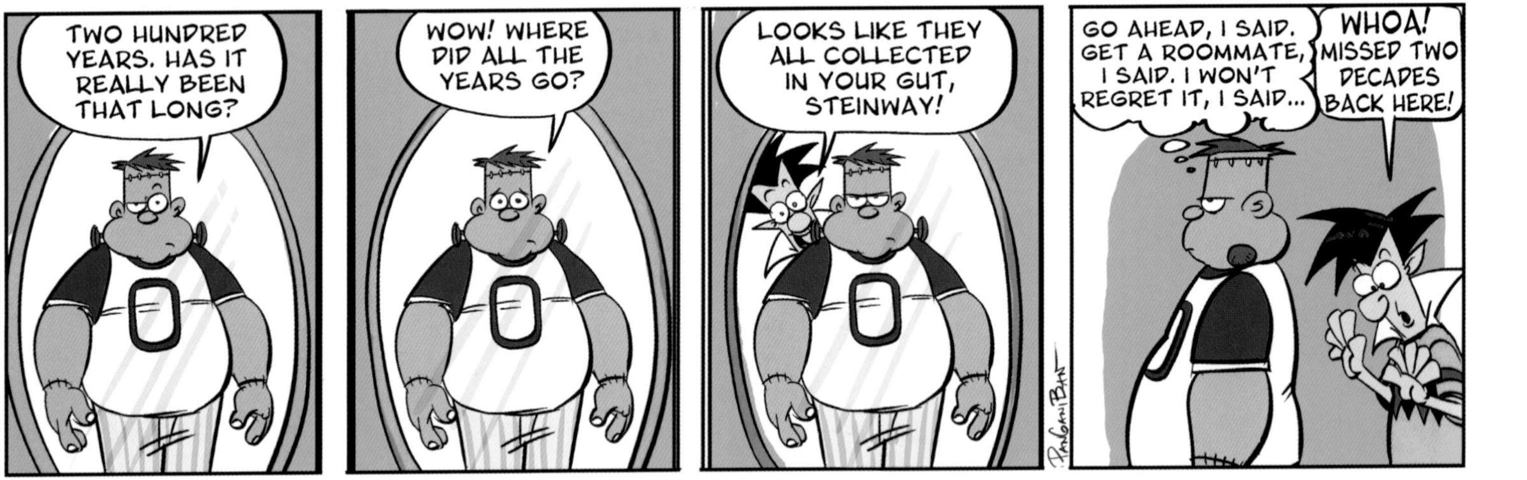
TWO HUNDRED YEARS. HAS IT REALLY BEEN THAT LONG?
WOW! WHERE DID ALL THE YEARS GO?
LOOKS LIKE THEY ALL COLLECTED IN YOUR GUT, STEINWAY!
GO AHEAD, I SAID. GET A ROOMMATE, I SAID. I WON'T REGRET IT, I SAID...
WHOA! MISSED TWO DECADES BACK HERE!

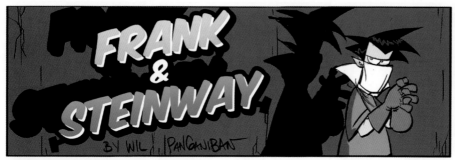

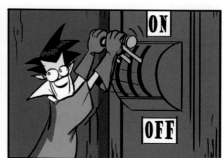

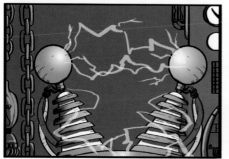

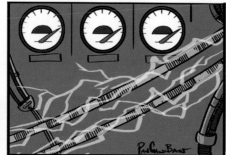

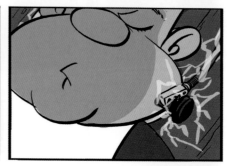

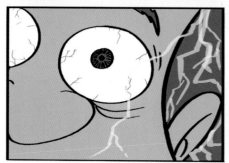

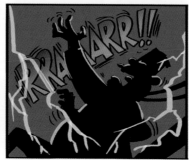

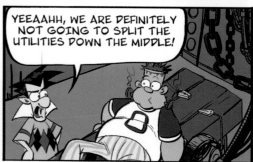

FRANK & STEINWAY
BY WIL PANGANIBAN
ON
OFF
PANGANIBAN
RRAAARR!!
YEEAAHH, WE ARE DEFINITELY NOT GOING TO SPLIT THE UTILITIES DOWN THE MIDDLE!

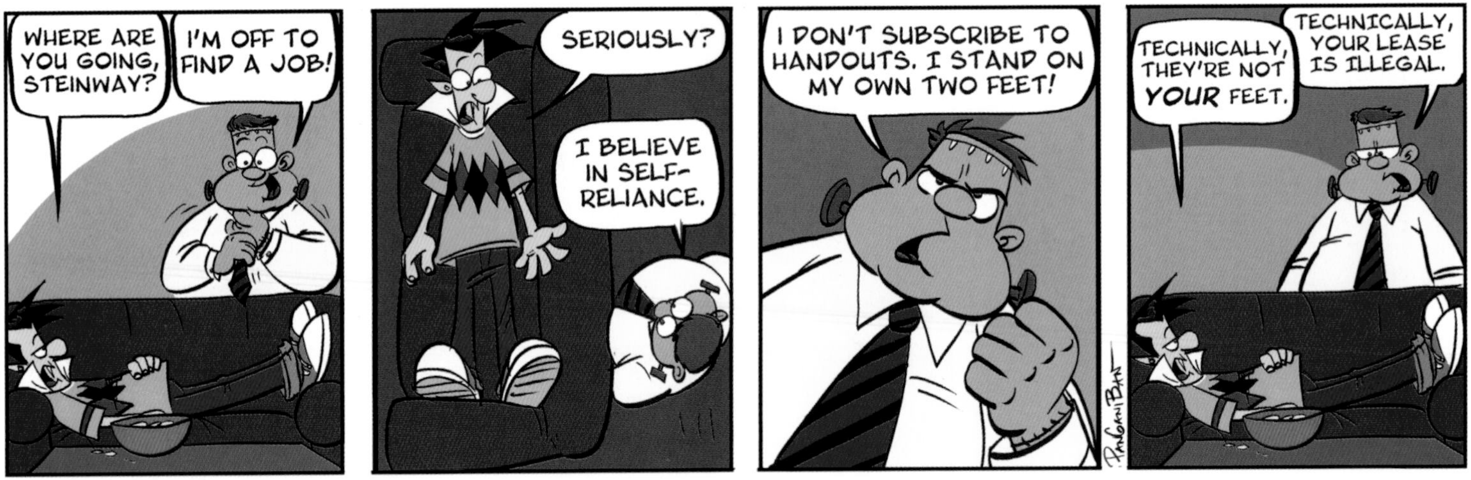
WHERE ARE YOU GOING, STEINWAY?
I'M OFF TO FIND A JOB!
SERIOUSLY?
I BELIEVE IN SELF-RELIANCE.
I DON'T SUBSCRIBE TO HANDOUTS. I STAND ON MY OWN TWO FEET!
TECHNICALLY, THEY'RE NOT **YOUR** FEET.
TECHNICALLY, YOUR LEASE IS ILLEGAL.

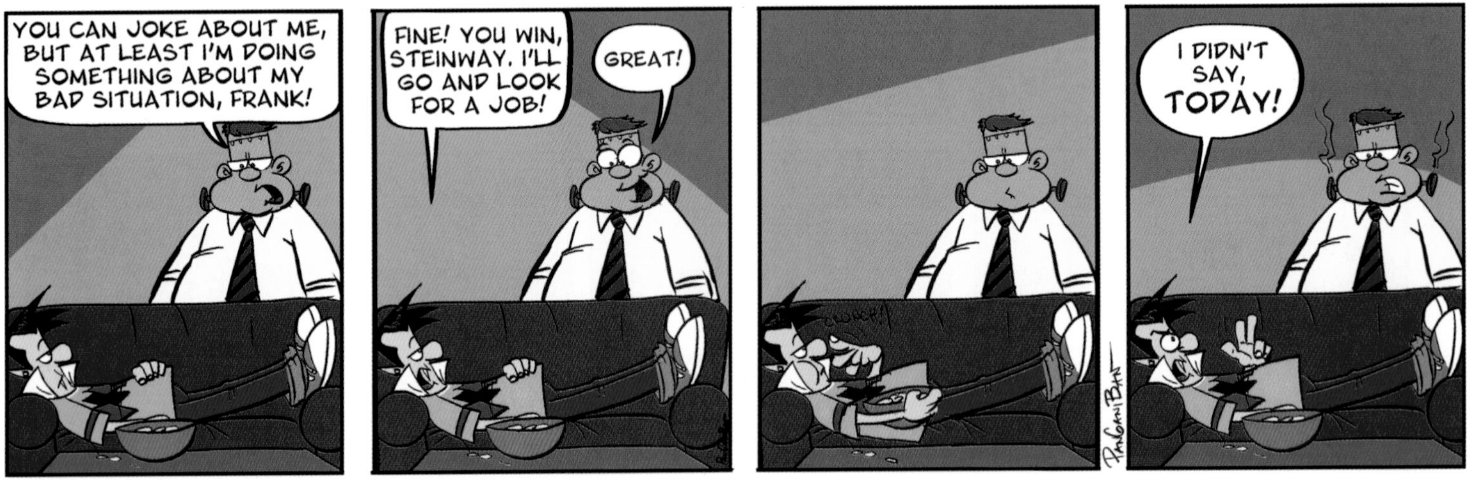
YOU CAN JOKE ABOUT ME, BUT AT LEAST I'M DOING SOMETHING ABOUT MY BAD SITUATION, FRANK!
FINE! YOU WIN, STEINWAY. I'LL GO AND LOOK FOR A JOB!
GREAT!
I DIDN'T SAY, **TODAY!**

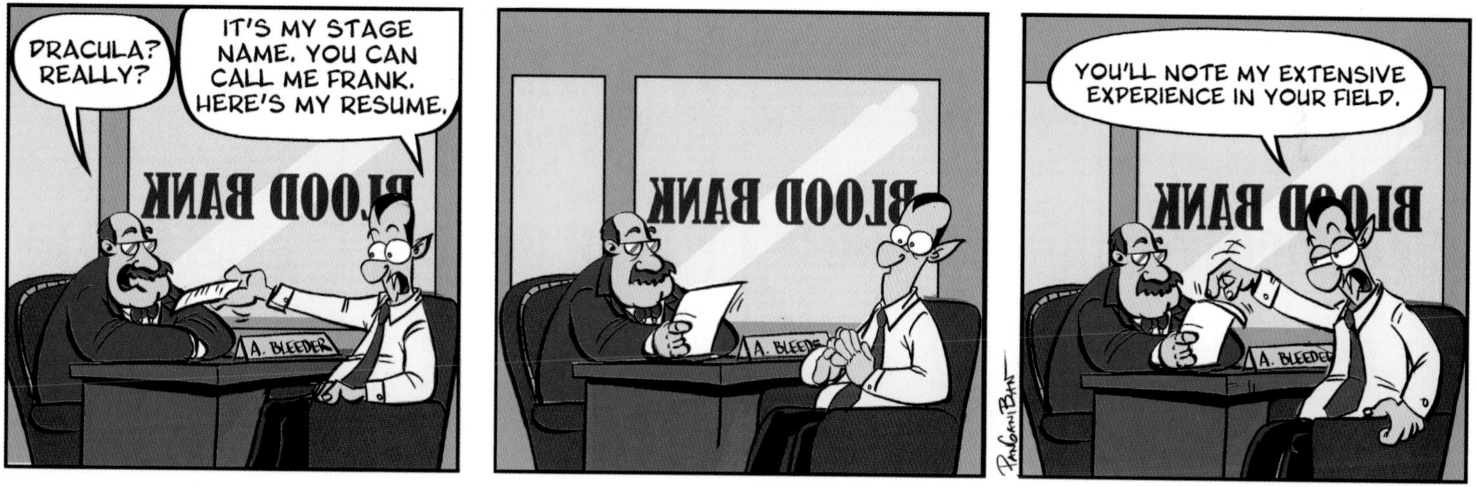
DRACULA? REALLY?
IT'S MY STAGE NAME. YOU CAN CALL ME FRANK. HERE'S MY RESUME.
BLOOD BANK
A. BLEEDER
YOU'LL NOTE MY EXTENSIVE EXPERIENCE IN YOUR FIELD.

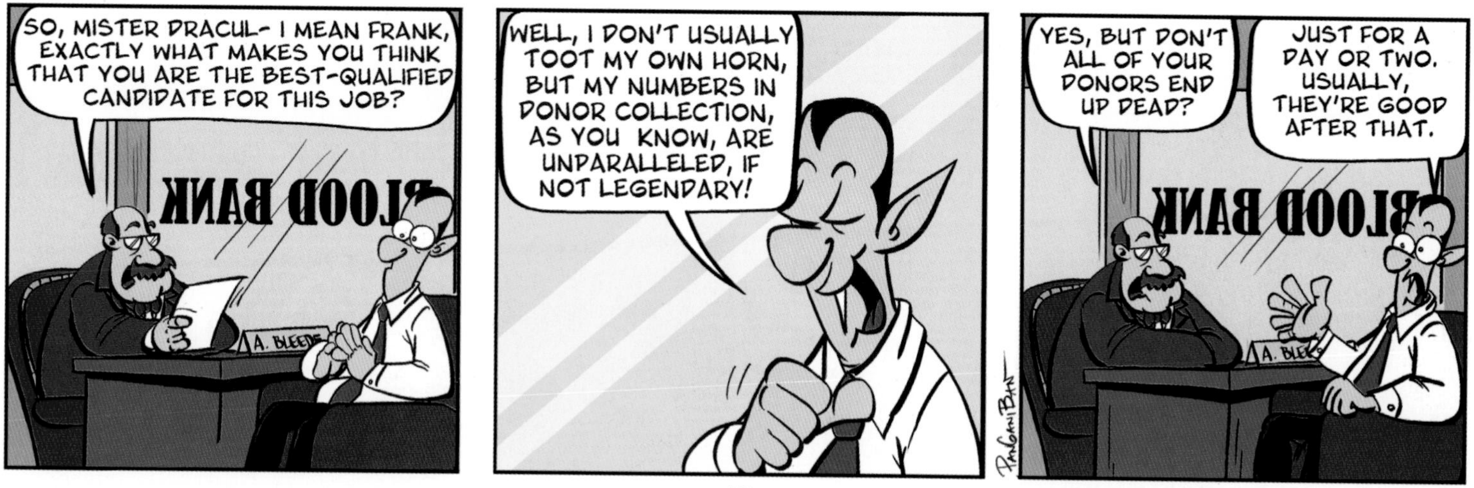
SO, MISTER DRACUL- I MEAN FRANK, EXACTLY WHAT MAKES YOU THINK THAT YOU ARE THE BEST-QUALIFIED CANDIDATE FOR THIS JOB?
BLOOD BANK
WELL, I DON'T USUALLY TOOT MY OWN HORN, BUT MY NUMBERS IN DONOR COLLECTION, AS YOU KNOW, ARE UNPARALLELED, IF NOT LEGENDARY!
YES, BUT DON'T ALL OF YOUR DONORS END UP DEAD?
JUST FOR A DAY OR TWO. USUALLY, THEY'RE GOOD AFTER THAT.

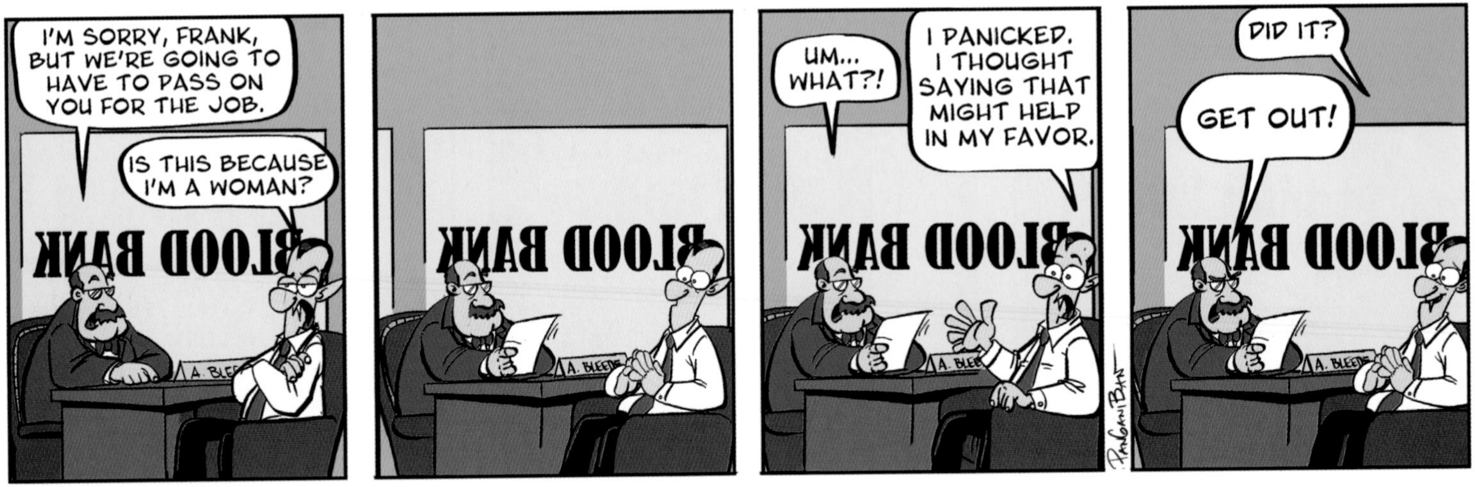
I'M SORRY, FRANK, BUT WE'RE GOING TO HAVE TO PASS ON YOU FOR THE JOB.
IS THIS BECAUSE I'M A WOMAN?
UM... WHAT?!
I PANICKED. I THOUGHT SAYING THAT MIGHT HELP IN MY FAVOR.
DID IT?
GET OUT!

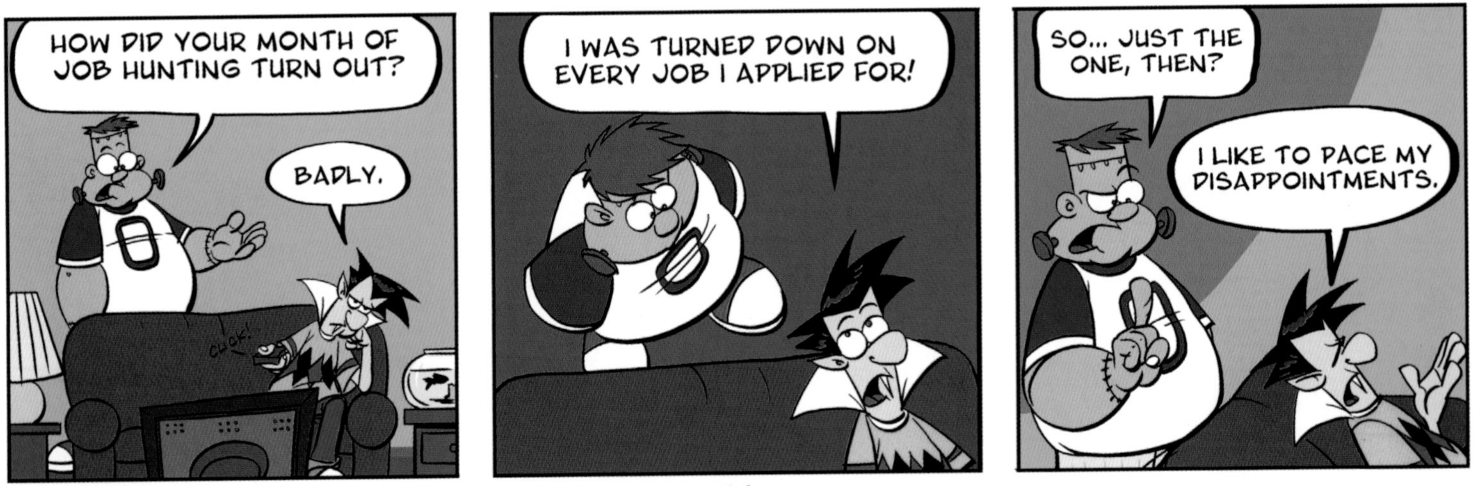
HOW DID YOUR MONTH OF JOB HUNTING TURN OUT?
BADLY.
CLICK!
I WAS TURNED DOWN ON EVERY JOB I APPLIED FOR!
SO... JUST THE ONE, THEN?
I LIKE TO PACE MY DISAPPOINTMENTS.

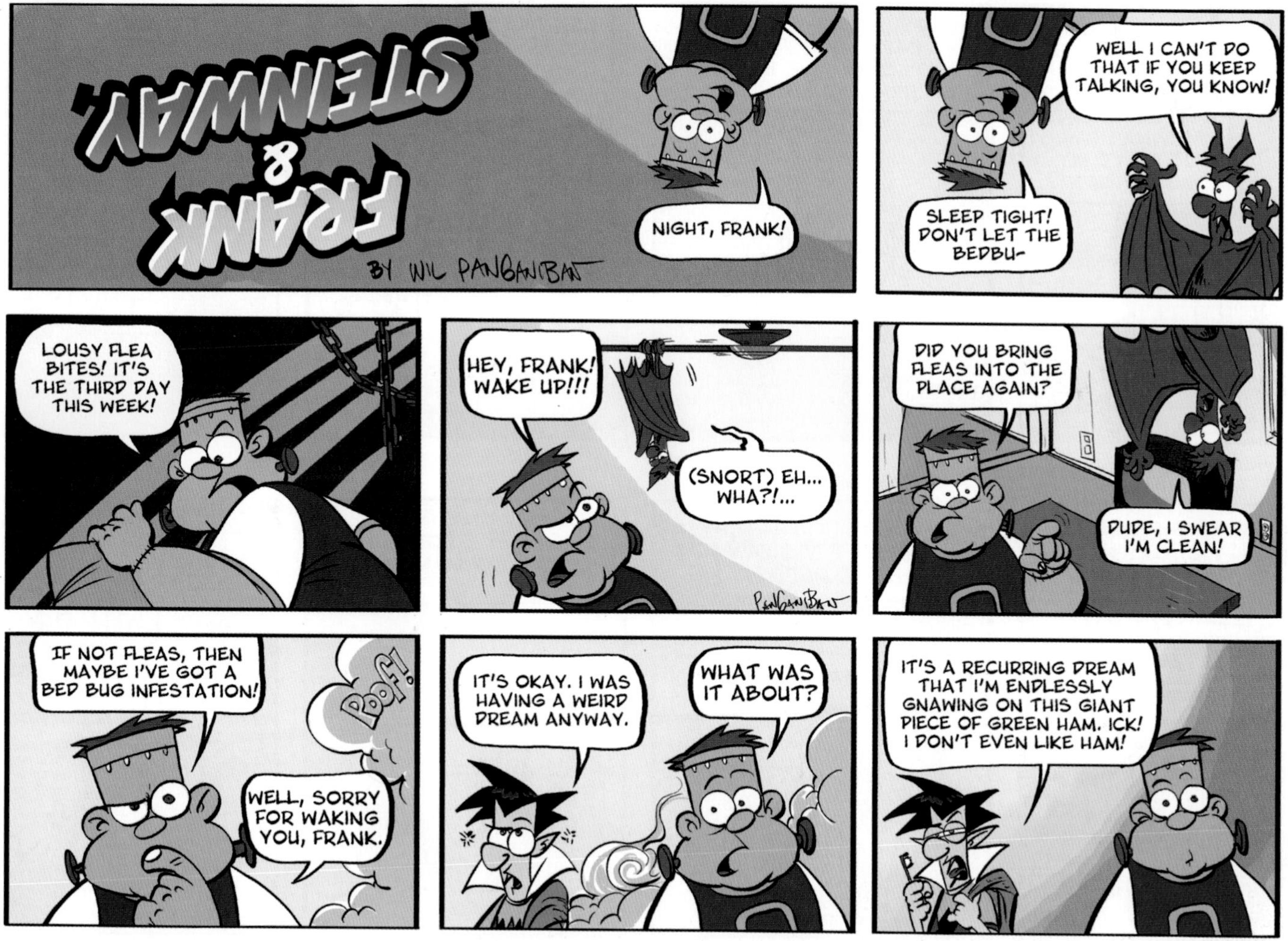
FRANK & STEINWAY
BY WIL PANGANIBAN
NIGHT, FRANK!
SLEEP TIGHT! DON'T LET THE BEDBU-
WELL I CAN'T DO THAT IF YOU KEEP TALKING, YOU KNOW!
LOUSY FLEA BITES! IT'S THE THIRD DAY THIS WEEK!
HEY, FRANK! WAKE UP!!!
(SNORT) EH... WHA?!...
PANGANIBAN
DID YOU BRING FLEAS INTO THE PLACE AGAIN?
DUDE, I SWEAR I'M CLEAN!
IF NOT FLEAS, THEN MAYBE I'VE GOT A BED BUG INFESTATION!
POOF!
WELL, SORRY FOR WAKING YOU, FRANK.
IT'S OKAY. I WAS HAVING A WEIRD DREAM ANYWAY.
WHAT WAS IT ABOUT?
IT'S A RECURRING DREAM THAT I'M ENDLESSLY GNAWING ON THIS GIANT PIECE OF GREEN HAM. ICK! I DON'T EVEN LIKE HAM!

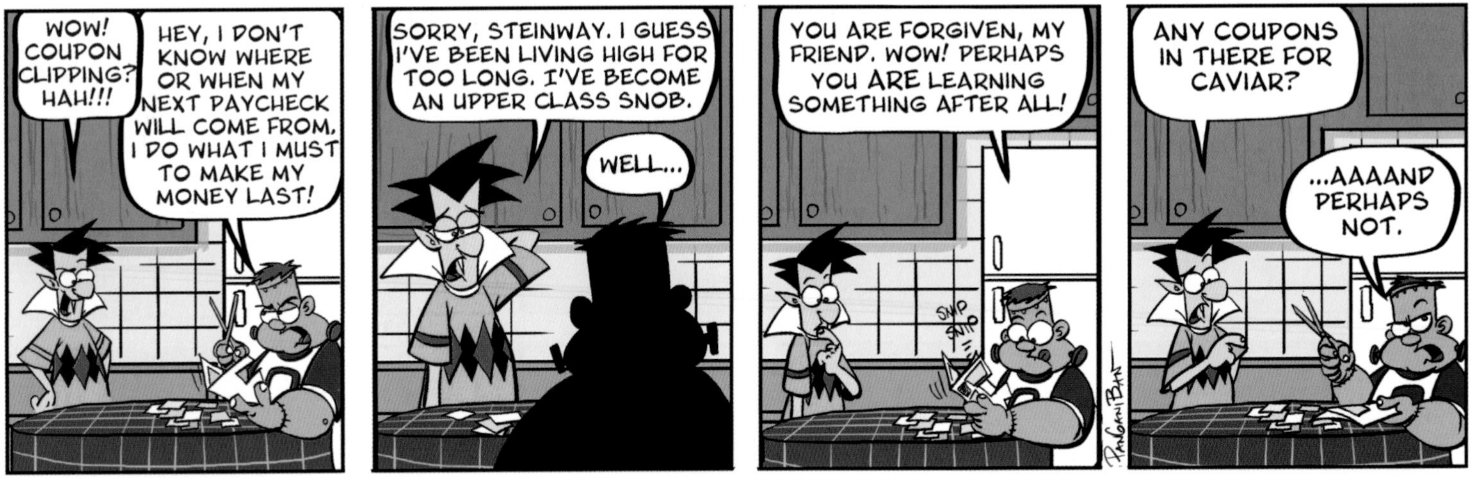
WOW! COUPON CLIPPING? HAH!!!
HEY, I DON'T KNOW WHERE OR WHEN MY NEXT PAYCHECK WILL COME FROM. I DO WHAT I MUST TO MAKE MY MONEY LAST!
SORRY, STEINWAY. I GUESS I'VE BEEN LIVING HIGH FOR TOO LONG. I'VE BECOME AN UPPER CLASS SNOB.
WELL...
YOU ARE FORGIVEN, MY FRIEND. WOW! PERHAPS YOU ARE LEARNING SOMETHING AFTER ALL!
SNIP SNIP
ANY COUPONS IN THERE FOR CAVIAR?
...AAAAND PERHAPS NOT.

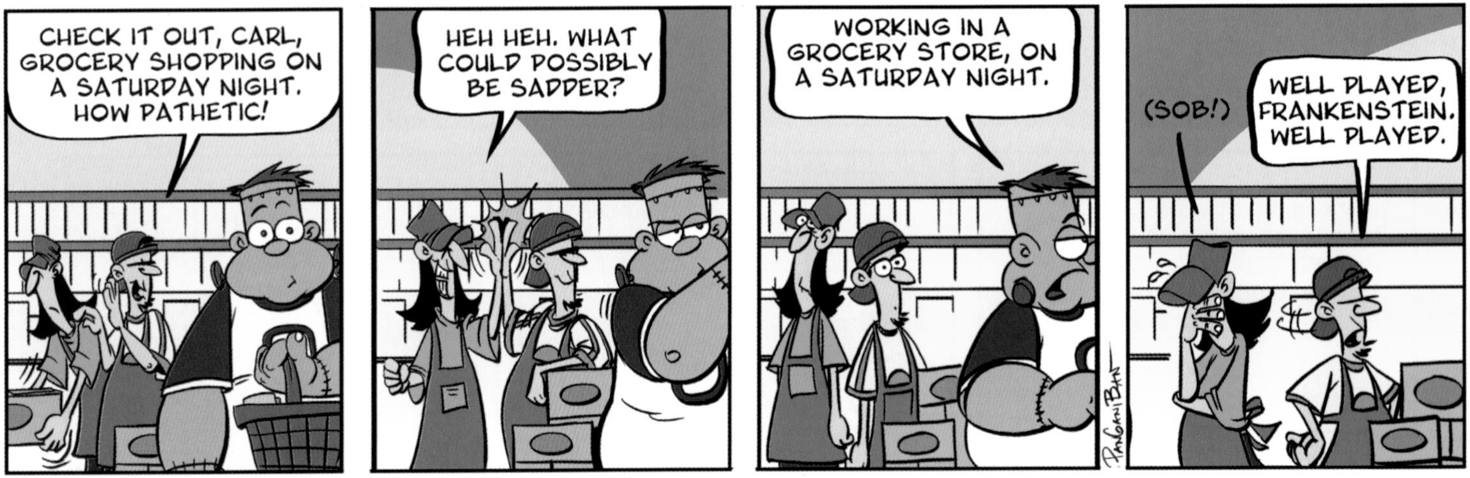
CHECK IT OUT, CARL, GROCERY SHOPPING ON A SATURDAY NIGHT. HOW PATHETIC!
HEH HEH. WHAT COULD POSSIBLY BE SADDER?
WORKING IN A GROCERY STORE, ON A SATURDAY NIGHT.
(SOB!)
WELL PLAYED, FRANKENSTEIN. WELL PLAYED.

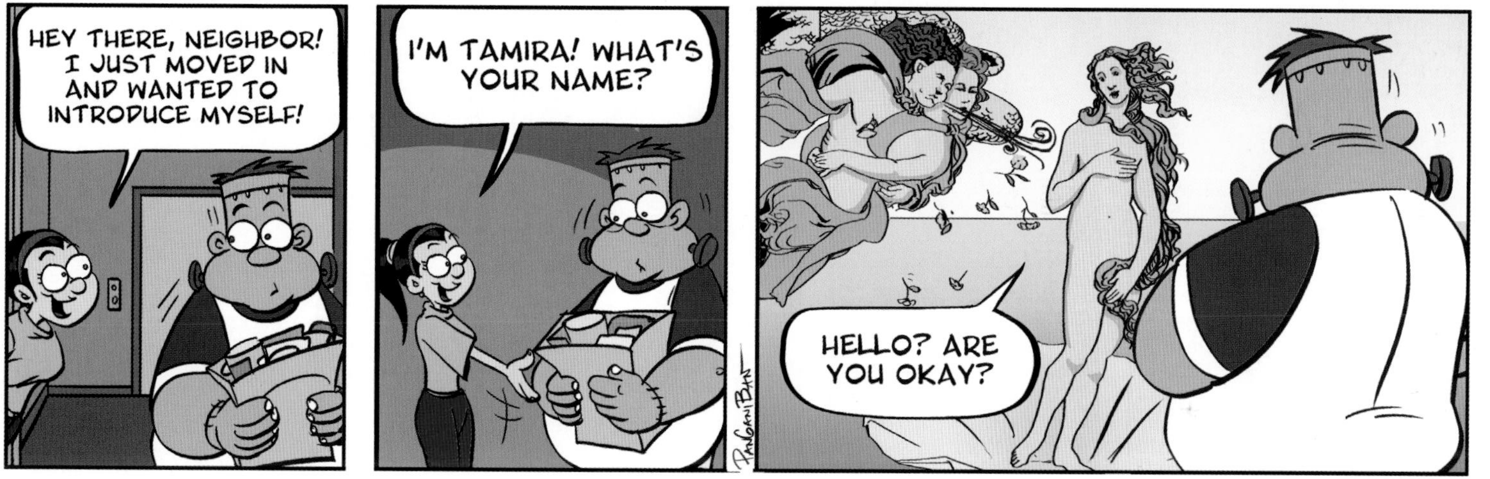
HEY THERE, NEIGHBOR! I JUST MOVED IN AND WANTED TO INTRODUCE MYSELF!
I'M TAMIRA! WHAT'S YOUR NAME?
HELLO? ARE YOU OKAY?

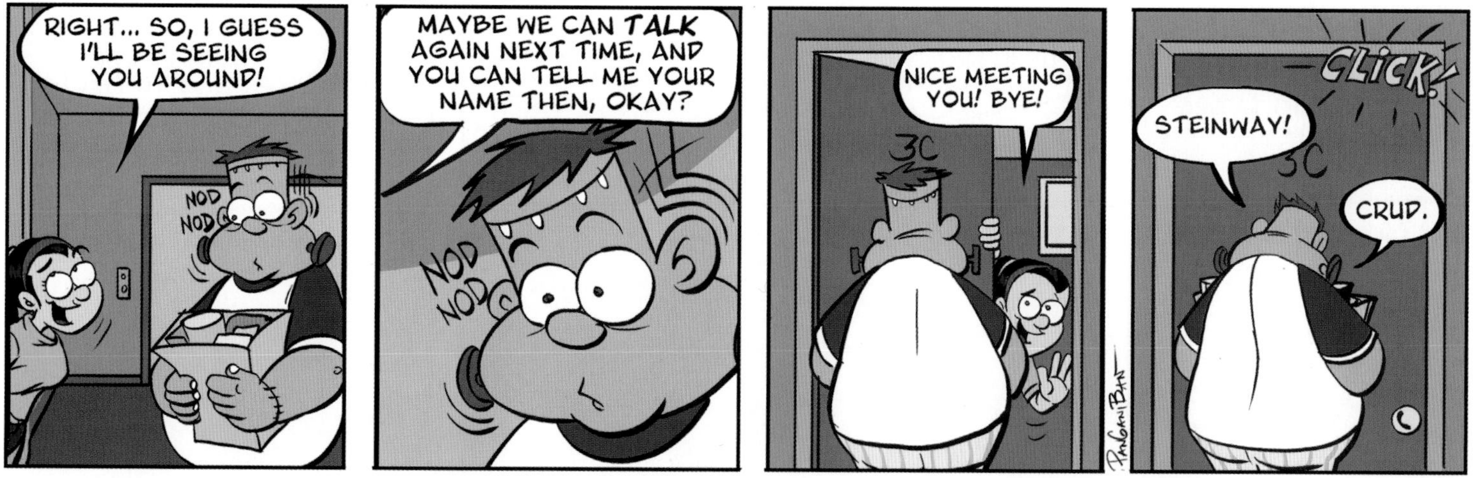
RIGHT... SO, I GUESS I'LL BE SEEING YOU AROUND!
NOD NOD
MAYBE WE CAN TALK AGAIN NEXT TIME, AND YOU CAN TELL ME YOUR NAME THEN, OKAY?
NOD NOD
NICE MEETING YOU! BYE!
3C
CLICK!
STEINWAY!
3C
CRUD.

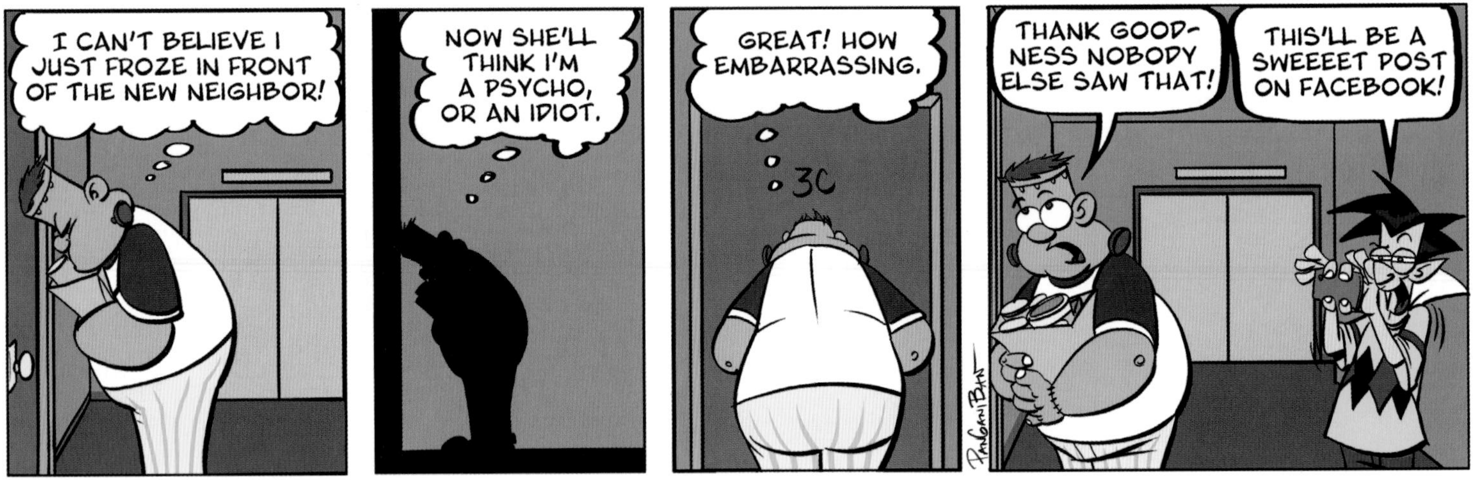
I CAN'T BELIEVE I JUST FROZE IN FRONT OF THE NEW NEIGHBOR!
NOW SHE'LL THINK I'M A PSYCHO, OR AN IDIOT.
3C
GREAT! HOW EMBARRASSING.
THANK GOODNESS NOBODY ELSE SAW THAT!
THIS'LL BE A SWEEEET POST ON FACEBOOK!

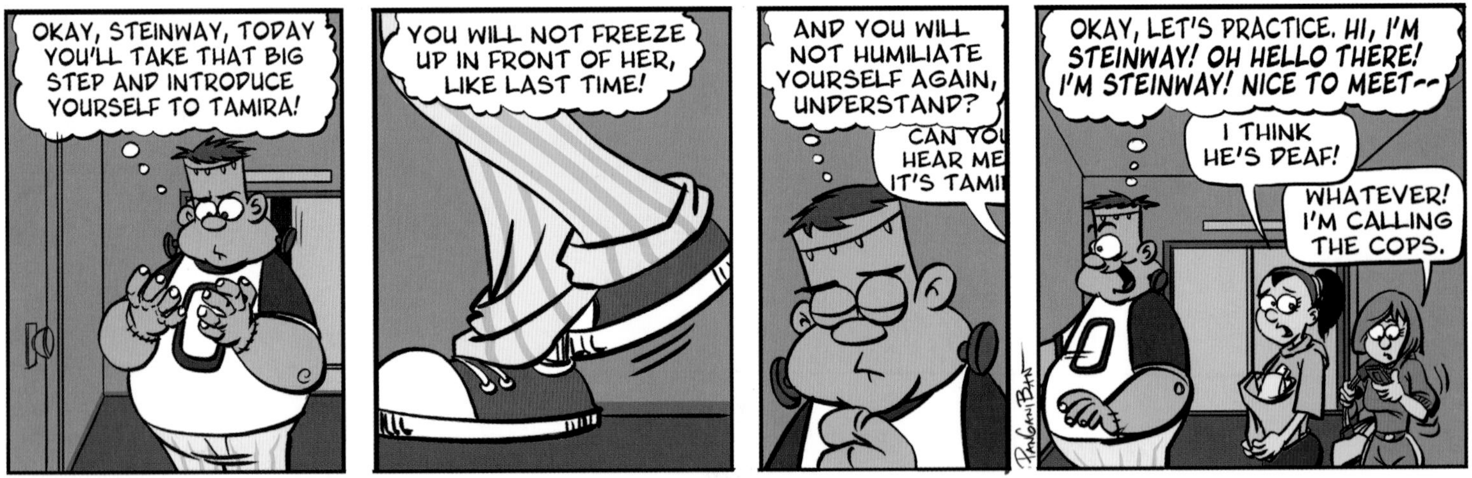
OKAY, STEINWAY, TODAY YOU'LL TAKE THAT BIG STEP AND INTRODUCE YOURSELF TO TAMIRA!
YOU WILL NOT FREEZE UP IN FRONT OF HER, LIKE LAST TIME!
AND YOU WILL NOT HUMILIATE YOURSELF AGAIN, UNDERSTAND?
CAN YO
HEAR ME
IT'S TAMI
OKAY, LET'S PRACTICE. HI, I'M STEINWAY! OH HELLO THERE! I'M STEINWAY! NICE TO MEET--
I THINK HE'S DEAF!
WHATEVER! I'M CALLING THE COPS.

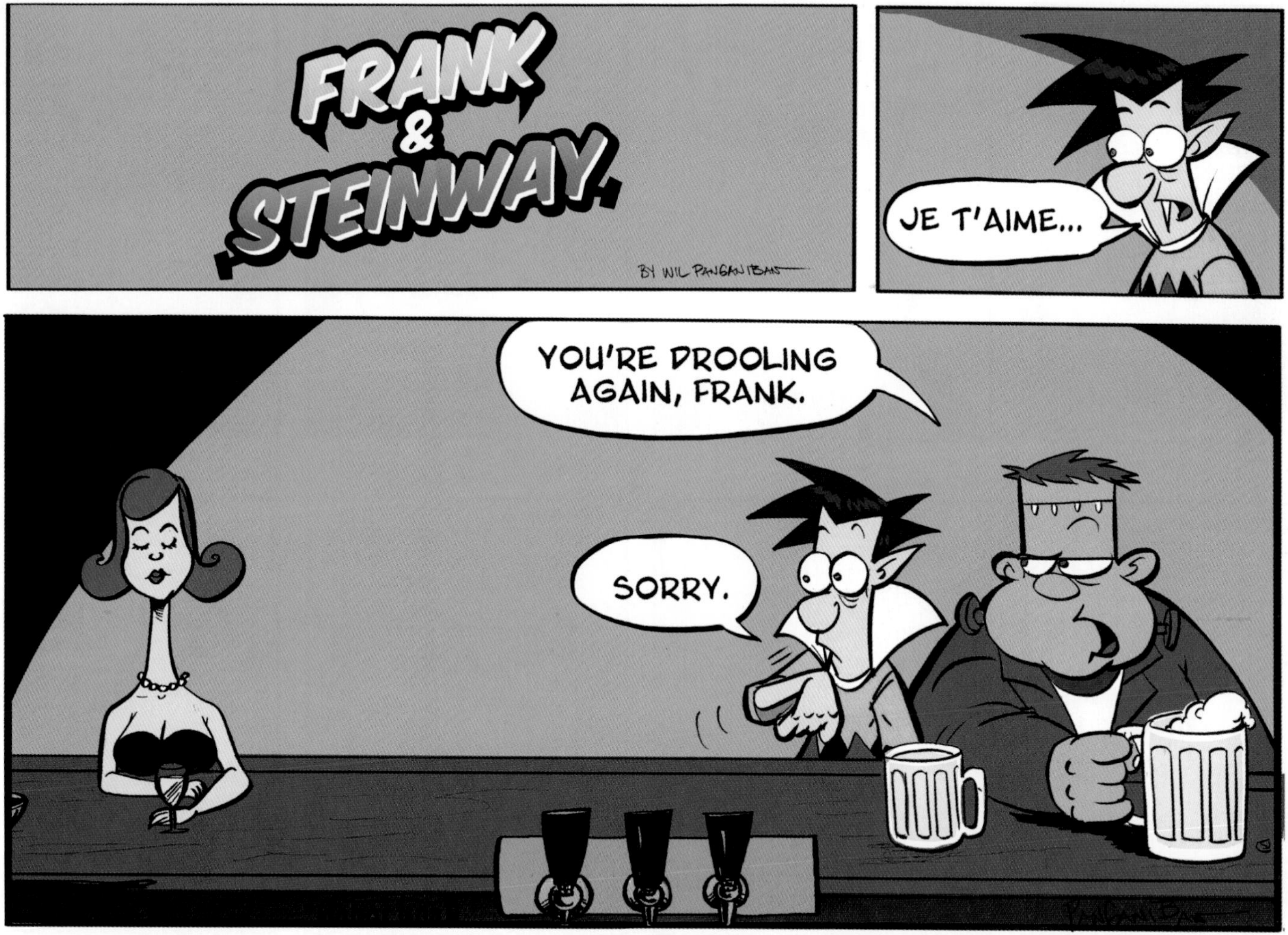
FRANK & STEINWAY
BY WIL PANGANIBAN
JE T'AIME...
YOU'RE DROOLING AGAIN, FRANK.
SORRY.

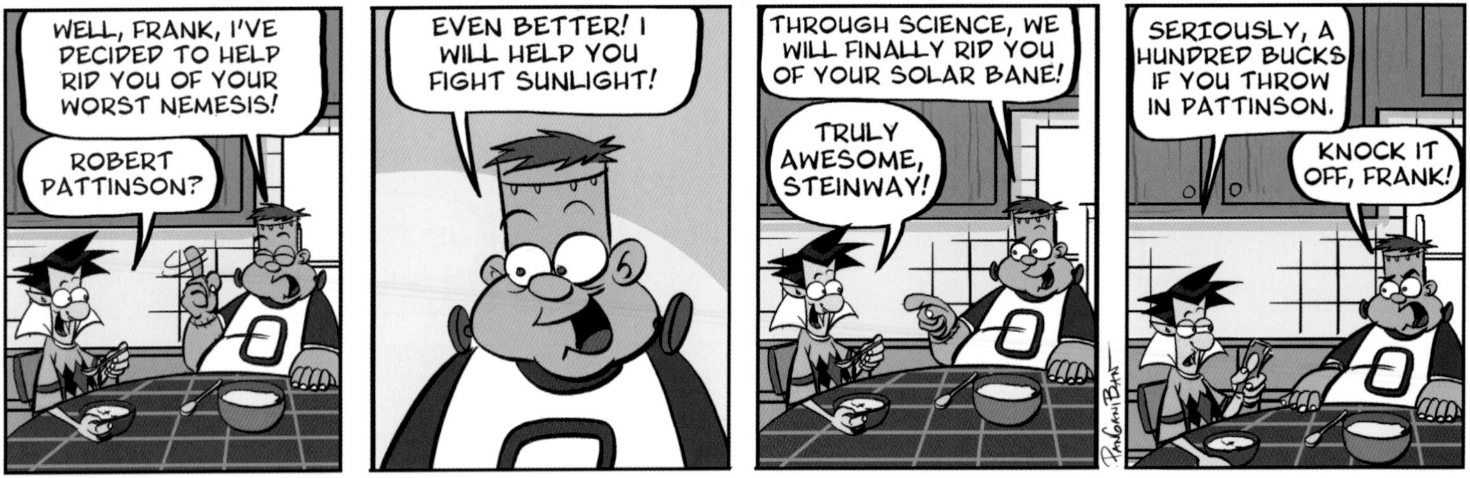
WELL, FRANK, I'VE DECIDED TO HELP RID YOU OF YOUR WORST NEMESIS!
ROBERT PATTINSON?
EVEN BETTER! I WILL HELP YOU FIGHT SUNLIGHT!
THROUGH SCIENCE, WE WILL FINALLY RID YOU OF YOUR SOLAR BANE!
TRULY AWESOME, STEINWAY!
SERIOUSLY, A HUNDRED BUCKS IF YOU THROW IN PATTINSON.
KNOCK IT OFF, FRANK!

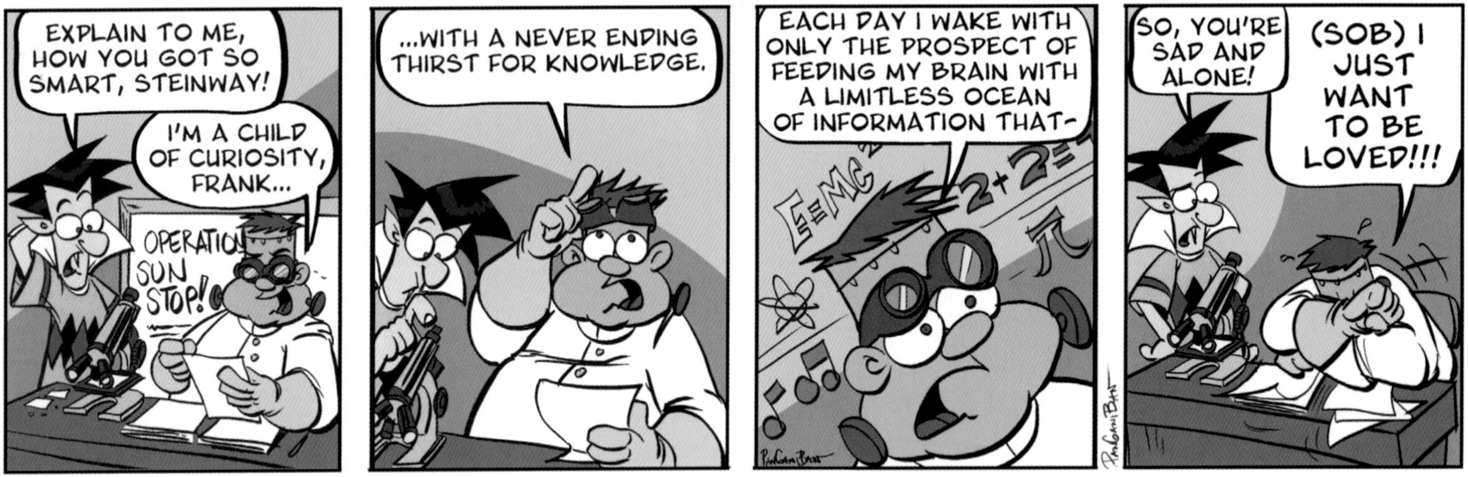
EXPLAIN TO ME, HOW YOU GOT SO SMART, STEINWAY!
I'M A CHILD OF CURIOSITY, FRANK...
OPERATION SUN STOP!
...WITH A NEVER ENDING THIRST FOR KNOWLEDGE.
EACH DAY I WAKE WITH ONLY THE PROSPECT OF FEEDING MY BRAIN WITH A LIMITLESS OCEAN OF INFORMATION THAT-
SO, YOU'RE SAD AND ALONE!
(SOB) I JUST WANT TO BE LOVED!!!

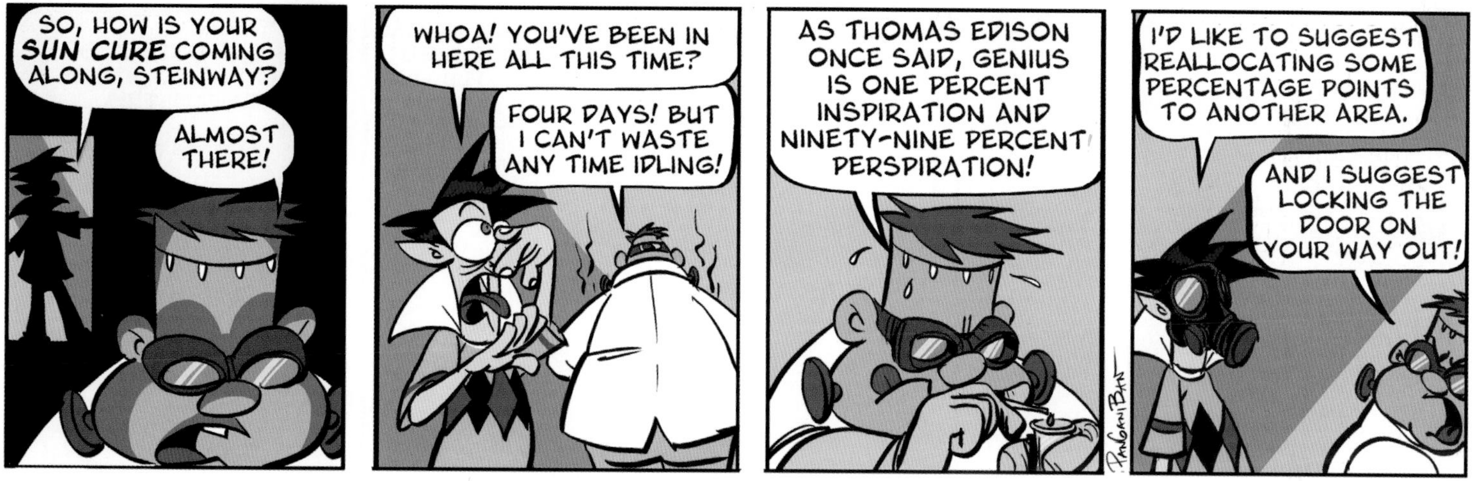
SO, HOW IS YOUR SUN CURE COMING ALONG, STEINWAY?
ALMOST THERE!
WHOA! YOU'VE BEEN IN HERE ALL THIS TIME?
FOUR DAYS! BUT I CAN'T WASTE ANY TIME IDLING!
AS THOMAS EDISON ONCE SAID, GENIUS IS ONE PERCENT INSPIRATION AND NINETY-NINE PERCENT PERSPIRATION!
I'D LIKE TO SUGGEST REALLOCATING SOME PERCENTAGE POINTS TO ANOTHER AREA.
AND I SUGGEST LOCKING THE DOOR ON YOUR WAY OUT!
PANGANIBAN

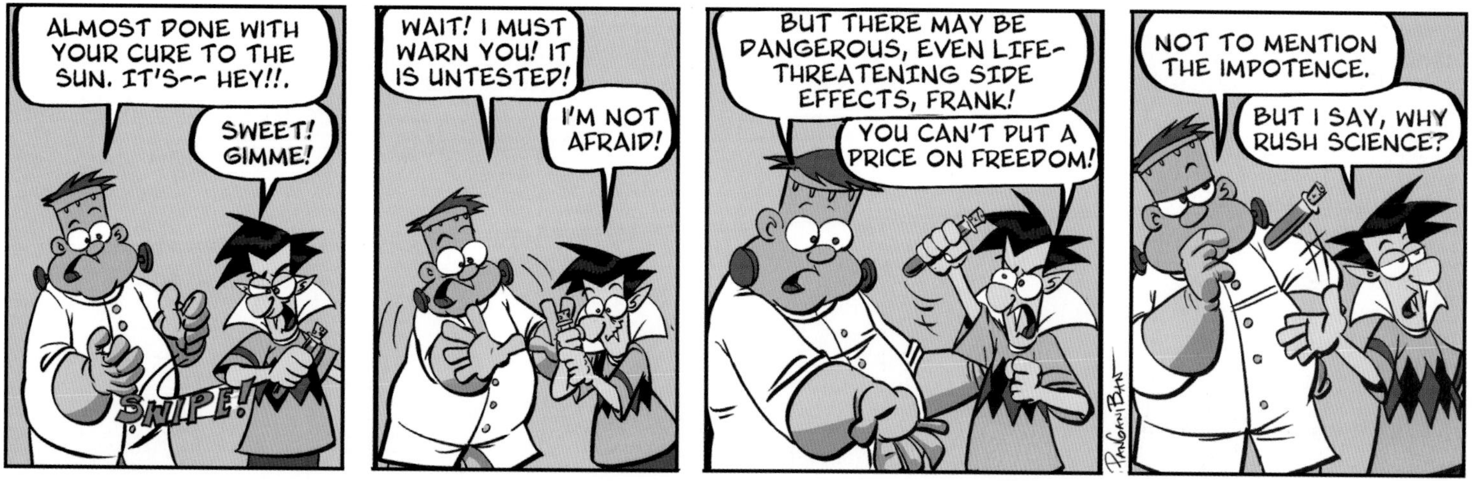
ALMOST DONE WITH YOUR CURE TO THE SUN. IT'S-- HEY!!.
SWEET! GIMME!
SWIPE!
WAIT! I MUST WARN YOU! IT IS UNTESTED!
I'M NOT AFRAID!
BUT THERE MAY BE DANGEROUS, EVEN LIFE-THREATENING SIDE EFFECTS, FRANK!
YOU CAN'T PUT A PRICE ON FREEDOM!
NOT TO MENTION THE IMPOTENCE.
BUT I SAY, WHY RUSH SCIENCE?
PANGANIBAN

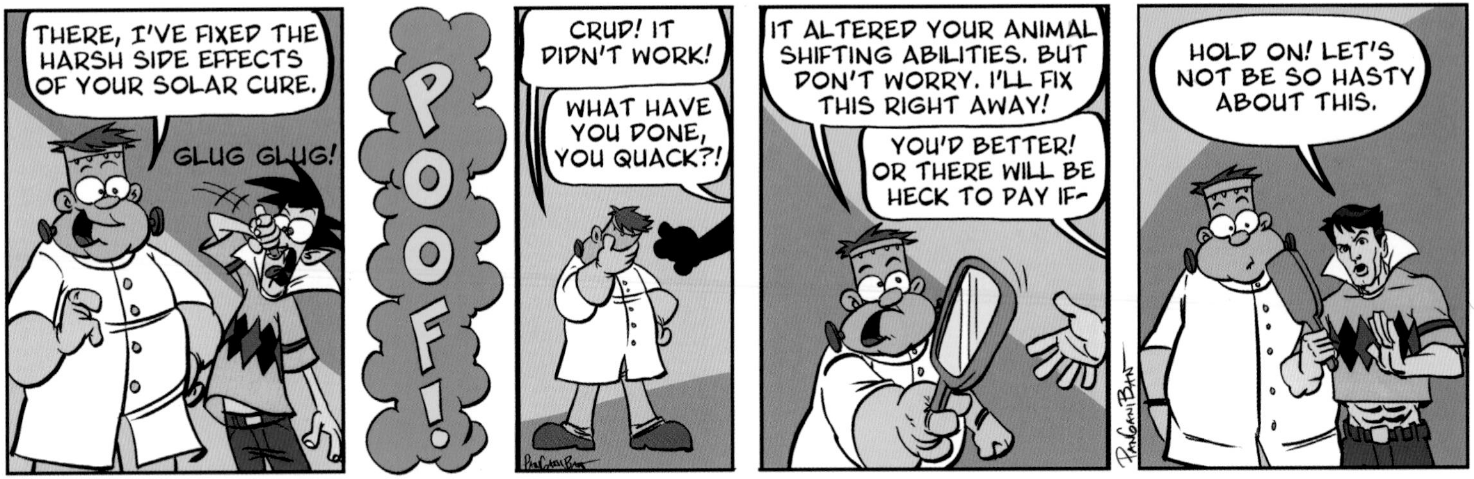
THERE, I'VE FIXED THE HARSH SIDE EFFECTS OF YOUR SOLAR CURE.
GLUG GLUG!
POOF!
CRUD! IT DIDN'T WORK!
WHAT HAVE YOU DONE, YOU QUACK?!
IT ALTERED YOUR ANIMAL SHIFTING ABILITIES. BUT DON'T WORRY. I'LL FIX THIS RIGHT AWAY!
YOU'D BETTER! OR THERE WILL BE HECK TO PAY IF-
HOLD ON! LET'S NOT BE SO HASTY ABOUT THIS.

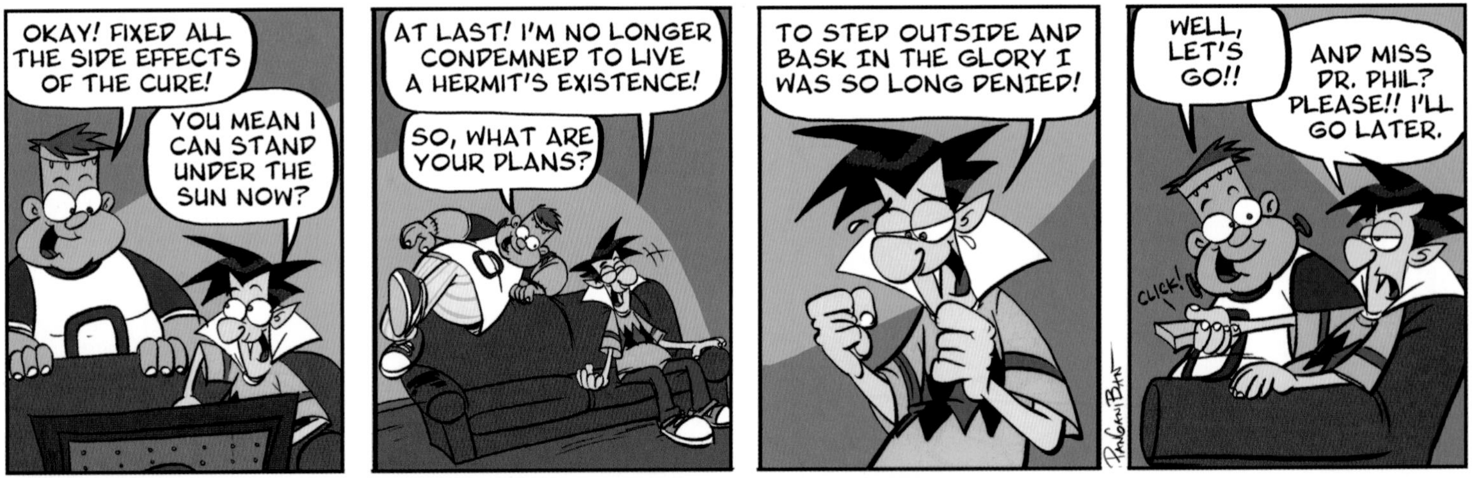
OKAY! FIXED ALL THE SIDE EFFECTS OF THE CURE!
YOU MEAN I CAN STAND UNDER THE SUN NOW?
AT LAST! I'M NO LONGER CONDEMNED TO LIVE A HERMIT'S EXISTENCE!
SO, WHAT ARE YOUR PLANS?
TO STEP OUTSIDE AND BASK IN THE GLORY I WAS SO LONG DENIED!
WELL, LET'S GO!!
AND MISS DR. PHIL? PLEASE!! I'LL GO LATER.
CLICK!

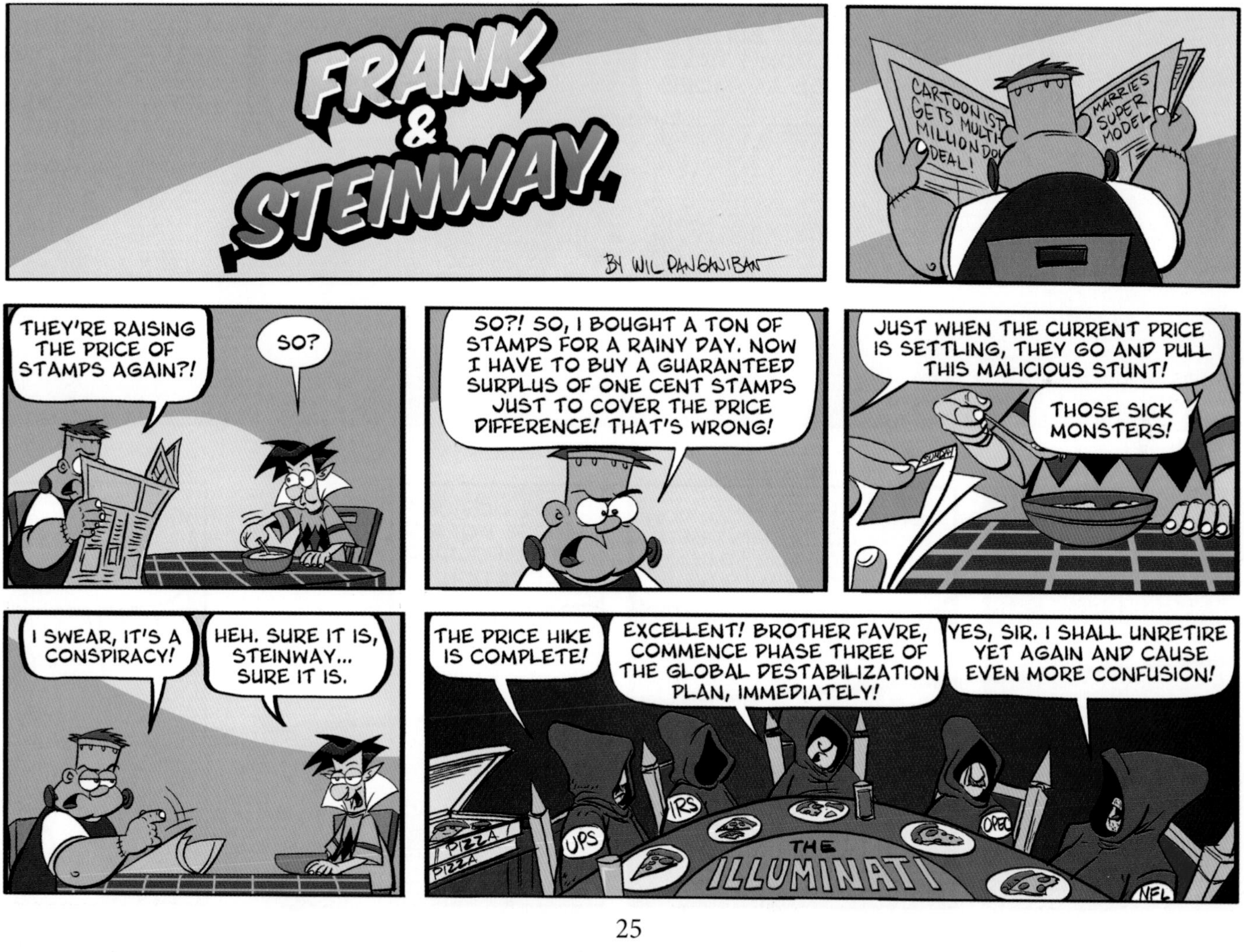
FRANK & STEINWAY
BY WIL PANGANIBAN
CARTOONIST GETS MULTI MILLION DO DEAL!
MARRIES SUPER MODEL
THEY'RE RAISING THE PRICE OF STAMPS AGAIN?!
SO?
SO?! SO, I BOUGHT A TON OF STAMPS FOR A RAINY DAY. NOW I HAVE TO BUY A GUARANTEED SURPLUS OF ONE CENT STAMPS JUST TO COVER THE PRICE DIFFERENCE! THAT'S WRONG!
JUST WHEN THE CURRENT PRICE IS SETTLING, THEY GO AND PULL THIS MALICIOUS STUNT!
THOSE SICK MONSTERS!
I SWEAR, IT'S A CONSPIRACY!
HEH. SURE IT IS, STEINWAY... SURE IT IS.
THE PRICE HIKE IS COMPLETE!
EXCELLENT! BROTHER FAVRE, COMMENCE PHASE THREE OF THE GLOBAL DESTABILIZATION PLAN, IMMEDIATELY!
YES, SIR. I SHALL UNRETIRE YET AGAIN AND CAUSE EVEN MORE CONFUSION!
PIZZA
PIZZA
UPS
IRS
OPEC
NFL
THE ILLUMINATI

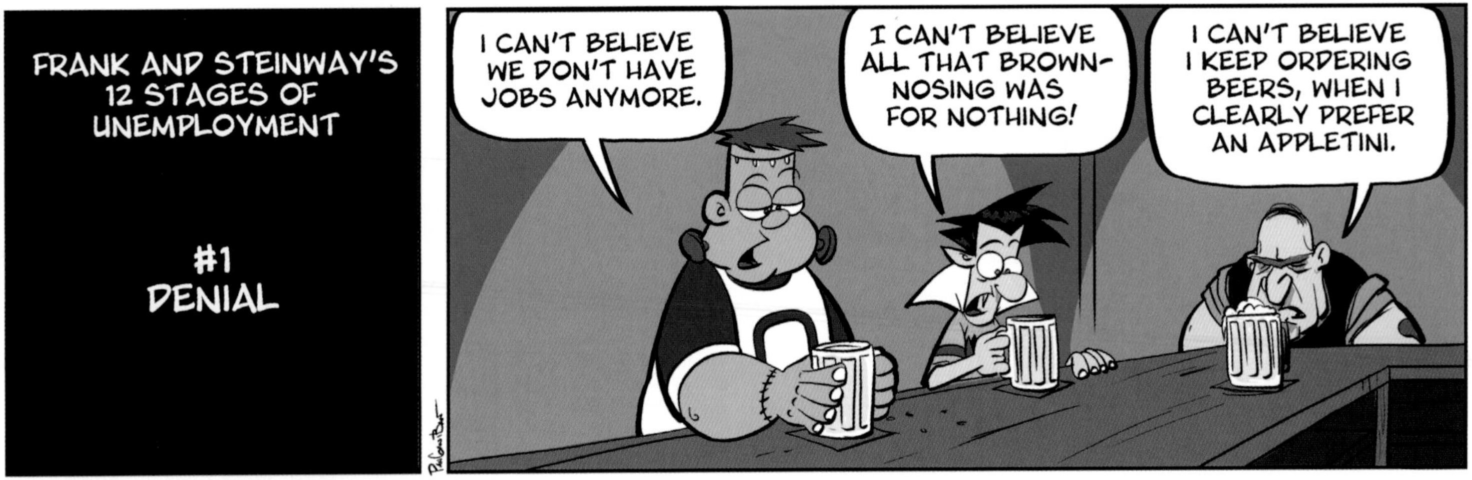
FRANK AND STEINWAY'S 12 STAGES OF UNEMPLOYMENT
#1 DENIAL
I CAN'T BELIEVE WE DON'T HAVE JOBS ANYMORE.
I CAN'T BELIEVE ALL THAT BROWN-NOSING WAS FOR NOTHING!
I CAN'T BELIEVE I KEEP ORDERING BEERS, WHEN I CLEARLY PREFER AN APPLETINI.

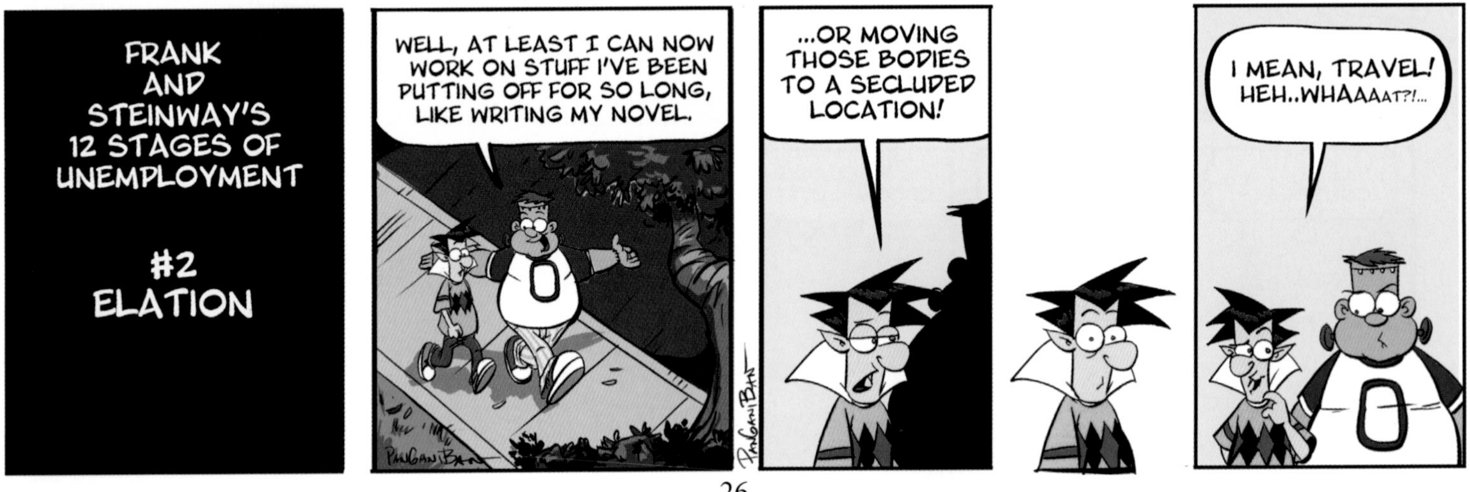
FRANK AND STEINWAY'S 12 STAGES OF UNEMPLOYMENT
#2 ELATION
WELL, AT LEAST I CAN NOW WORK ON STUFF I'VE BEEN PUTTING OFF FOR SO LONG, LIKE WRITING MY NOVEL.
...OR MOVING THOSE BODIES TO A SECLUDED LOCATION!
I MEAN, TRAVEL! HEH..WHAAAAT?!...

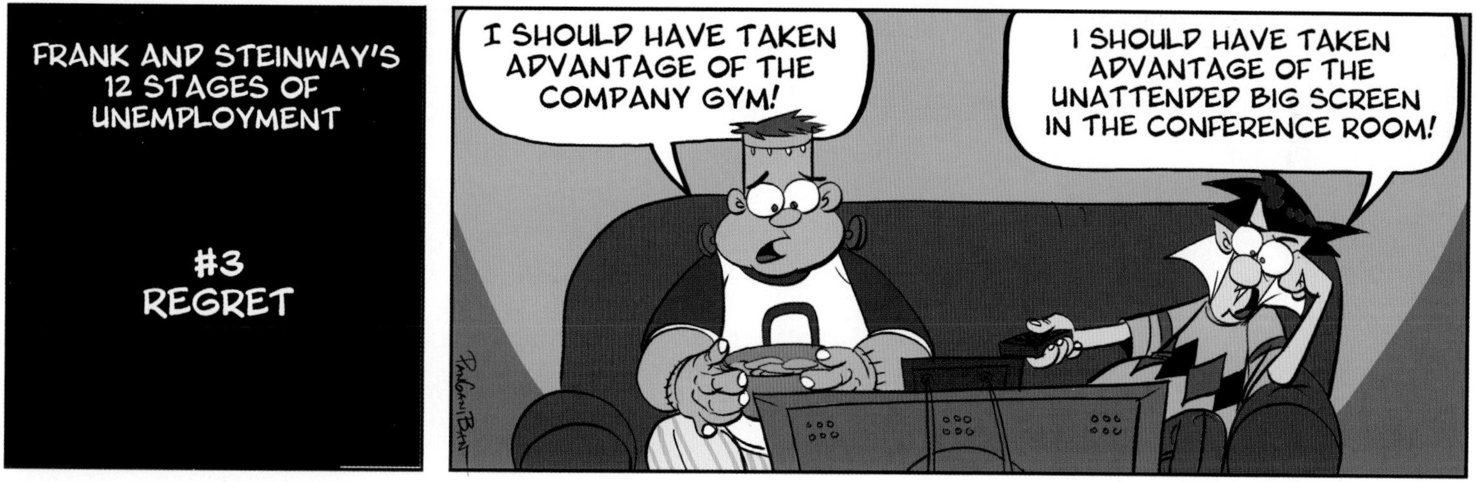
FRANK AND STEINWAY'S 12 STAGES OF UNEMPLOYMENT
#3 REGRET
I SHOULD HAVE TAKEN ADVANTAGE OF THE COMPANY GYM!
I SHOULD HAVE TAKEN ADVANTAGE OF THE UNATTENDED BIG SCREEN IN THE CONFERENCE ROOM!

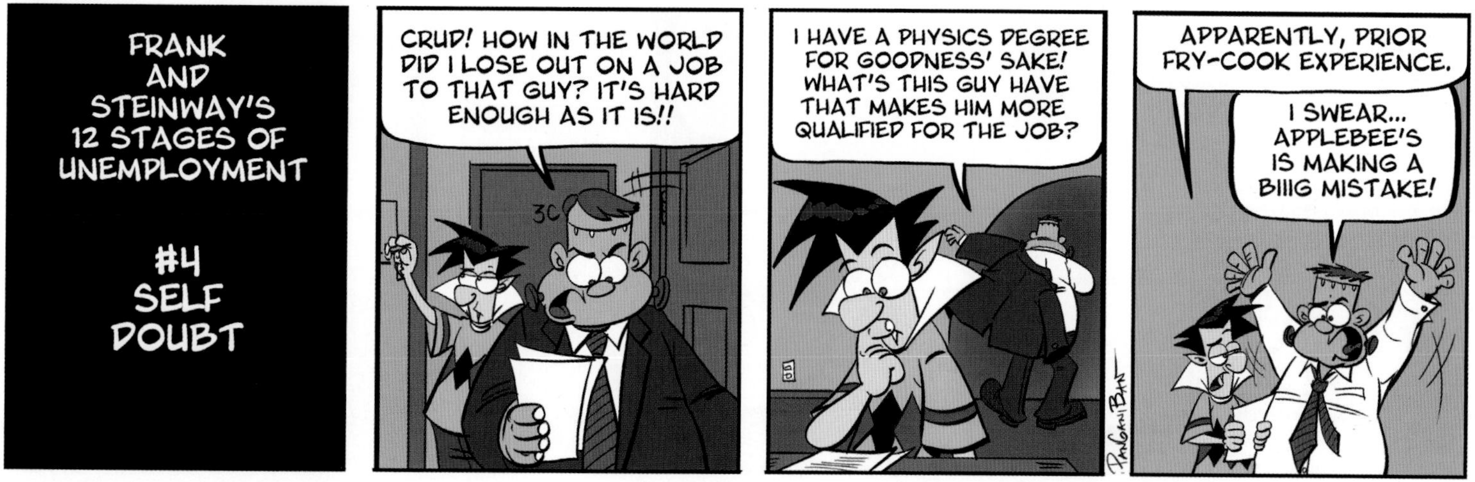
FRANK AND STEINWAY'S 12 STAGES OF UNEMPLOYMENT
#4 SELF DOUBT
CRUD! HOW IN THE WORLD DID I LOSE OUT ON A JOB TO THAT GUY? IT'S HARD ENOUGH AS IT IS!!
3C
I HAVE A PHYSICS DEGREE FOR GOODNESS' SAKE! WHAT'S THIS GUY HAVE THAT MAKES HIM MORE QUALIFIED FOR THE JOB?
APPARENTLY, PRIOR FRY-COOK EXPERIENCE.
I SWEAR... APPLEBEE'S IS MAKING A BIIIG MISTAKE!

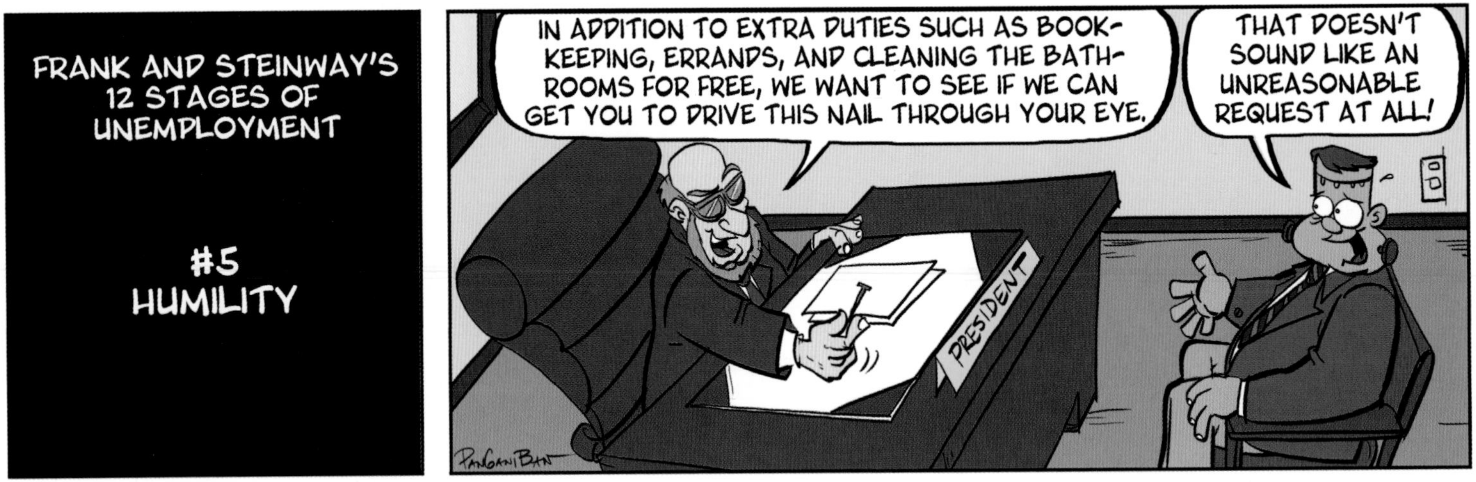
FRANK AND STEINWAY'S 12 STAGES OF UNEMPLOYMENT
#5 HUMILITY
IN ADDITION TO EXTRA DUTIES SUCH AS BOOK-KEEPING, ERRANDS, AND CLEANING THE BATH-ROOMS FOR FREE, WE WANT TO SEE IF WE CAN GET YOU TO DRIVE THIS NAIL THROUGH YOUR EYE.
THAT DOESN'T SOUND LIKE AN UNREASONABLE REQUEST AT ALL!
PRESIDENT

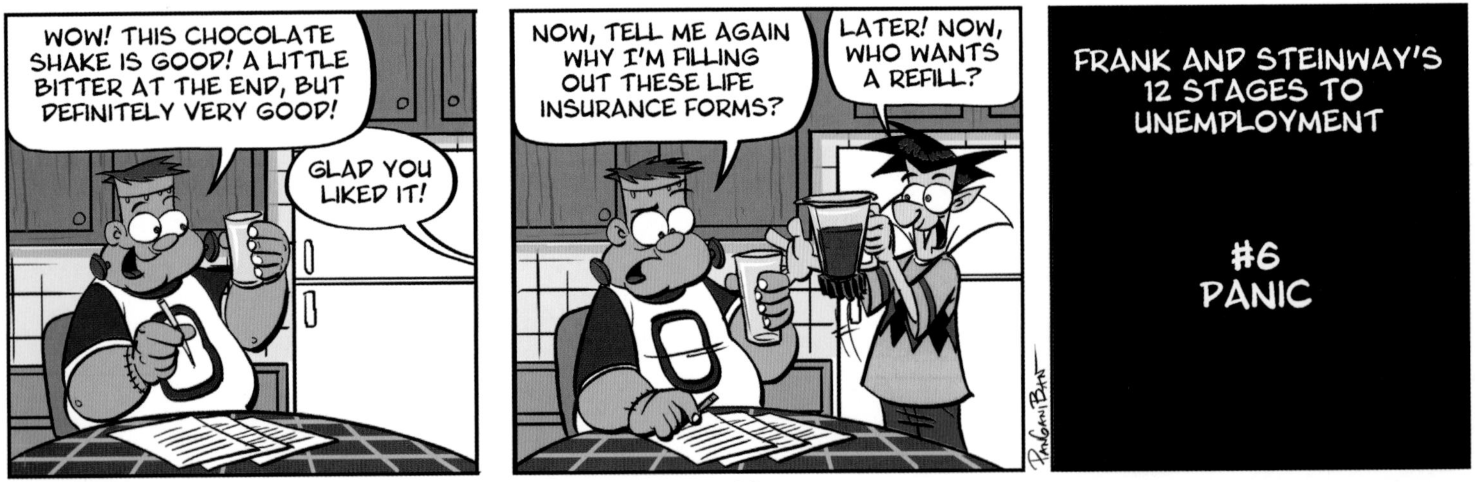
WOW! THIS CHOCOLATE SHAKE IS GOOD! A LITTLE BITTER AT THE END, BUT DEFINITELY VERY GOOD!
GLAD YOU LIKED IT!
NOW, TELL ME AGAIN WHY I'M FILLING OUT THESE LIFE INSURANCE FORMS?
LATER! NOW, WHO WANTS A REFILL?
FRANK AND STEINWAY'S 12 STAGES TO UNEMPLOYMENT
#6 PANIC

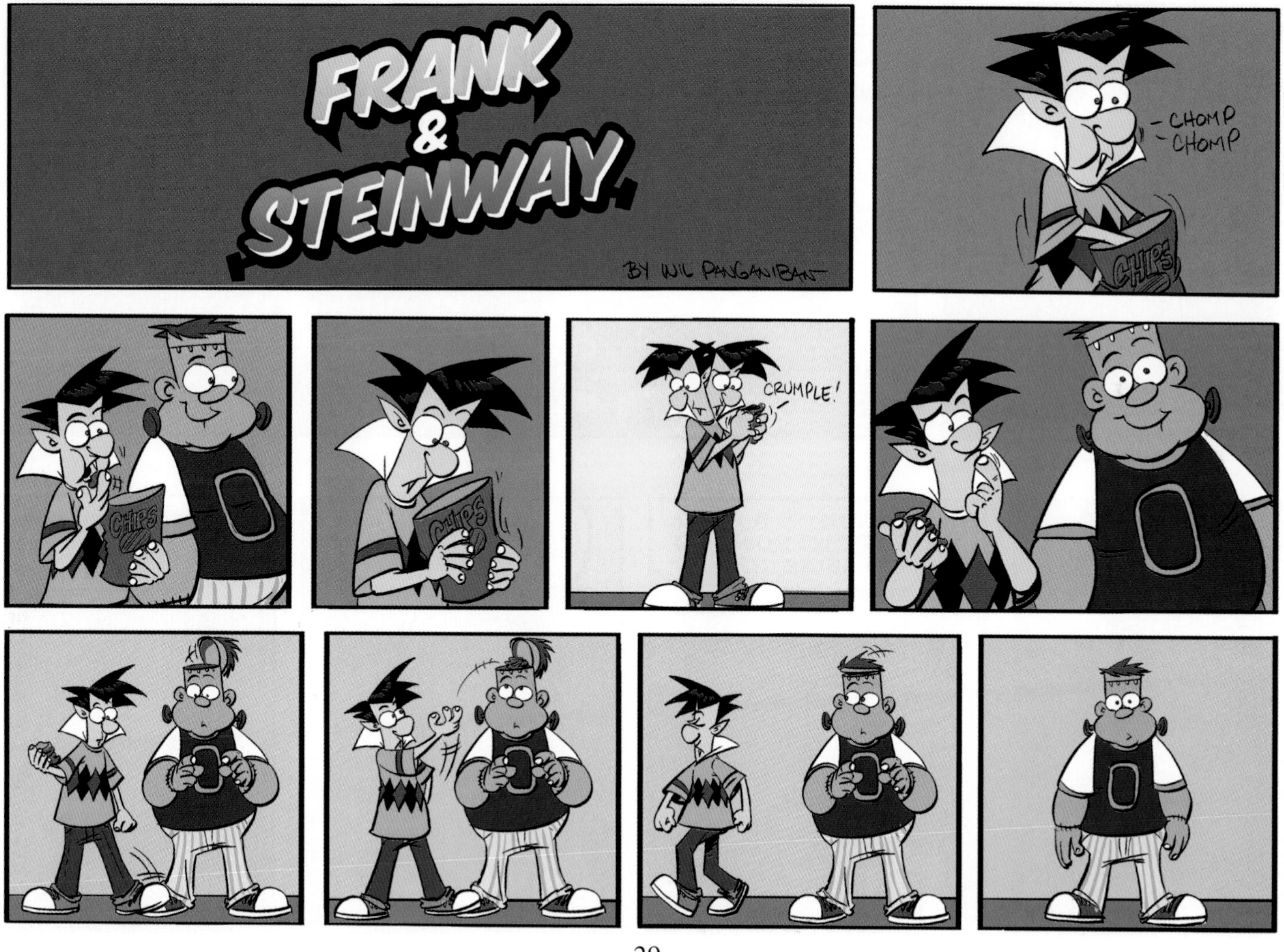
FRANK & STEINWAY
BY WIL PANGANIBAN
CHOMP
CHOMP
CHIPS
CHIPS
CHIPS
CRUMPLE!

FRANK AND STEINWAY'S
12 STAGES OF
UNEMPLOYMENT

#7
IRONY

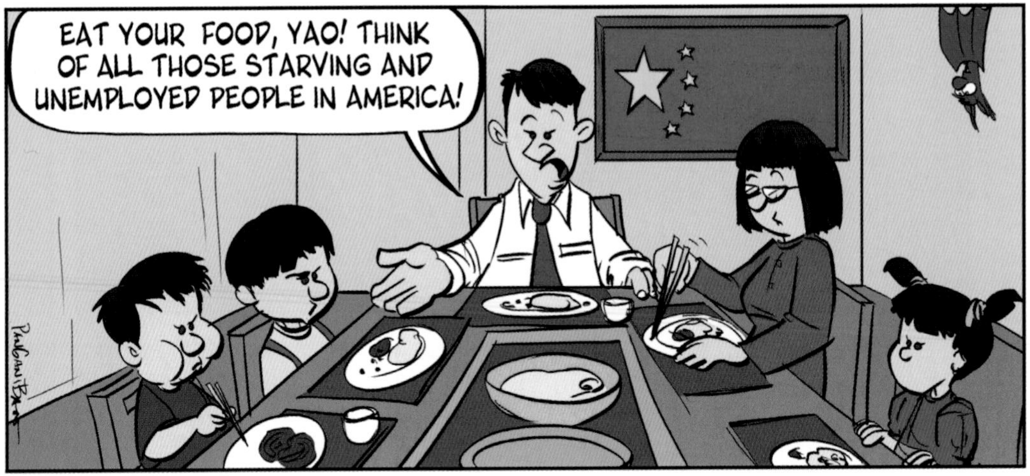
EAT YOUR FOOD, YAO! THINK OF ALL THOSE STARVING AND UNEMPLOYED PEOPLE IN AMERICA!

FRANK
AND
STEINWAY'S
12 STAGES OF
UNEMPLOYMENT

#8
ANGER

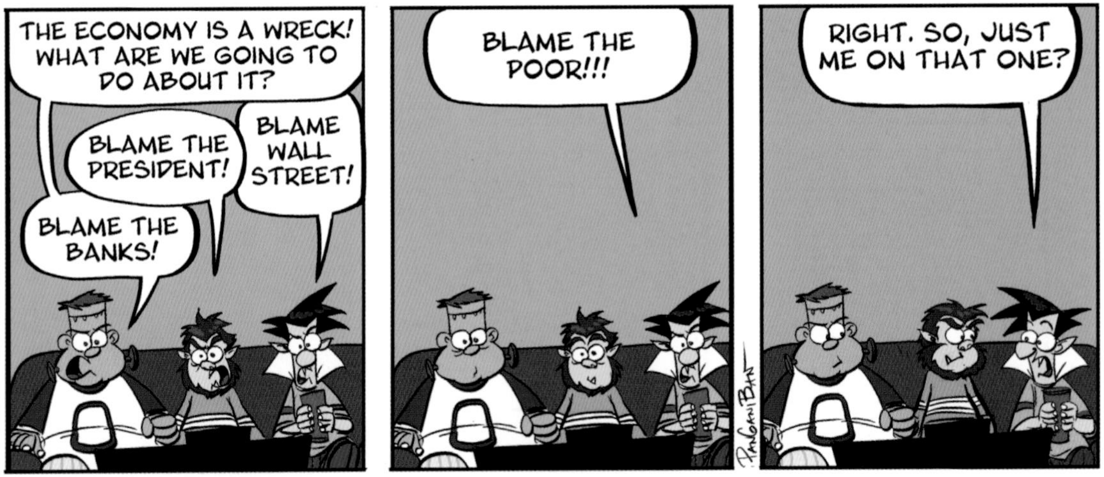
THE ECONOMY IS A WRECK! WHAT ARE WE GOING TO DO ABOUT IT?
BLAME THE BANKS!
BLAME THE PRESIDENT!
BLAME WALL STREET!
BLAME THE POOR!!!
RIGHT. SO, JUST ME ON THAT ONE?

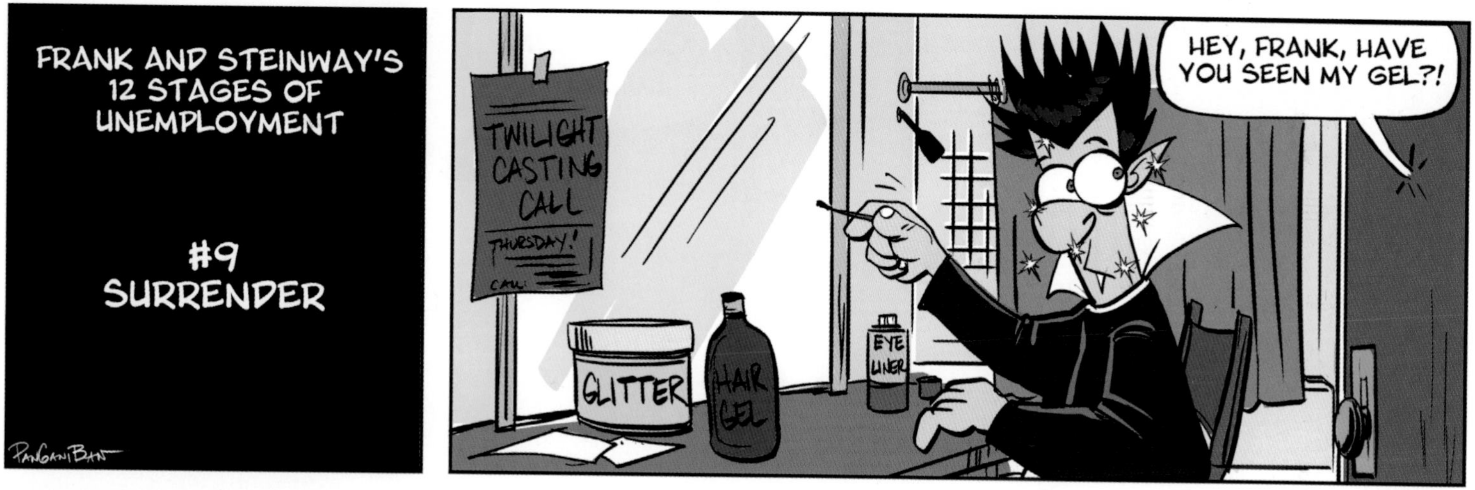
FRANK AND STEINWAY'S 12 STAGES OF UNEMPLOYMENT
#9 SURRENDER
PANGANIBAN
TWILIGHT CASTING CALL
THURSDAY!
GLITTER
HAIR GEL
EYE LINER
HEY, FRANK, HAVE YOU SEEN MY GEL?!

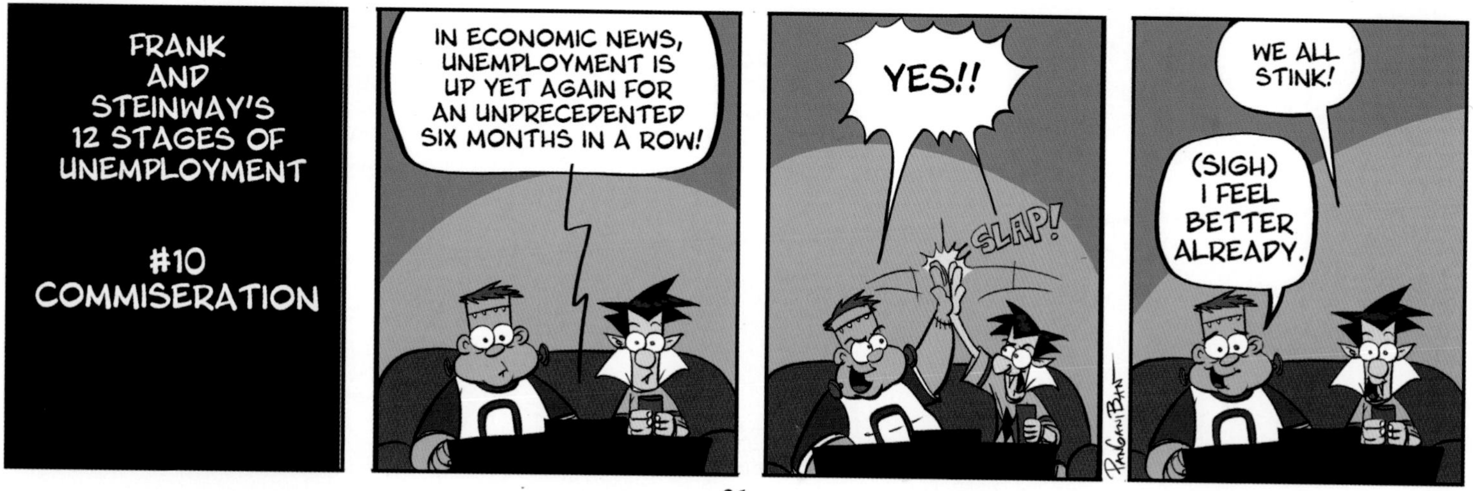
FRANK AND STEINWAY'S 12 STAGES OF UNEMPLOYMENT
#10 COMMISERATION
IN ECONOMIC NEWS, UNEMPLOYMENT IS UP YET AGAIN FOR AN UNPRECEDENTED SIX MONTHS IN A ROW!
YES!!
SLAP!
PANGANIBAN
WE ALL STINK!
(SIGH) I FEEL BETTER ALREADY.

FRANK AND STEINWAY'S 12 STAGES OF UNEMPLOYMENT

#11 HOPE

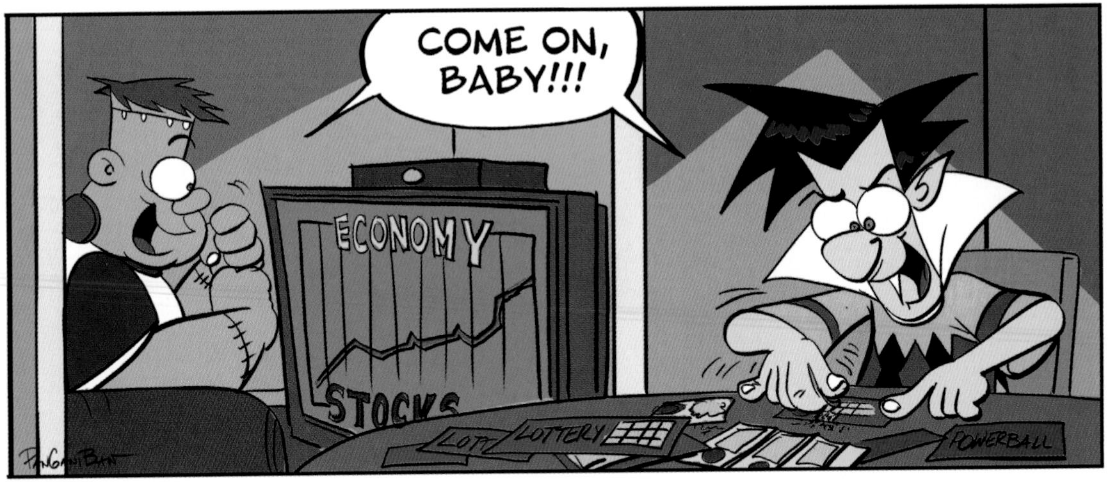
COME ON, BABY!!!
ECONOMY
LOTTERY
POWERBALL
PANGANIBAN

FRANK AND STEINWAY'S 12 STAGES OF UNEMPLOYMENT

#12 SARDONIC WIT

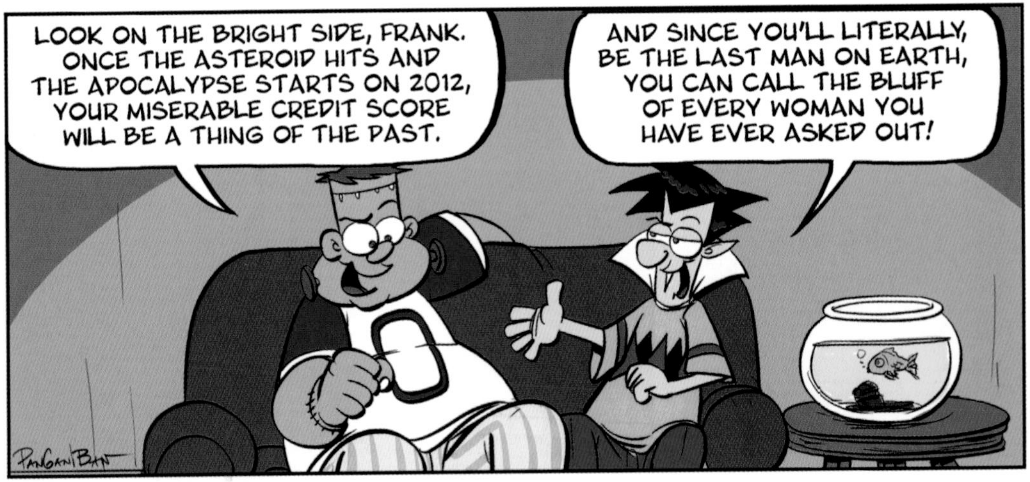
LOOK ON THE BRIGHT SIDE, FRANK. ONCE THE ASTEROID HITS AND THE APOCALYPSE STARTS ON 2012, YOUR MISERABLE CREDIT SCORE WILL BE A THING OF THE PAST.
AND SINCE YOU'LL LITERALLY, BE THE LAST MAN ON EARTH, YOU CAN CALL THE BLUFF OF EVERY WOMAN YOU HAVE EVER ASKED OUT!
PANGANIBAN

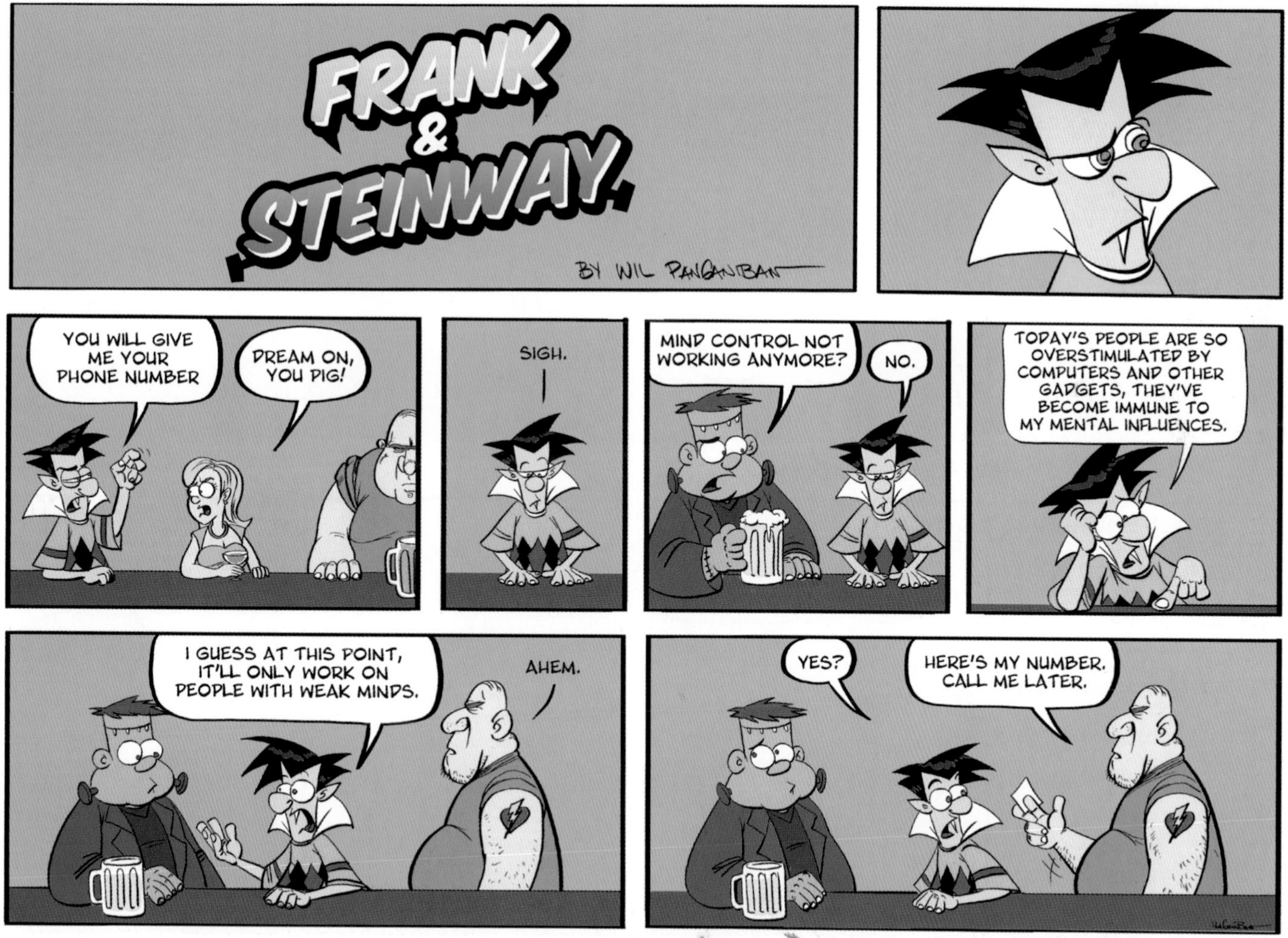
FRANK & STEINWAY
BY WIL PANGANIBAN
YOU WILL GIVE ME YOUR PHONE NUMBER
DREAM ON, YOU PIG!
SIGH.
MIND CONTROL NOT WORKING ANYMORE?
NO.
TODAY'S PEOPLE ARE SO OVERSTIMULATED BY COMPUTERS AND OTHER GADGETS, THEY'VE BECOME IMMUNE TO MY MENTAL INFLUENCES.
I GUESS AT THIS POINT, IT'LL ONLY WORK ON PEOPLE WITH WEAK MINDS.
AHEM.
YES?
HERE'S MY NUMBER. CALL ME LATER.

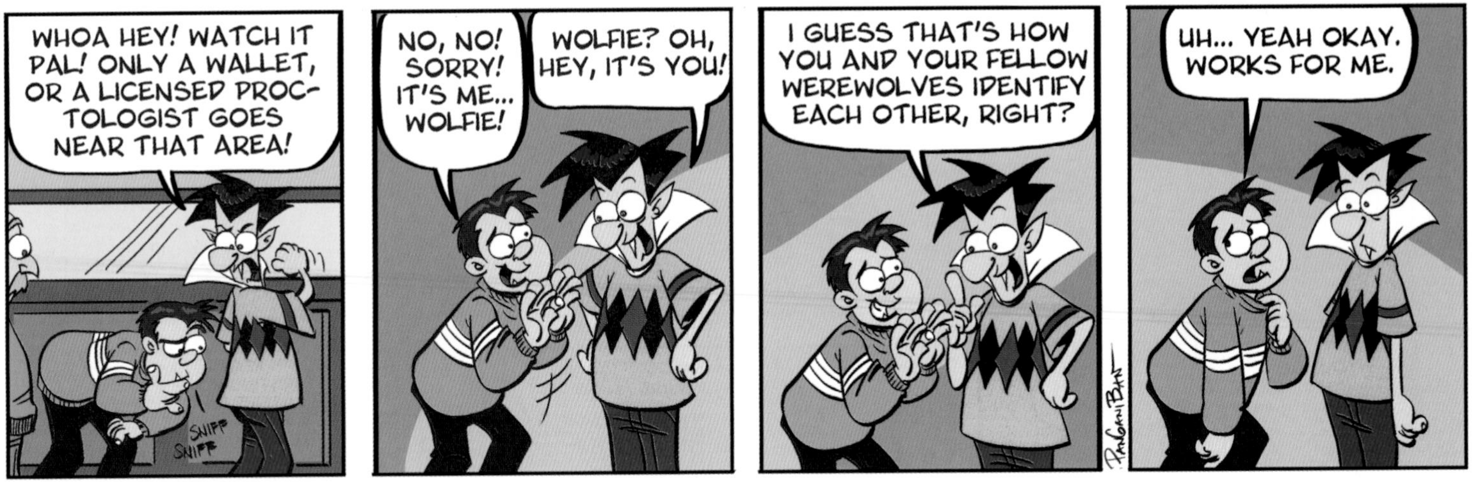
WHOA HEY! WATCH IT PAL! ONLY A WALLET, OR A LICENSED PROCTOLOGIST GOES NEAR THAT AREA!
SNIFF
SNIFF
NO, NO! SORRY! IT'S ME... WOLFIE!
WOLFIE? OH, HEY, IT'S YOU!
I GUESS THAT'S HOW YOU AND YOUR FELLOW WEREWOLVES IDENTIFY EACH OTHER, RIGHT?
UH... YEAH OKAY. WORKS FOR ME.

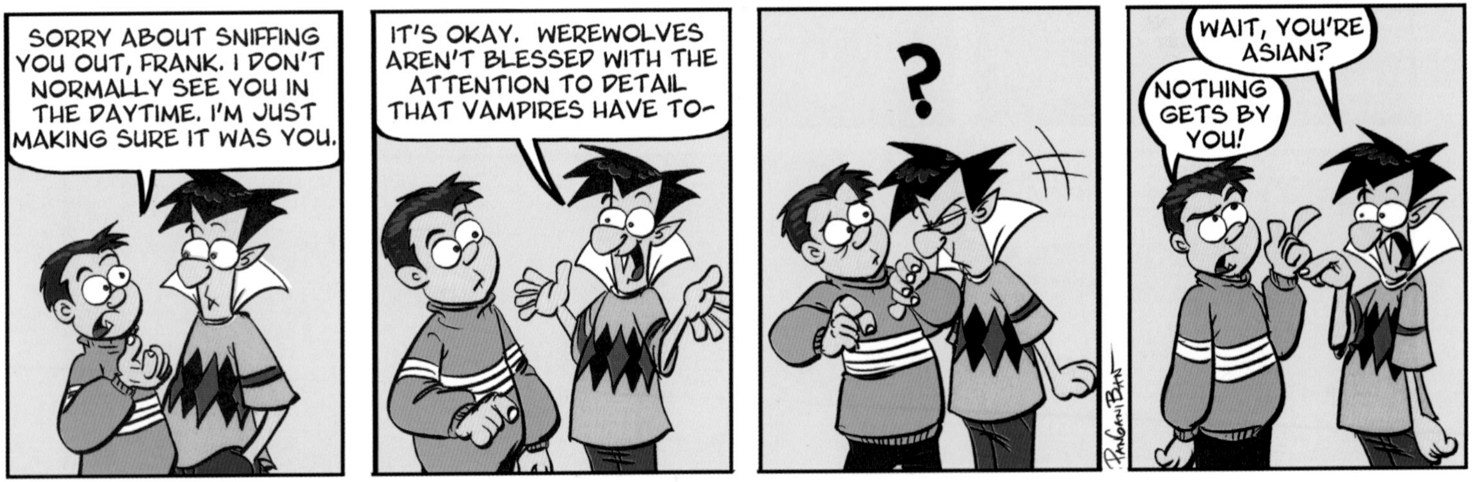
SORRY ABOUT SNIFFING YOU OUT, FRANK. I DON'T NORMALLY SEE YOU IN THE DAYTIME. I'M JUST MAKING SURE IT WAS YOU.
IT'S OKAY. WEREWOLVES AREN'T BLESSED WITH THE ATTENTION TO DETAIL THAT VAMPIRES HAVE TO-
?
WAIT, YOU'RE ASIAN?
NOTHING GETS BY YOU!

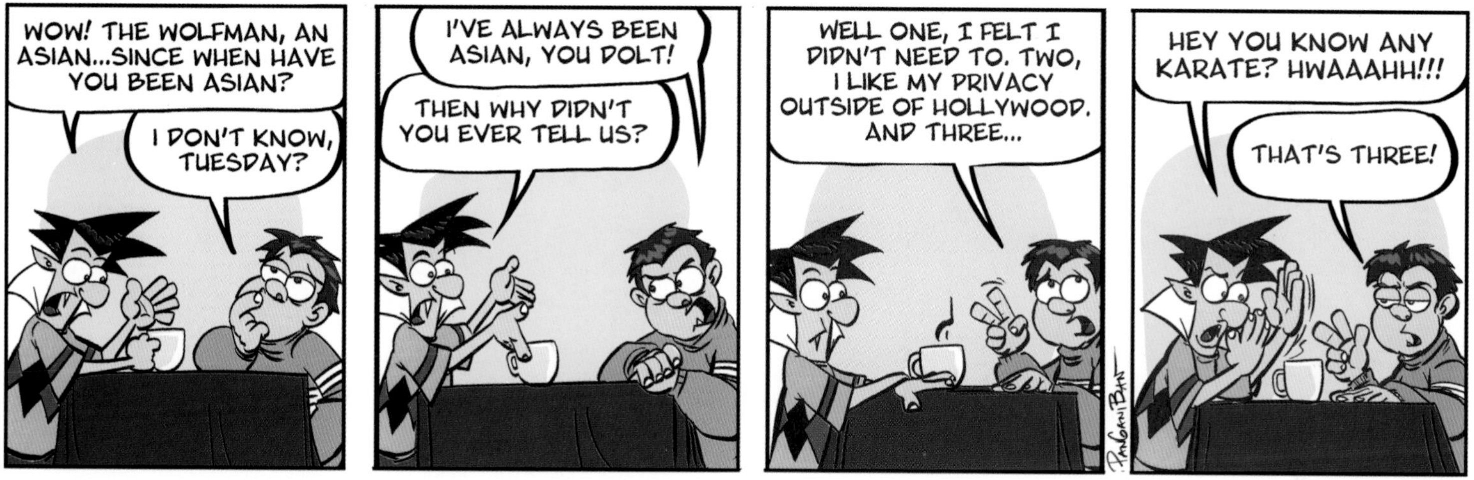
WOW! THE WOLFMAN, AN ASIAN...SINCE WHEN HAVE YOU BEEN ASIAN?
I DON'T KNOW, TUESDAY?
I'VE ALWAYS BEEN ASIAN, YOU DOLT!
THEN WHY DIDN'T YOU EVER TELL US?
WELL ONE, I FELT I DIDN'T NEED TO. TWO, I LIKE MY PRIVACY OUTSIDE OF HOLLYWOOD. AND THREE...
HEY YOU KNOW ANY KARATE? HWAAAHH!!!
THAT'S THREE!

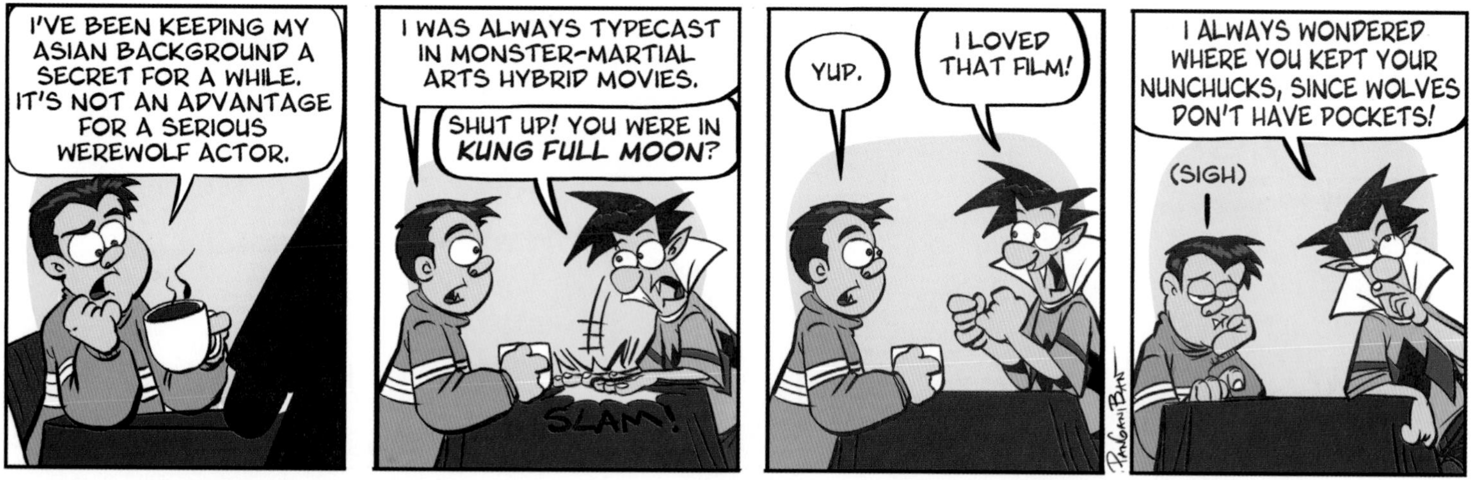
I'VE BEEN KEEPING MY ASIAN BACKGROUND A SECRET FOR A WHILE. IT'S NOT AN ADVANTAGE FOR A SERIOUS WEREWOLF ACTOR.
I WAS ALWAYS TYPECAST IN MONSTER-MARTIAL ARTS HYBRID MOVIES.
SHUT UP! YOU WERE IN *KUNG FULL MOON*?
SLAM!
YUP.
I LOVED THAT FILM!
I ALWAYS WONDERED WHERE YOU KEPT YOUR NUNCHUCKS, SINCE WOLVES DON'T HAVE POCKETS!
(SIGH)

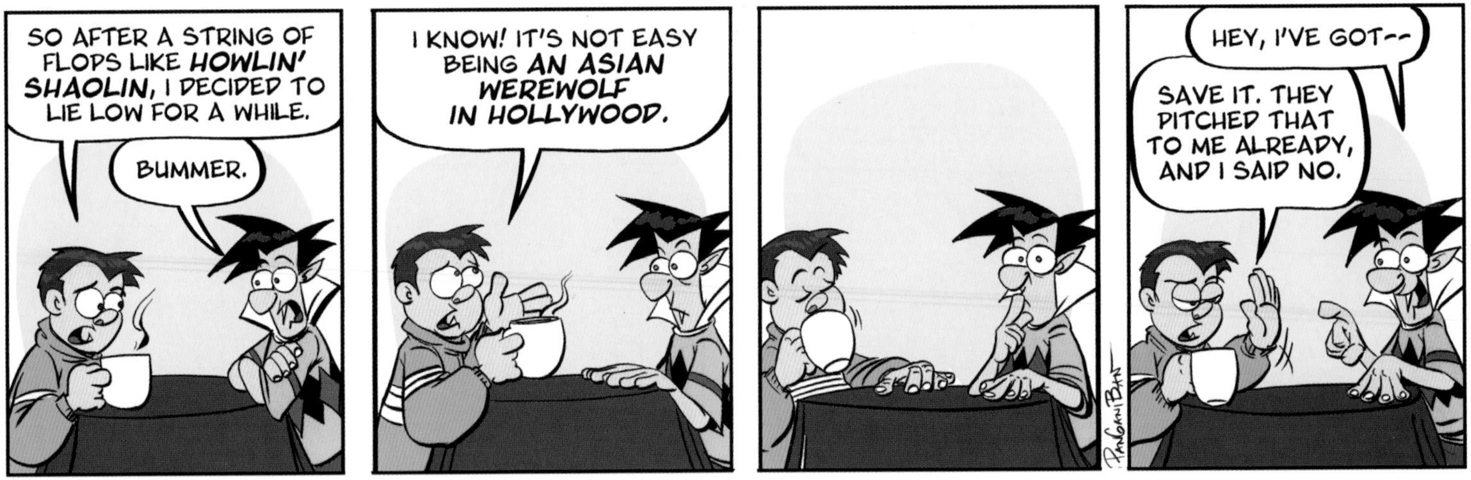
SO AFTER A STRING OF FLOPS LIKE **HOWLIN' SHAOLIN**, I DECIDED TO LIE LOW FOR A WHILE.
BUMMER.
I KNOW! IT'S NOT EASY BEING **AN ASIAN WEREWOLF IN HOLLYWOOD**.
HEY, I'VE GOT--
SAVE IT. THEY PITCHED THAT TO ME ALREADY, AND I SAID NO.

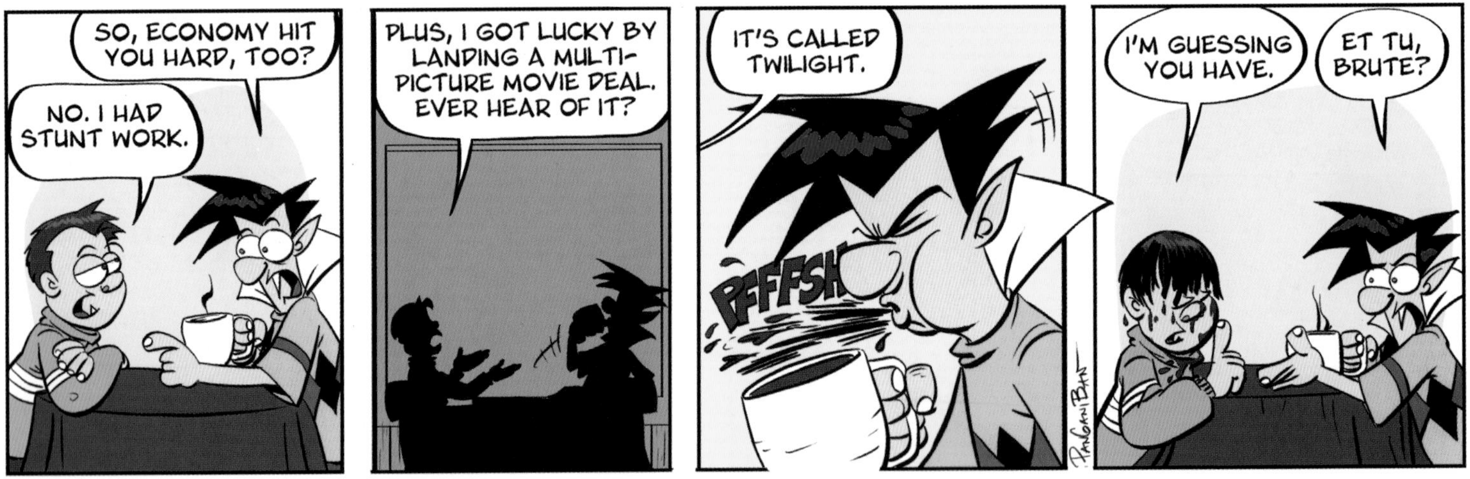
SO, ECONOMY HIT YOU HARD, TOO?
NO. I HAD STUNT WORK.
PLUS, I GOT LUCKY BY LANDING A MULTI-PICTURE MOVIE DEAL. EVER HEAR OF IT?
IT'S CALLED TWILIGHT.
PFFFSH
I'M GUESSING YOU HAVE.
ET TU, BRUTE?

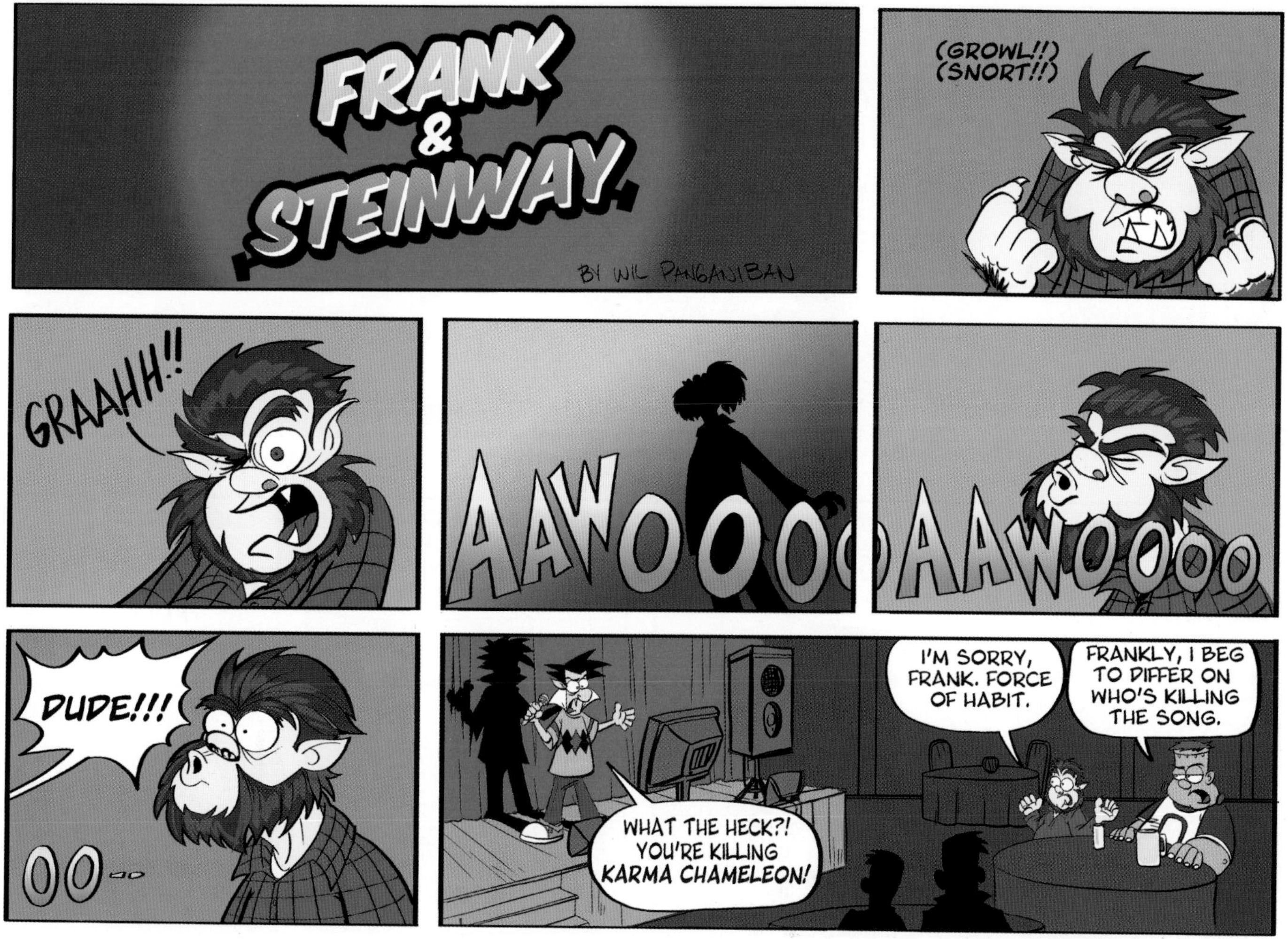
FRANK & STEINWAY
BY WIL PANGANIBAN
(GROWL!!)
(SNORT!!)
GRAAHH!!
AAWOOOO
AAWOOOO
DUDE!!!
OO--
WHAT THE HECK?! YOU'RE KILLING KARMA CHAMELEON!
I'M SORRY, FRANK. FORCE OF HABIT.
FRANKLY, I BEG TO DIFFER ON WHO'S KILLING THE SONG.

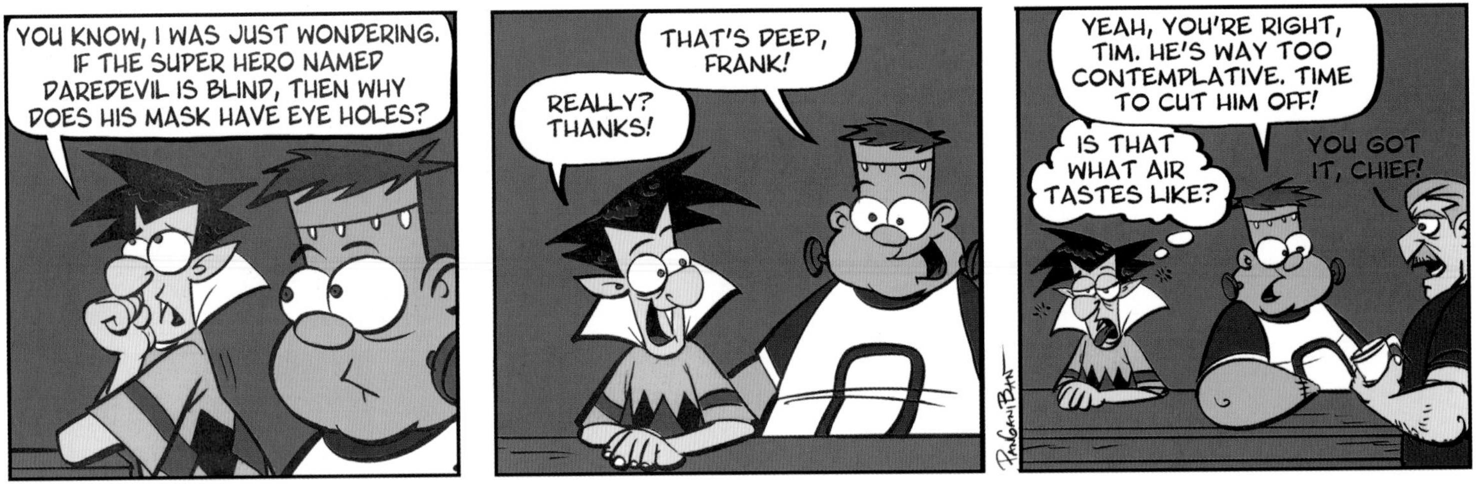
YOU KNOW, I WAS JUST WONDERING. IF THE SUPER HERO NAMED DAREDEVIL IS BLIND, THEN WHY DOES HIS MASK HAVE EYE HOLES?
THAT'S DEEP, FRANK!
REALLY? THANKS!
YEAH, YOU'RE RIGHT, TIM. HE'S WAY TOO CONTEMPLATIVE. TIME TO CUT HIM OFF!
IS THAT WHAT AIR TASTES LIKE?
YOU GOT IT, CHIEF!

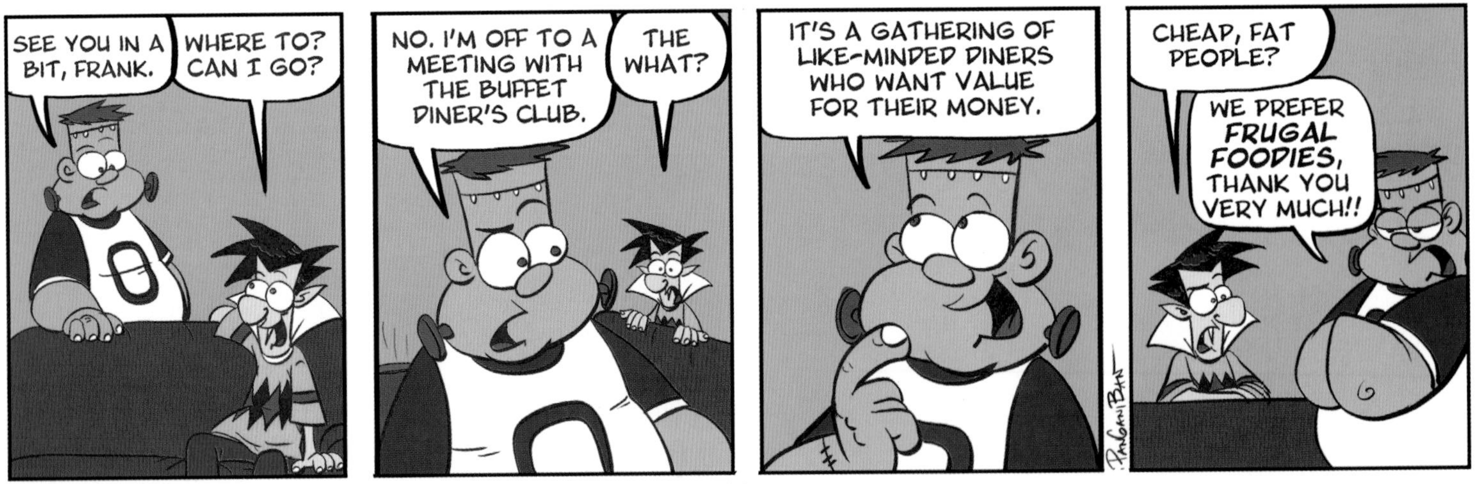
SEE YOU IN A BIT, FRANK.
WHERE TO? CAN I GO?
NO. I'M OFF TO A MEETING WITH THE BUFFET DINER'S CLUB.
THE WHAT?
IT'S A GATHERING OF LIKE-MINDED DINERS WHO WANT VALUE FOR THEIR MONEY.
CHEAP, FAT PEOPLE?
WE PREFER FRUGAL FOODIES, THANK YOU VERY MUCH!!

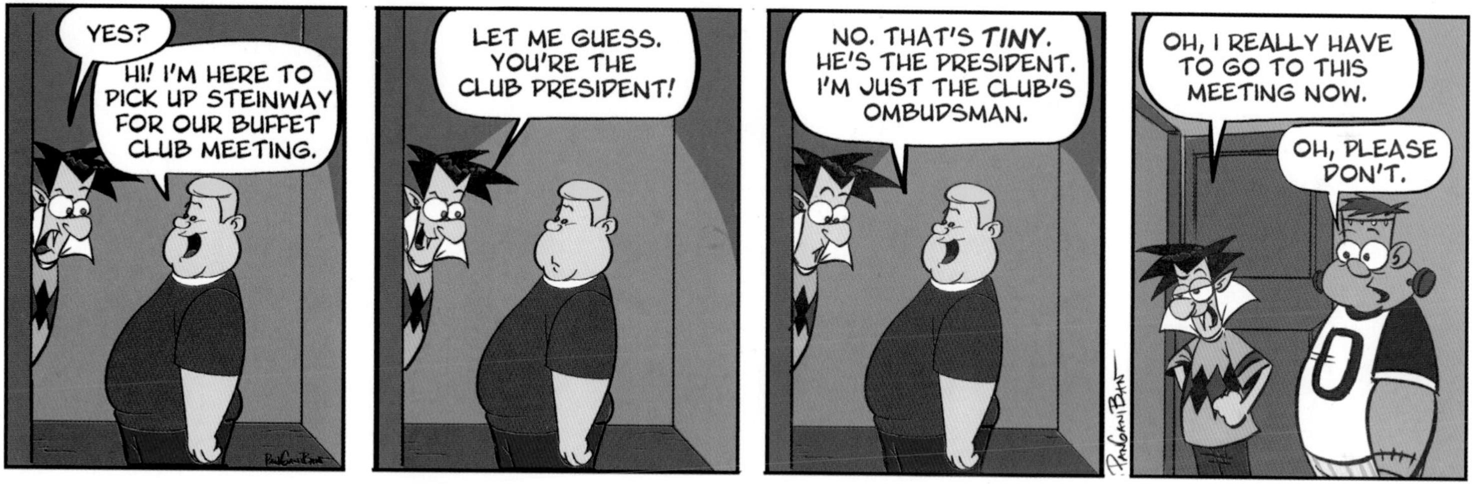
YES?
HI! I'M HERE TO PICK UP STEINWAY FOR OUR BUFFET CLUB MEETING.
LET ME GUESS. YOU'RE THE CLUB PRESIDENT!
NO. THAT'S TINY. HE'S THE PRESIDENT. I'M JUST THE CLUB'S OMBUDSMAN.
OH, I REALLY HAVE TO GO TO THIS MEETING NOW.
OH, PLEASE DON'T.

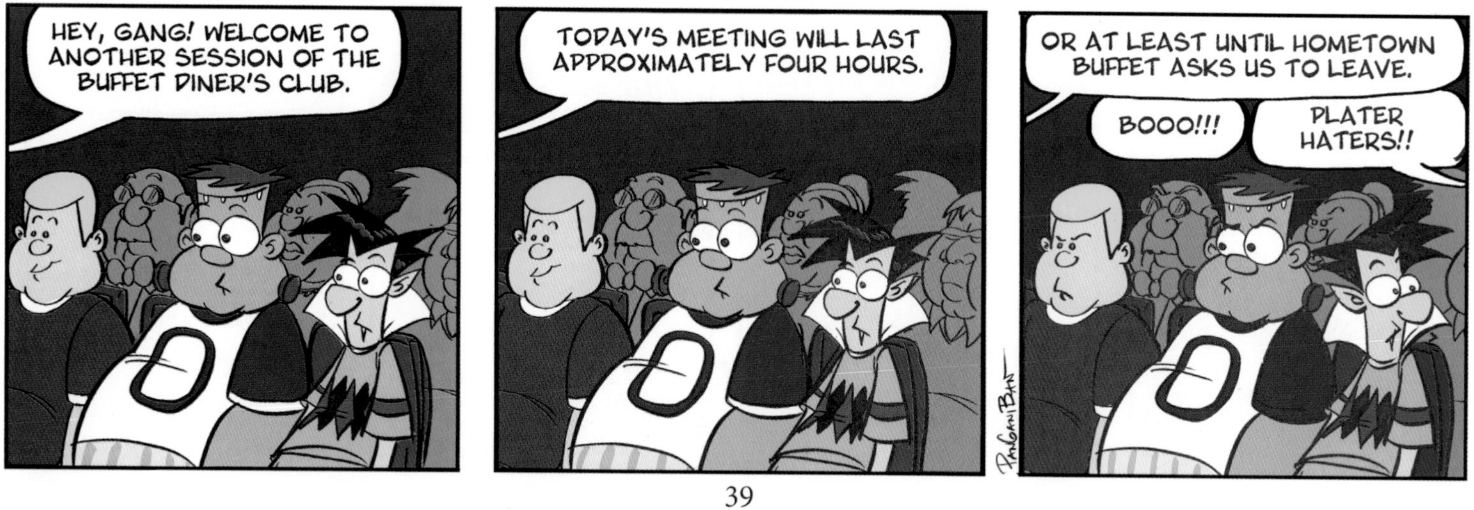
HEY, GANG! WELCOME TO ANOTHER SESSION OF THE BUFFET DINER'S CLUB.
TODAY'S MEETING WILL LAST APPROXIMATELY FOUR HOURS.
OR AT LEAST UNTIL HOMETOWN BUFFET ASKS US TO LEAVE.
BOOO!!!
PLATER HATERS!!

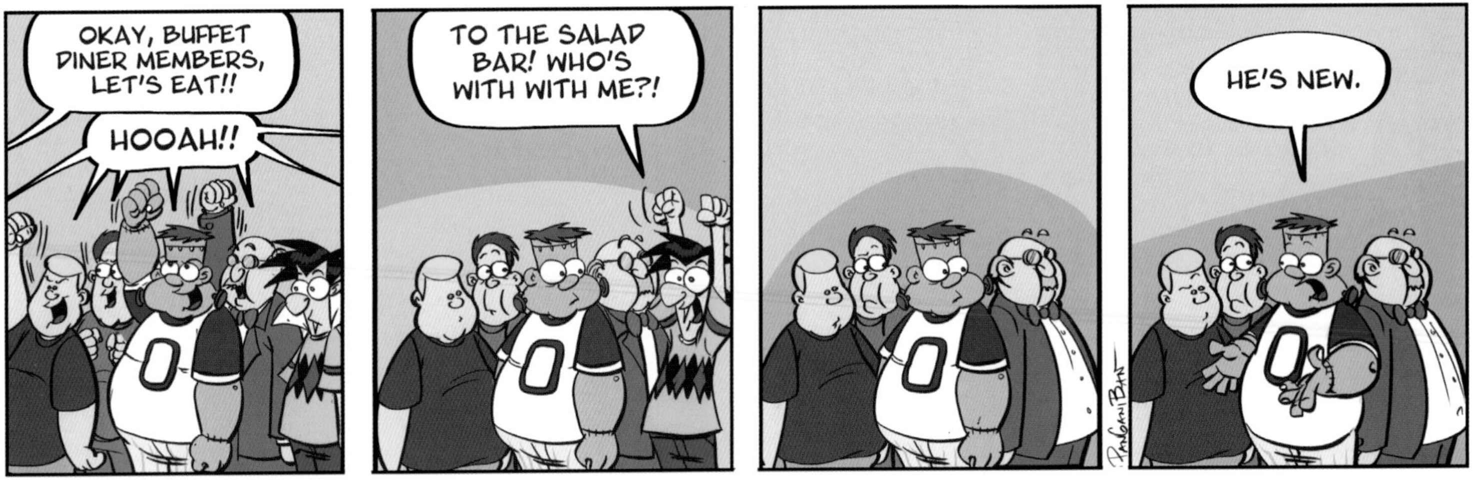
OKAY, BUFFET DINER MEMBERS, LET'S EAT!!
HOOAH!!
TO THE SALAD BAR! WHO'S WITH WITH ME?!
HE'S NEW.

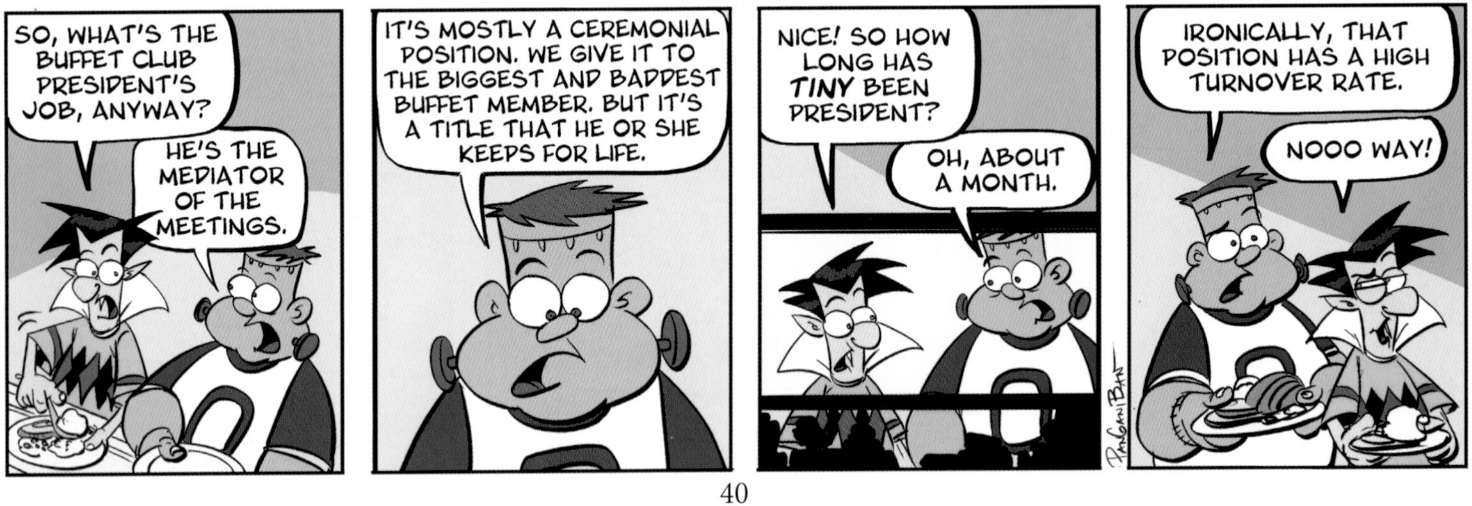
SO, WHAT'S THE BUFFET CLUB PRESIDENT'S JOB, ANYWAY?
HE'S THE MEDIATOR OF THE MEETINGS.
IT'S MOSTLY A CEREMONIAL POSITION. WE GIVE IT TO THE BIGGEST AND BADDEST BUFFET MEMBER. BUT IT'S A TITLE THAT HE OR SHE KEEPS FOR LIFE.
NICE! SO HOW LONG HAS TINY BEEN PRESIDENT?
OH, ABOUT A MONTH.
IRONICALLY, THAT POSITION HAS A HIGH TURNOVER RATE.
NOOO WAY!

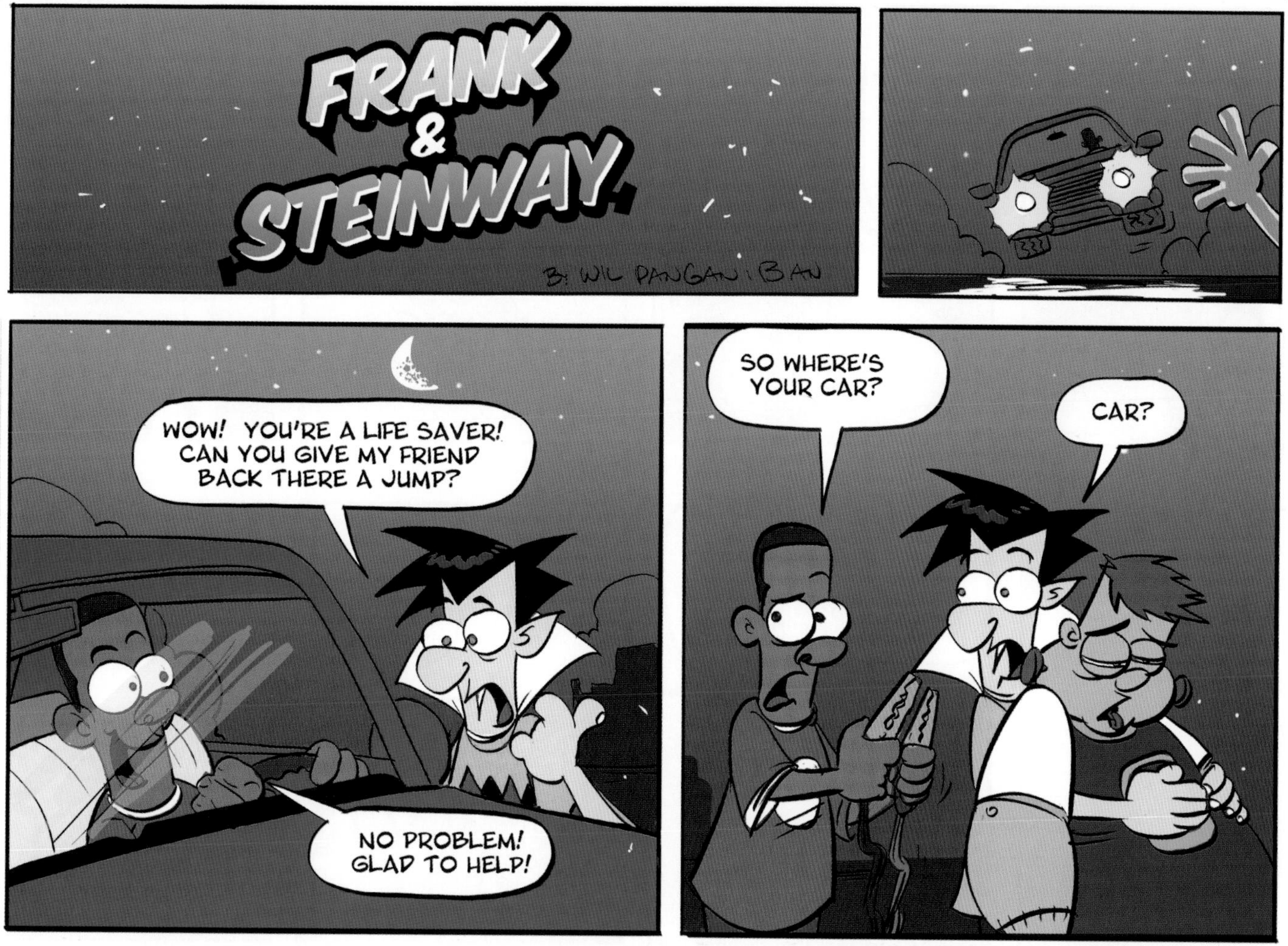
FRANK & STEINWAY
B: WIL PANGANIBAN
WOW! YOU'RE A LIFE SAVER! CAN YOU GIVE MY FRIEND BACK THERE A JUMP?
NO PROBLEM! GLAD TO HELP!
SO WHERE'S YOUR CAR?
CAR?

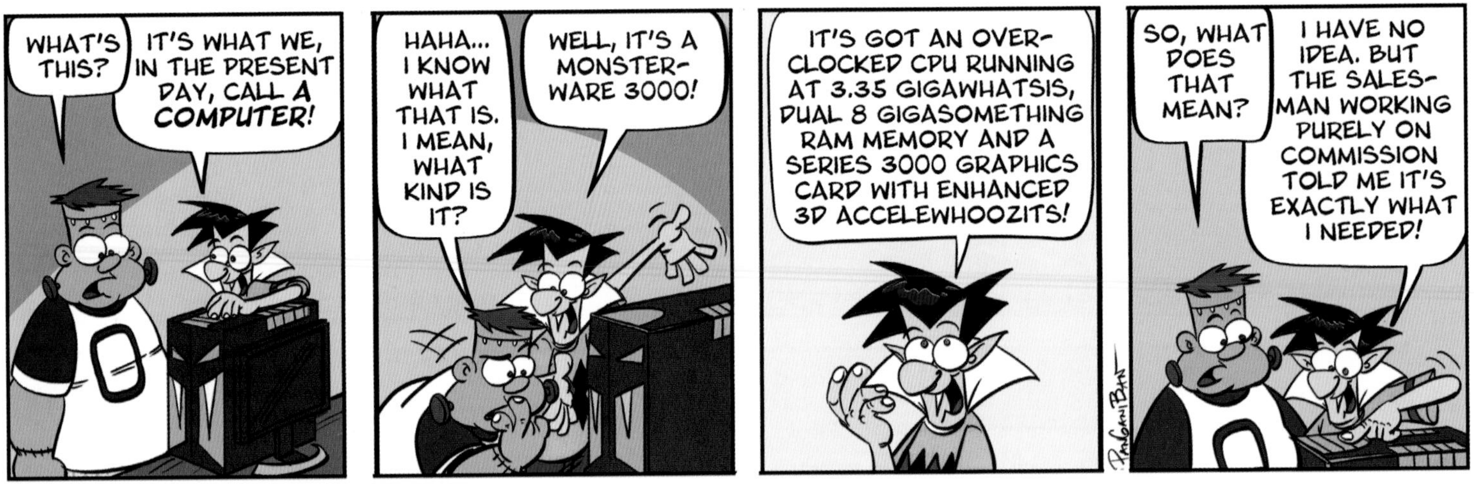
WHAT'S THIS?
IT'S WHAT WE, IN THE PRESENT DAY, CALL A COMPUTER!
HAHA... I KNOW WHAT THAT IS. I MEAN, WHAT KIND IS IT?
WELL, IT'S A MONSTER-WARE 3000!
IT'S GOT AN OVER-CLOCKED CPU RUNNING AT 3.35 GIGAWHATSIS, DUAL 8 GIGASOMETHING RAM MEMORY AND A SERIES 3000 GRAPHICS CARD WITH ENHANCED 3D ACCELEWHOOZITS!
SO, WHAT DOES THAT MEAN?
I HAVE NO IDEA. BUT THE SALES-MAN WORKING PURELY ON COMMISSION TOLD ME IT'S EXACTLY WHAT I NEEDED!

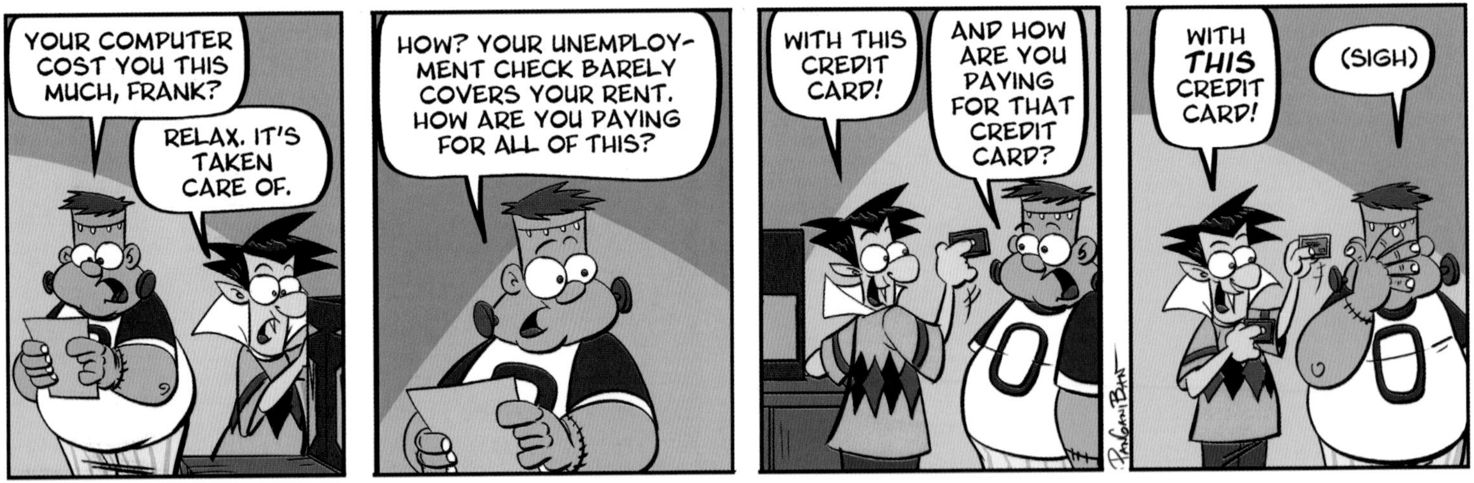
YOUR COMPUTER COST YOU THIS MUCH, FRANK?
RELAX. IT'S TAKEN CARE OF.
HOW? YOUR UNEMPLOY-MENT CHECK BARELY COVERS YOUR RENT. HOW ARE YOU PAYING FOR ALL OF THIS?
WITH THIS CREDIT CARD!
AND HOW ARE YOU PAYING FOR THAT CREDIT CARD?
WITH THIS CREDIT CARD!
(SIGH)

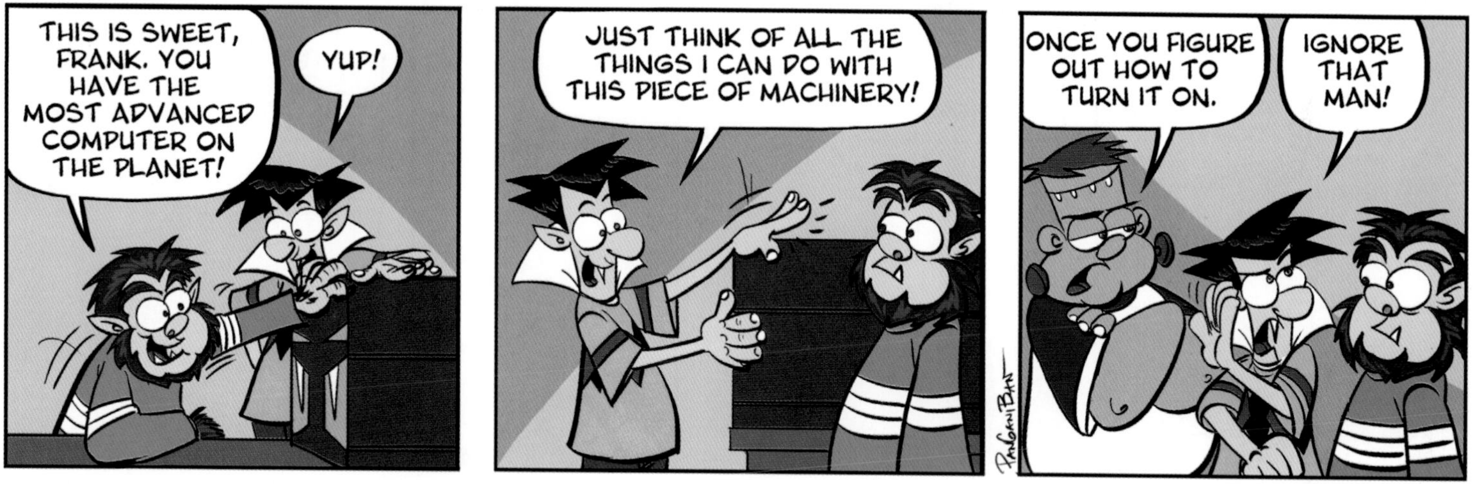
THIS IS SWEET, FRANK. YOU HAVE THE MOST ADVANCED COMPUTER ON THE PLANET!
YUP!
JUST THINK OF ALL THE THINGS I CAN DO WITH THIS PIECE OF MACHINERY!
ONCE YOU FIGURE OUT HOW TO TURN IT ON.
IGNORE THAT MAN!

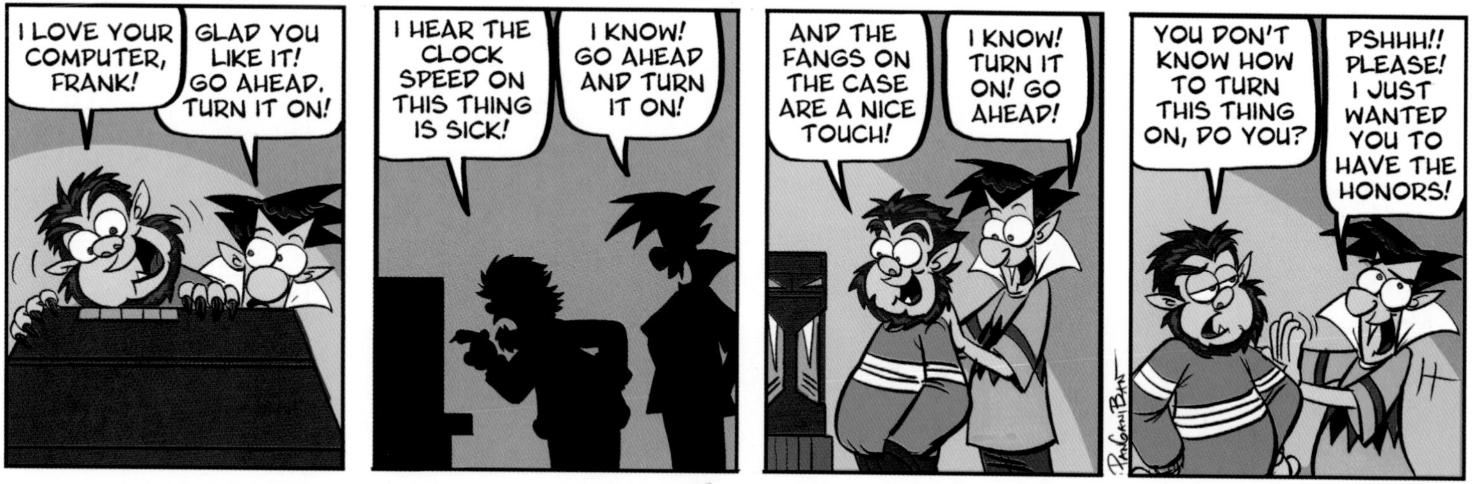
I LOVE YOUR COMPUTER, FRANK!
GLAD YOU LIKE IT! GO AHEAD. TURN IT ON!
I HEAR THE CLOCK SPEED ON THIS THING IS SICK!
I KNOW! GO AHEAD AND TURN IT ON!
AND THE FANGS ON THE CASE ARE A NICE TOUCH!
I KNOW! TURN IT ON! GO AHEAD!
YOU DON'T KNOW HOW TO TURN THIS THING ON, DO YOU?
PSHHH!! PLEASE! I JUST WANTED YOU TO HAVE THE HONORS!

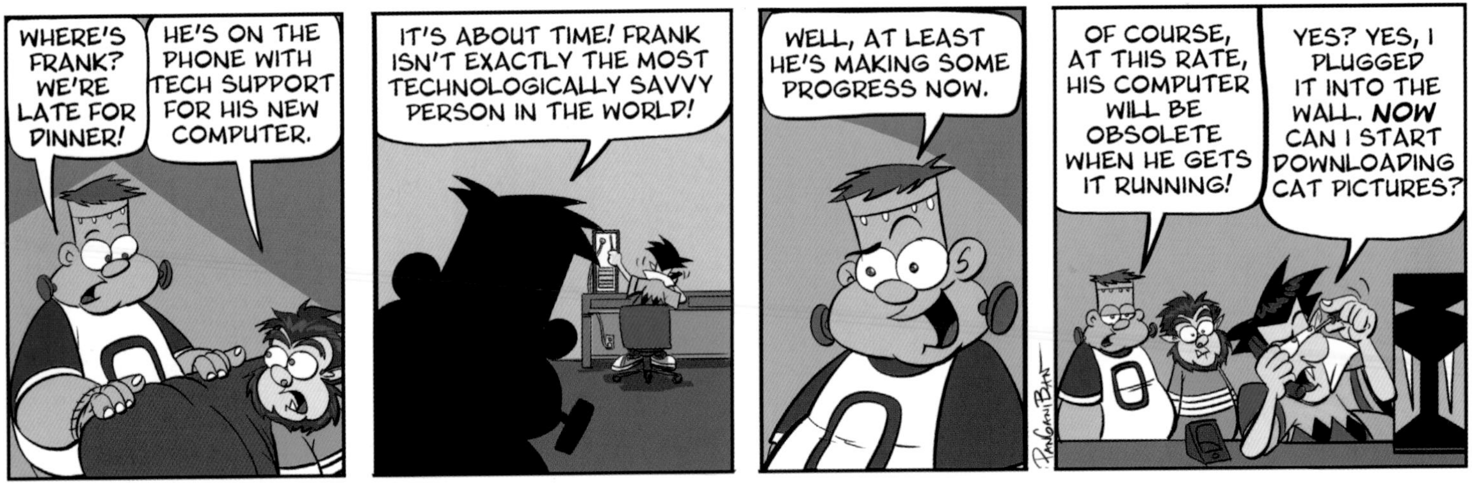
WHERE'S FRANK? WE'RE LATE FOR DINNER!
HE'S ON THE PHONE WITH TECH SUPPORT FOR HIS NEW COMPUTER.
IT'S ABOUT TIME! FRANK ISN'T EXACTLY THE MOST TECHNOLOGICALLY SAVVY PERSON IN THE WORLD!
WELL, AT LEAST HE'S MAKING SOME PROGRESS NOW.
OF COURSE, AT THIS RATE, HIS COMPUTER WILL BE OBSOLETE WHEN HE GETS IT RUNNING!
YES? YES, I PLUGGED IT INTO THE WALL. **NOW** CAN I START DOWNLOADING CAT PICTURES?

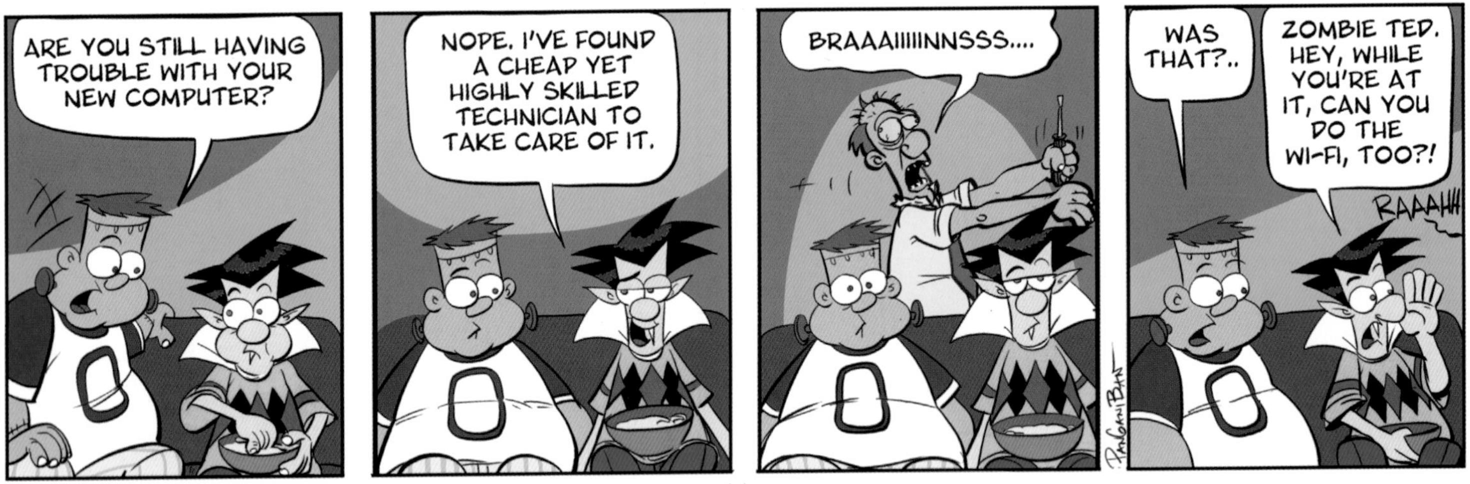
ARE YOU STILL HAVING TROUBLE WITH YOUR NEW COMPUTER?
NOPE. I'VE FOUND A CHEAP YET HIGHLY SKILLED TECHNICIAN TO TAKE CARE OF IT.
BRAAAIIIIINNSSS....
WAS THAT?..
ZOMBIE TED. HEY, WHILE YOU'RE AT IT, CAN YOU DO THE WI-FI, TOO?!
RAAAHH

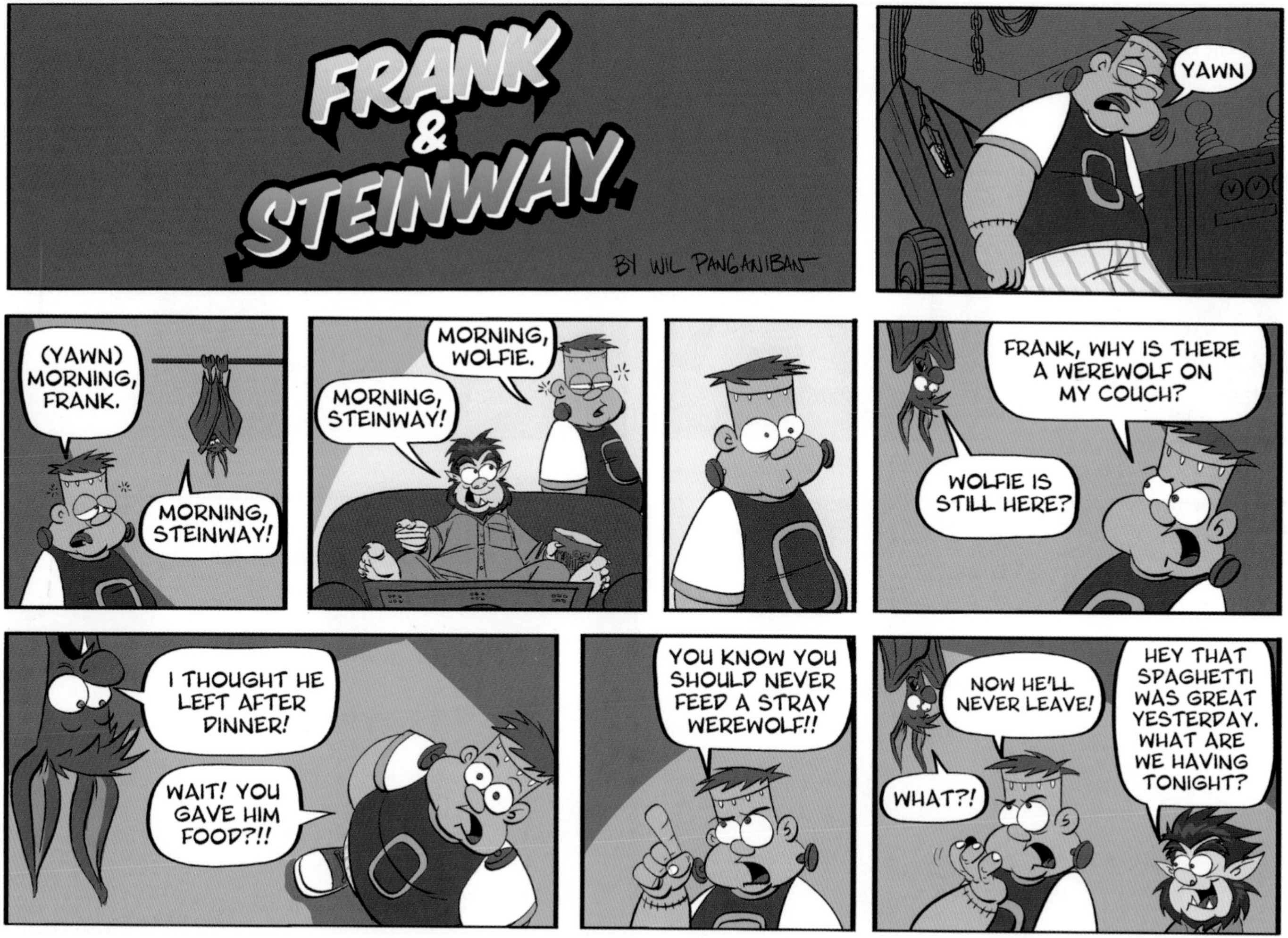
FRANK & STEINWAY
BY WIL PANGANIBAN
YAWN
(YAWN) MORNING, FRANK.
MORNING, STEINWAY!
MORNING, STEINWAY!
MORNING, WOLFIE.
FRANK, WHY IS THERE A WEREWOLF ON MY COUCH?
WOLFIE IS STILL HERE?
I THOUGHT HE LEFT AFTER DINNER!
WAIT! YOU GAVE HIM FOOD?!!
YOU KNOW YOU SHOULD NEVER FEED A STRAY WEREWOLF!!
NOW HE'LL NEVER LEAVE!
WHAT?!
HEY THAT SPAGHETTI WAS GREAT YESTERDAY. WHAT ARE WE HAVING TONIGHT?

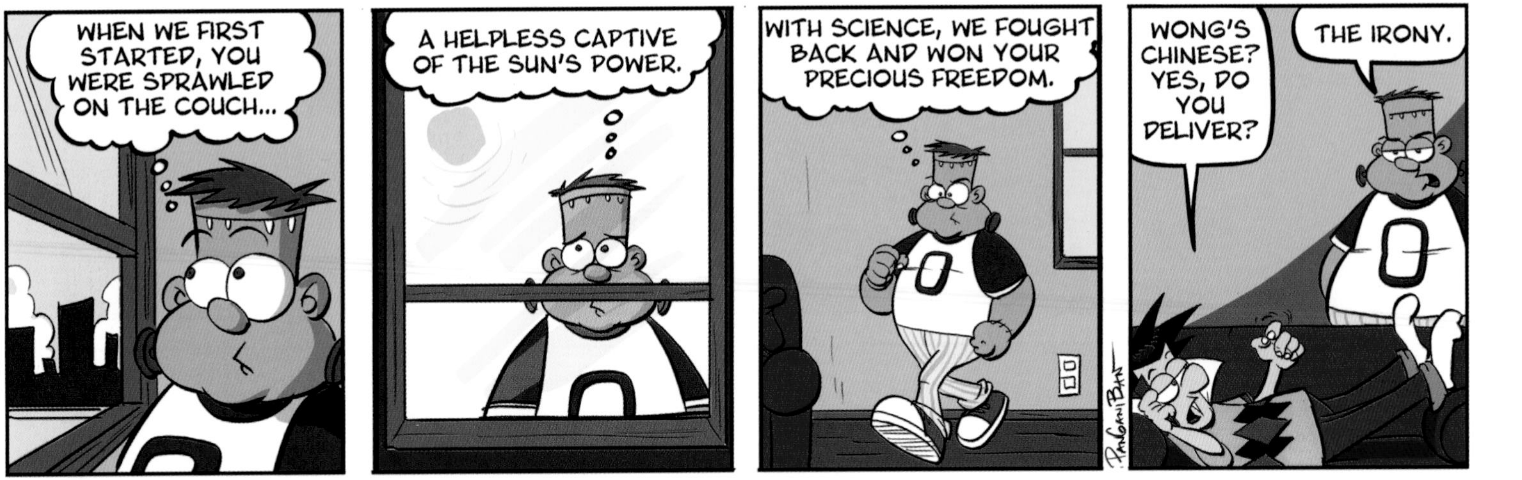
WHEN WE FIRST STARTED, YOU WERE SPRAWLED ON THE COUCH...
A HELPLESS CAPTIVE OF THE SUN'S POWER.
WITH SCIENCE, WE FOUGHT BACK AND WON YOUR PRECIOUS FREEDOM.
WONG'S CHINESE? YES, DO YOU DELIVER?
THE IRONY.

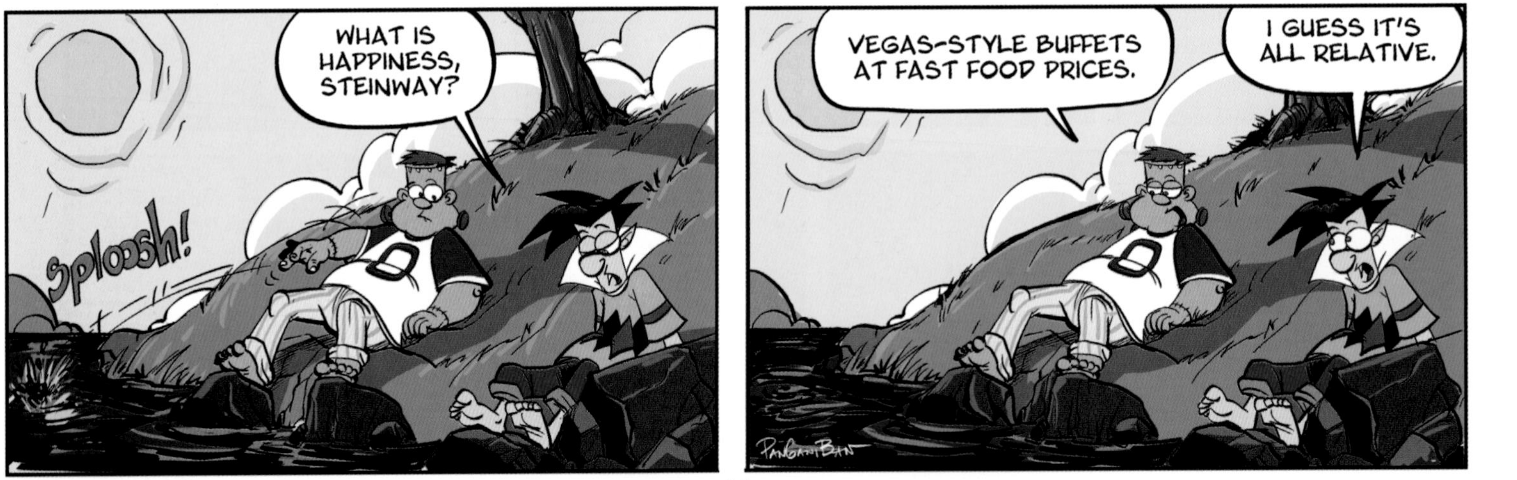
WHAT IS HAPPINESS, STEINWAY?
Sploosh!
VEGAS-STYLE BUFFETS AT FAST FOOD PRICES.
I GUESS IT'S ALL RELATIVE.

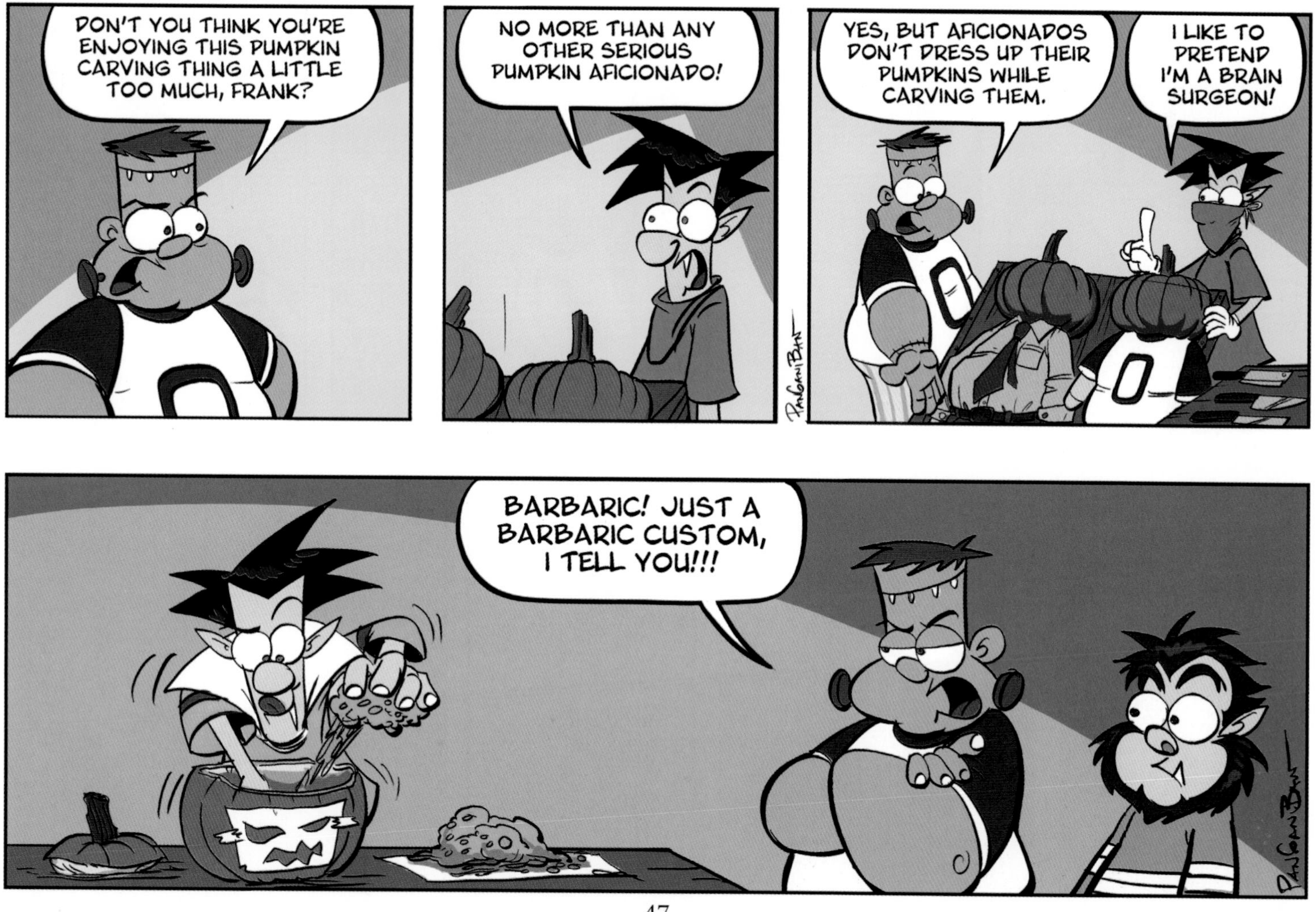
DON'T YOU THINK YOU'RE ENJOYING THIS PUMPKIN CARVING THING A LITTLE TOO MUCH, FRANK?
NO MORE THAN ANY OTHER SERIOUS PUMPKIN AFICIONADO!
YES, BUT AFICIONADOS DON'T DRESS UP THEIR PUMPKINS WHILE CARVING THEM.
I LIKE TO PRETEND I'M A BRAIN SURGEON!
BARBARIC! JUST A BARBARIC CUSTOM, I TELL YOU!!!

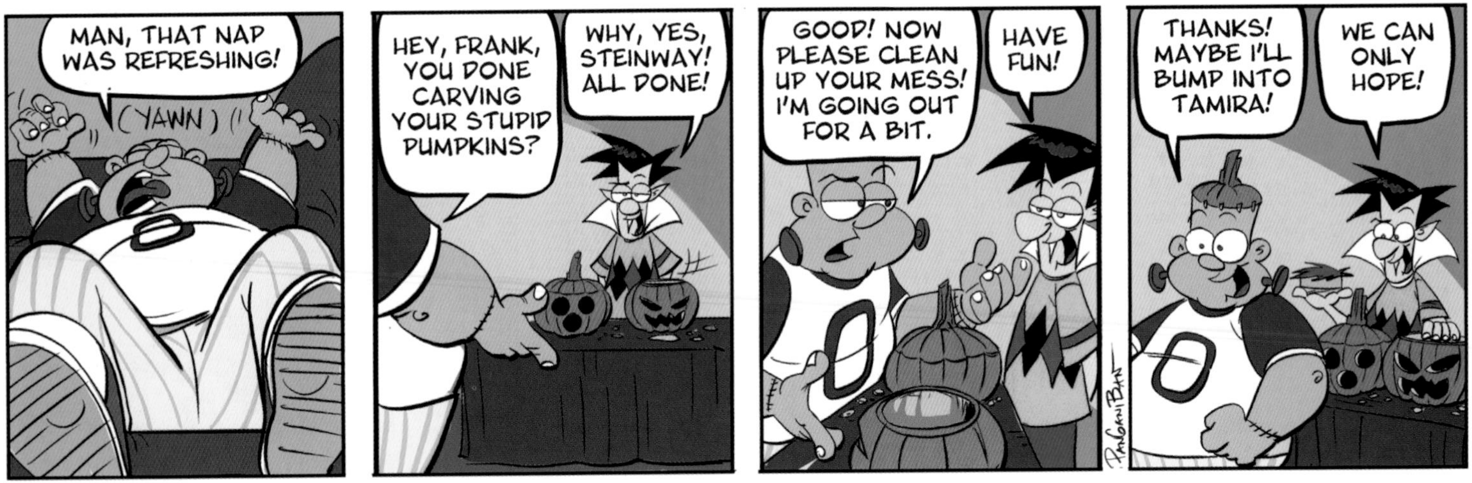
MAN, THAT NAP WAS REFRESHING!
(YAWN)
HEY, FRANK, YOU DONE CARVING YOUR STUPID PUMPKINS?
WHY, YES, STEINWAY! ALL DONE!
GOOD! NOW PLEASE CLEAN UP YOUR MESS! I'M GOING OUT FOR A BIT.
HAVE FUN!
THANKS! MAYBE I'LL BUMP INTO TAMIRA!
WE CAN ONLY HOPE!

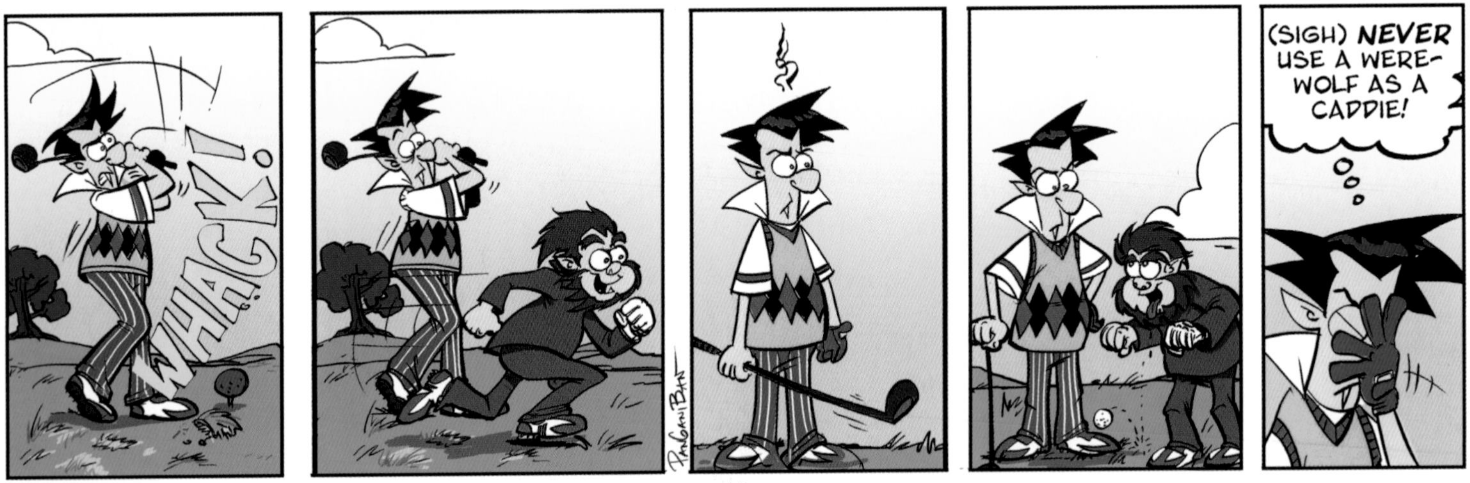
WHACK!
(SIGH) **NEVER** USE A WERE-WOLF AS A CADDIE!

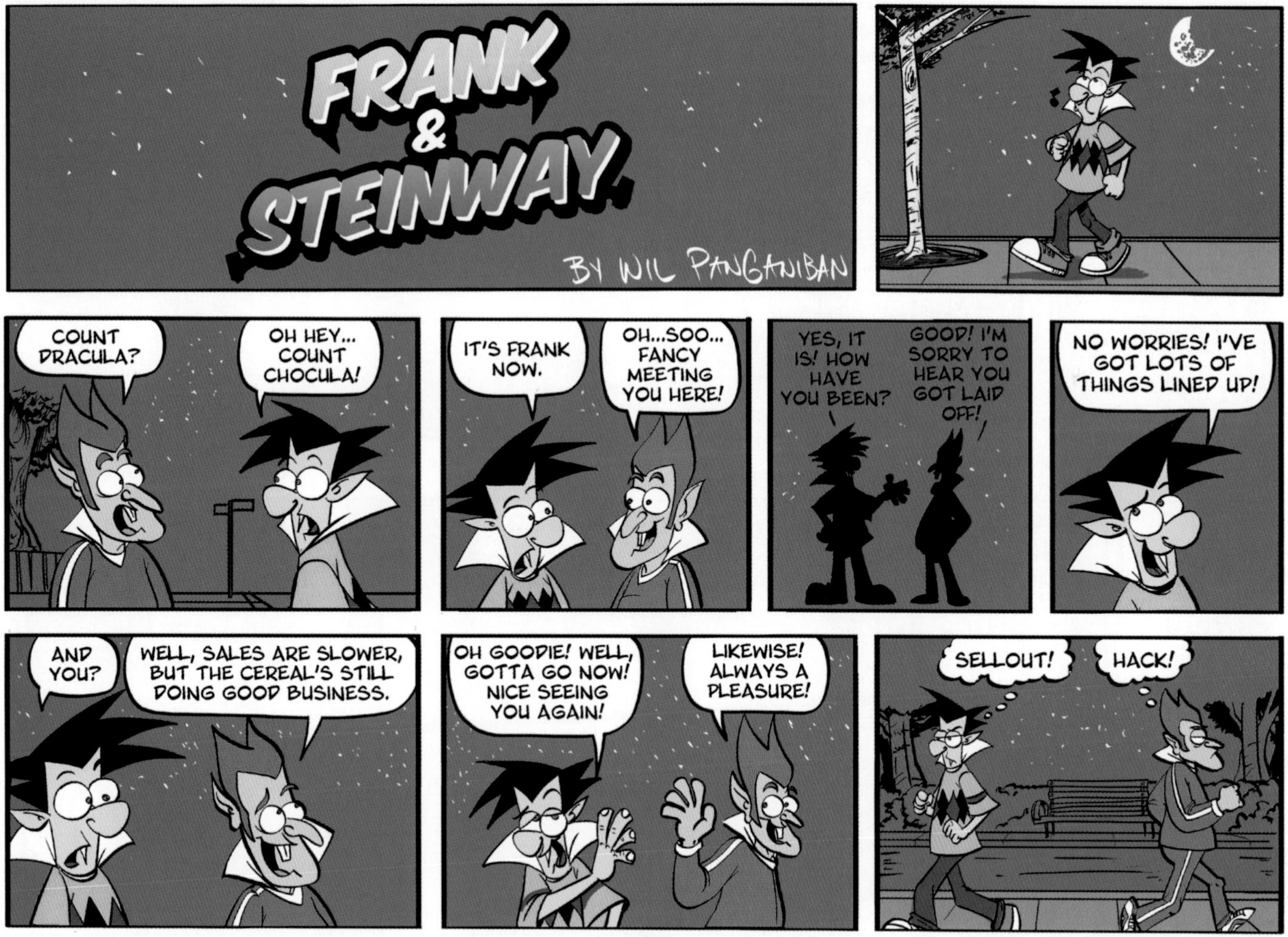
FRANK & STEINWAY
BY WIL PANGANIBAN
COUNT DRACULA?
OH HEY... COUNT CHOCULA!
IT'S FRANK NOW.
OH...SOO... FANCY MEETING YOU HERE!
YES, IT IS! HOW HAVE YOU BEEN?
GOOD! I'M SORRY TO HEAR YOU GOT LAID OFF!
NO WORRIES! I'VE GOT LOTS OF THINGS LINED UP!
AND YOU?
WELL, SALES ARE SLOWER, BUT THE CEREAL'S STILL DOING GOOD BUSINESS.
OH GOODIE! WELL, GOTTA GO NOW! NICE SEEING YOU AGAIN!
LIKEWISE! ALWAYS A PLEASURE!
SELLOUT!
HACK!

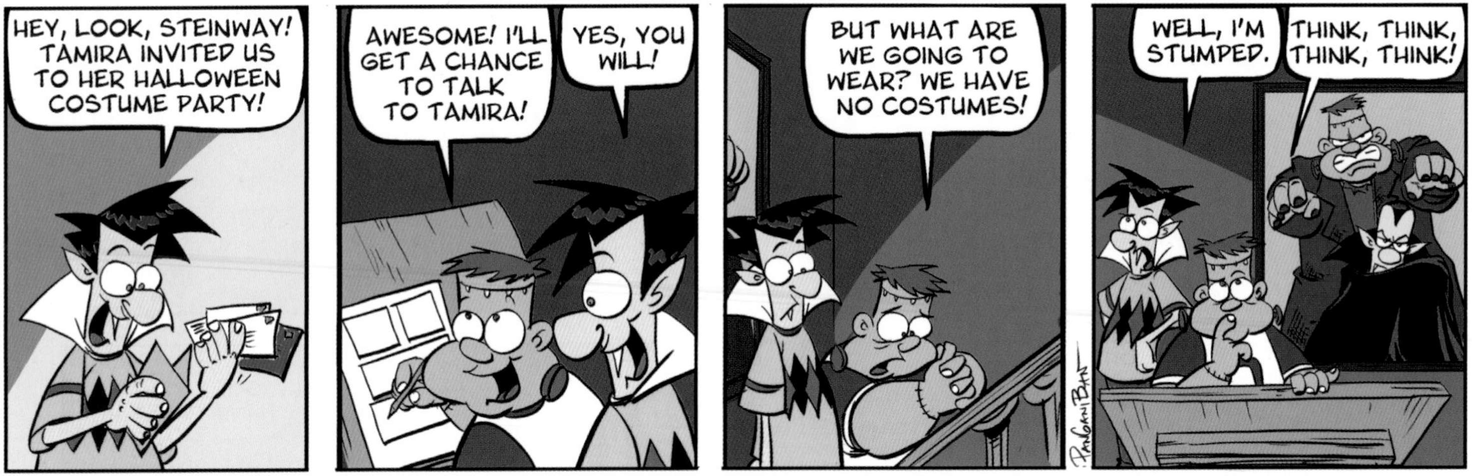
HEY, LOOK, STEINWAY! TAMIRA INVITED US TO HER HALLOWEEN COSTUME PARTY!
AWESOME! I'LL GET A CHANCE TO TALK TO TAMIRA!
YES, YOU WILL!
BUT WHAT ARE WE GOING TO WEAR? WE HAVE NO COSTUMES!
WELL, I'M STUMPED.
THINK, THINK, THINK, THINK!
PANGANIBAN

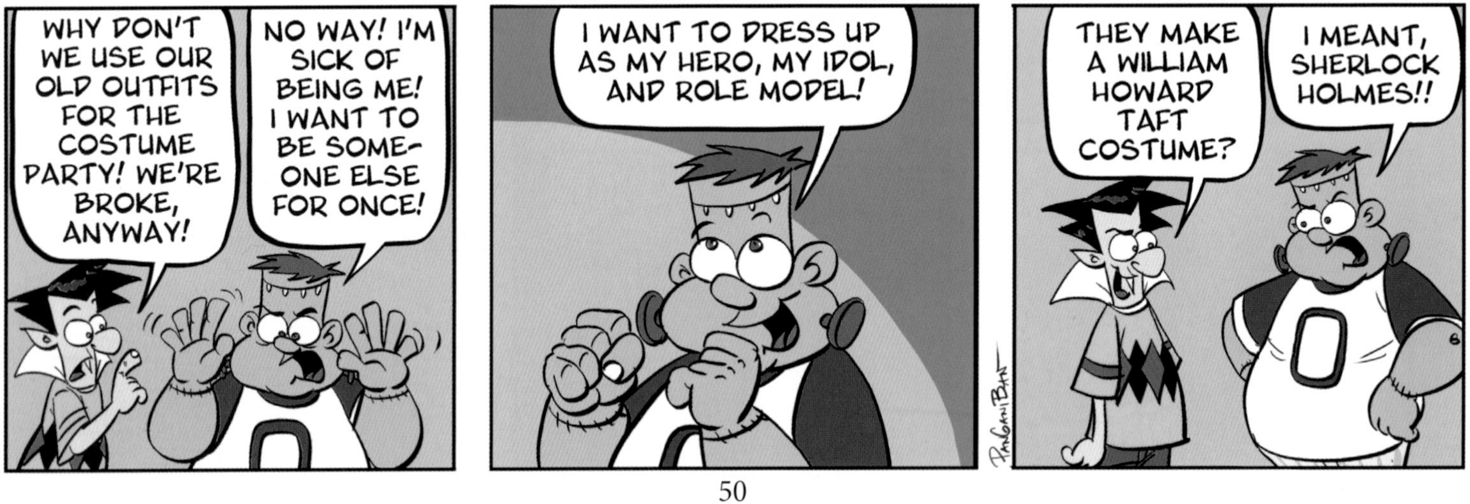
WHY DON'T WE USE OUR OLD OUTFITS FOR THE COSTUME PARTY! WE'RE BROKE, ANYWAY!
NO WAY! I'M SICK OF BEING ME! I WANT TO BE SOME-ONE ELSE FOR ONCE!
I WANT TO DRESS UP AS MY HERO, MY IDOL, AND ROLE MODEL!
PANGANIBAN
THEY MAKE A WILLIAM HOWARD TAFT COSTUME?
I MEANT, SHERLOCK HOLMES!!

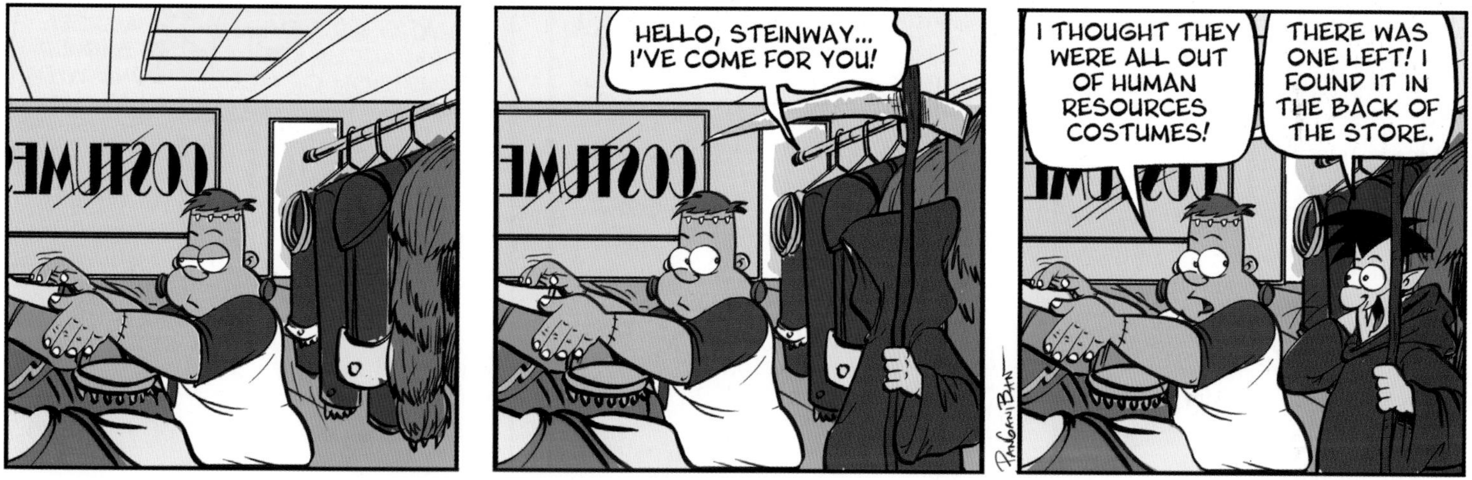
HELLO, STEINWAY... I'VE COME FOR YOU!
I THOUGHT THEY WERE ALL OUT OF HUMAN RESOURCES COSTUMES!
THERE WAS ONE LEFT! I FOUND IT IN THE BACK OF THE STORE.

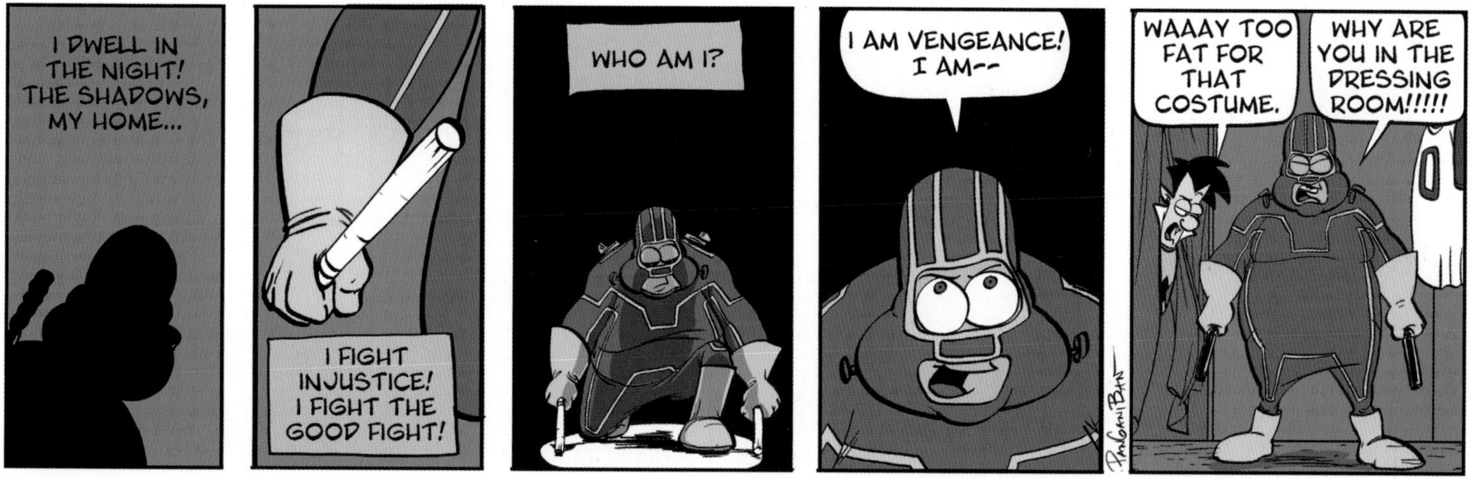
I DWELL IN THE NIGHT! THE SHADOWS, MY HOME...
I FIGHT INJUSTICE! I FIGHT THE GOOD FIGHT!
WHO AM I?
I AM VENGEANCE! I AM--
WAAAY TOO FAT FOR THAT COSTUME.
WHY ARE YOU IN THE DRESSING ROOM!!!!!

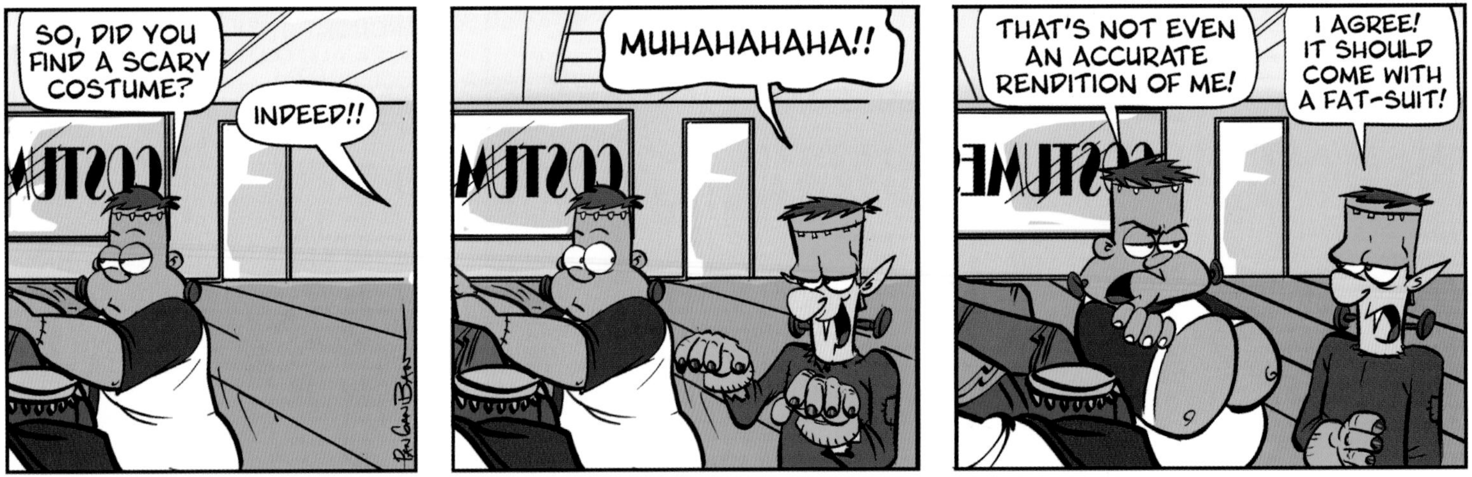
SO, DID YOU FIND A SCARY COSTUME?
INDEED!!
MUHAHAHAHA!!
THAT'S NOT EVEN AN ACCURATE RENDITION OF ME!
I AGREE! IT SHOULD COME WITH A FAT-SUIT!

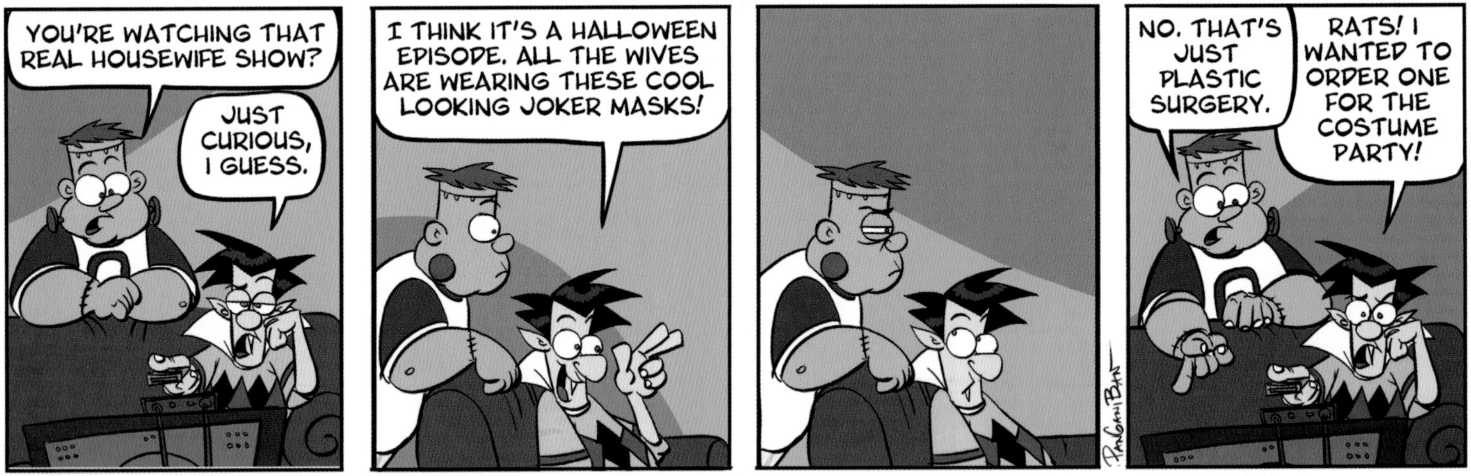
YOU'RE WATCHING THAT REAL HOUSEWIFE SHOW?
JUST CURIOUS, I GUESS.
I THINK IT'S A HALLOWEEN EPISODE. ALL THE WIVES ARE WEARING THESE COOL LOOKING JOKER MASKS!
NO. THAT'S JUST PLASTIC SURGERY.
RATS! I WANTED TO ORDER ONE FOR THE COSTUME PARTY!

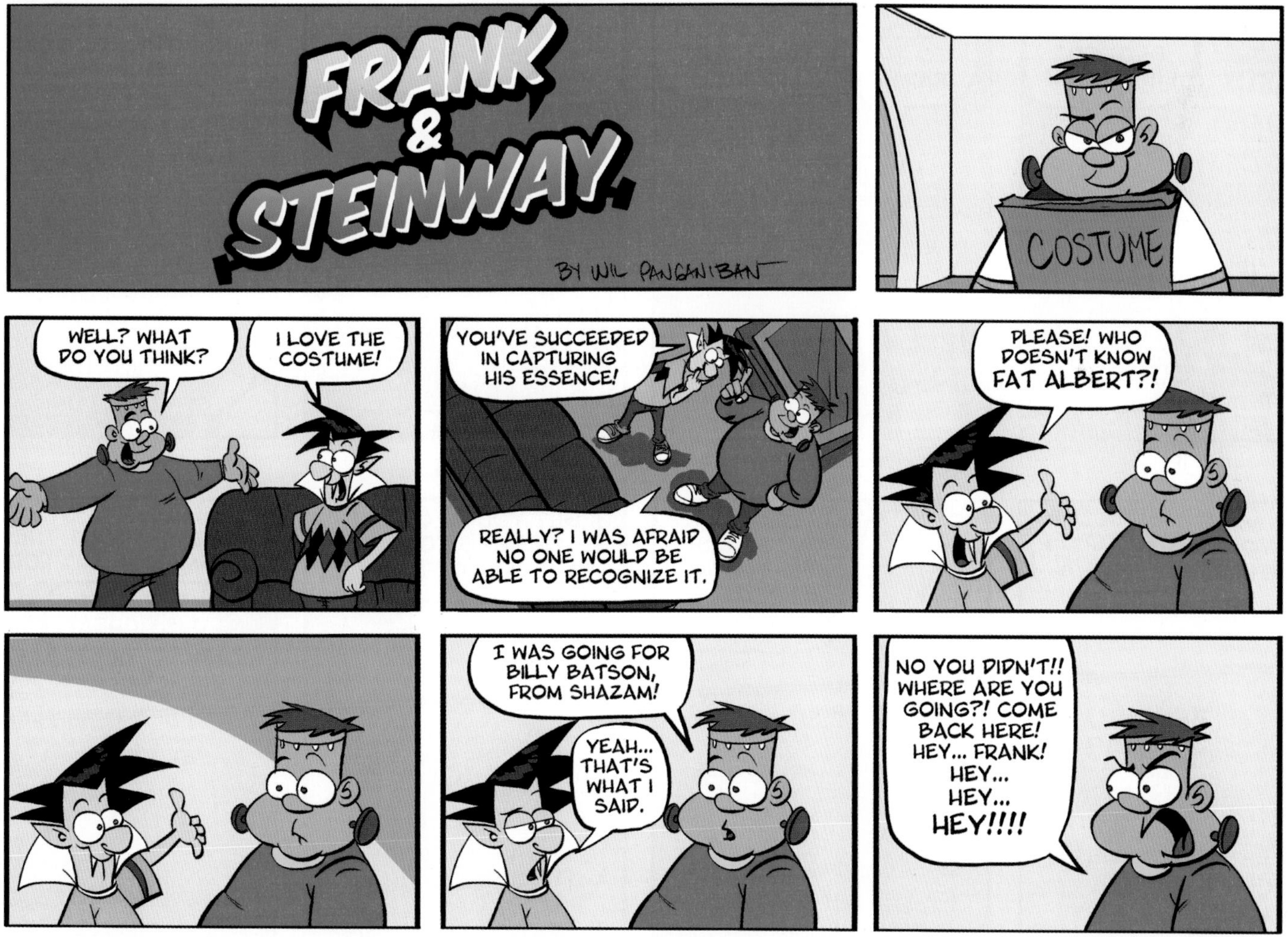
FRANK & STEINWAY
BY WIL PANGANIBAN
COSTUME
WELL? WHAT DO YOU THINK?
I LOVE THE COSTUME!
YOU'VE SUCCEEDED IN CAPTURING HIS ESSENCE!
REALLY? I WAS AFRAID NO ONE WOULD BE ABLE TO RECOGNIZE IT.
PLEASE! WHO DOESN'T KNOW FAT ALBERT?!
I WAS GOING FOR BILLY BATSON, FROM SHAZAM!
YEAH... THAT'S WHAT I SAID.
NO YOU DIDN'T!! WHERE ARE YOU GOING?! COME BACK HERE! HEY... FRANK! HEY... HEY... HEY!!!!

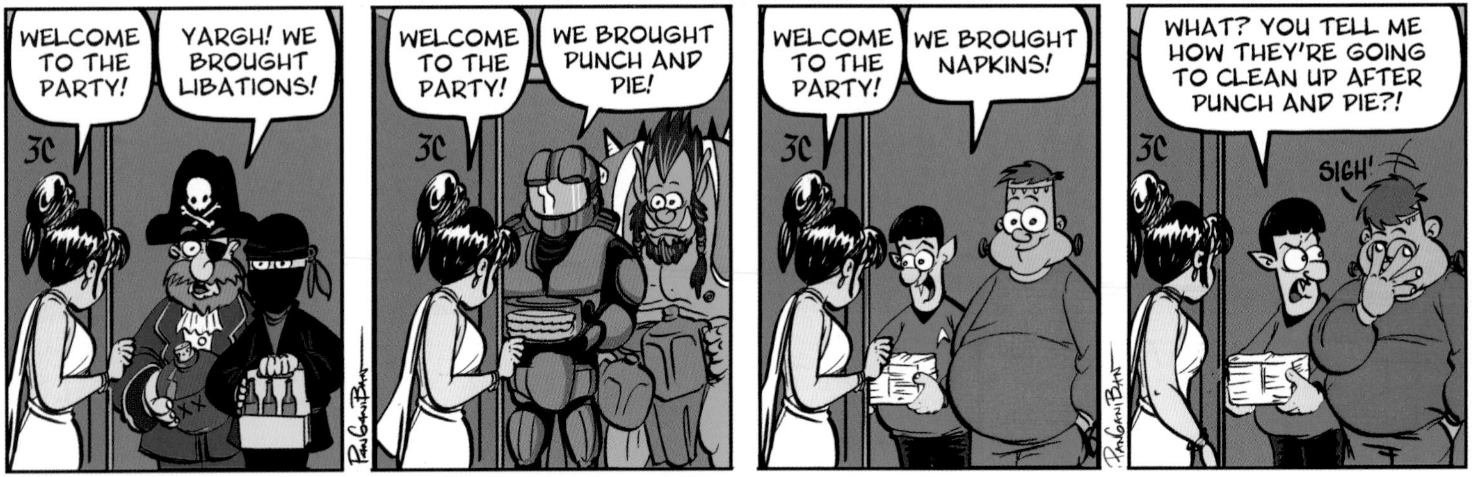
WELCOME TO THE PARTY!
YARGH! WE BROUGHT LIBATIONS!
WELCOME TO THE PARTY!
WE BROUGHT PUNCH AND PIE!
WELCOME TO THE PARTY!
WE BROUGHT NAPKINS!
WHAT? YOU TELL ME HOW THEY'RE GOING TO CLEAN UP AFTER PUNCH AND PIE?!
SIGH!

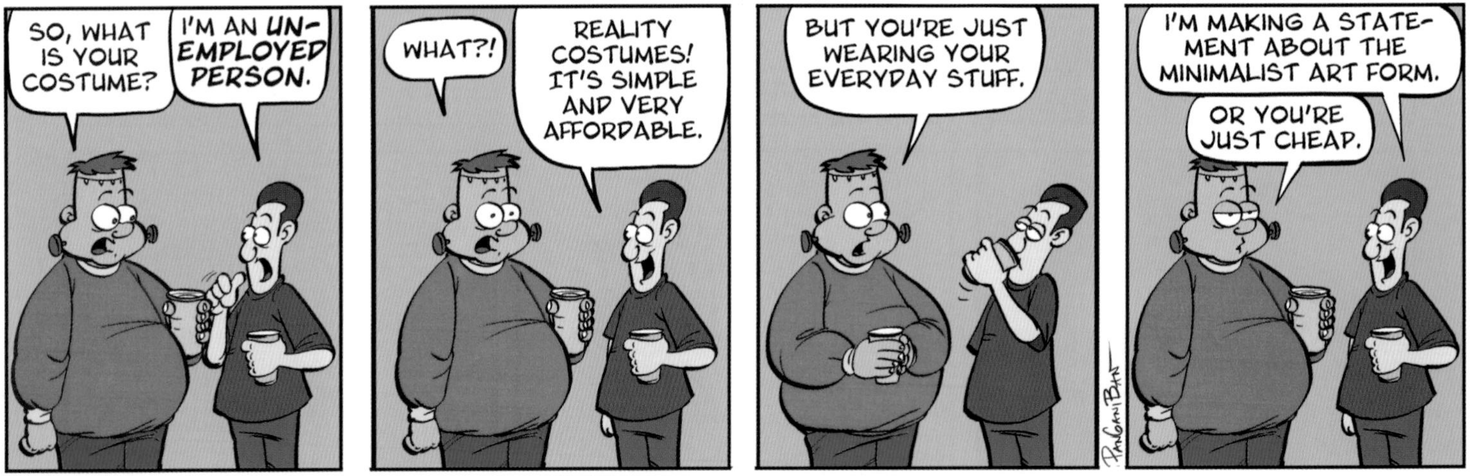
SO, WHAT IS YOUR COSTUME?
I'M AN **UN-EMPLOYED PERSON**.
WHAT?!
REALITY COSTUMES! IT'S SIMPLE AND VERY AFFORDABLE.
BUT YOU'RE JUST WEARING YOUR EVERYDAY STUFF.
I'M MAKING A STATE-MENT ABOUT THE MINIMALIST ART FORM.
OR YOU'RE JUST CHEAP.

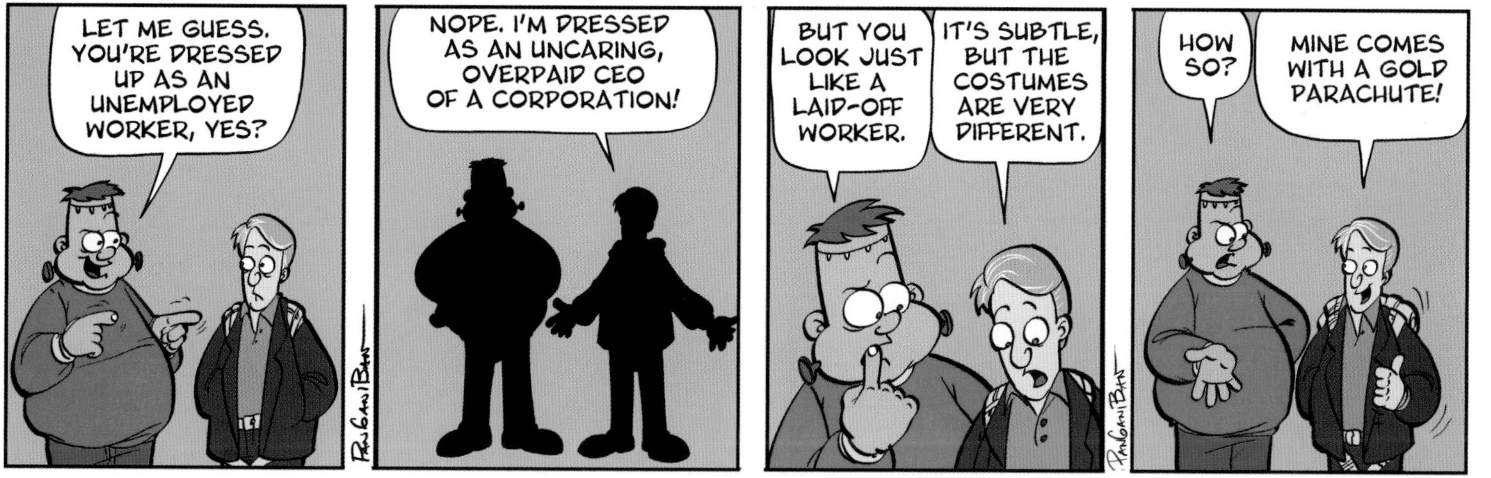
LET ME GUESS. YOU'RE DRESSED UP AS AN UNEMPLOYED WORKER, YES?
NOPE. I'M DRESSED AS AN UNCARING, OVERPAID CEO OF A CORPORATION!
BUT YOU LOOK JUST LIKE A LAID-OFF WORKER.
IT'S SUBTLE, BUT THE COSTUMES ARE VERY DIFFERENT.
HOW SO?
MINE COMES WITH A GOLD PARACHUTE!

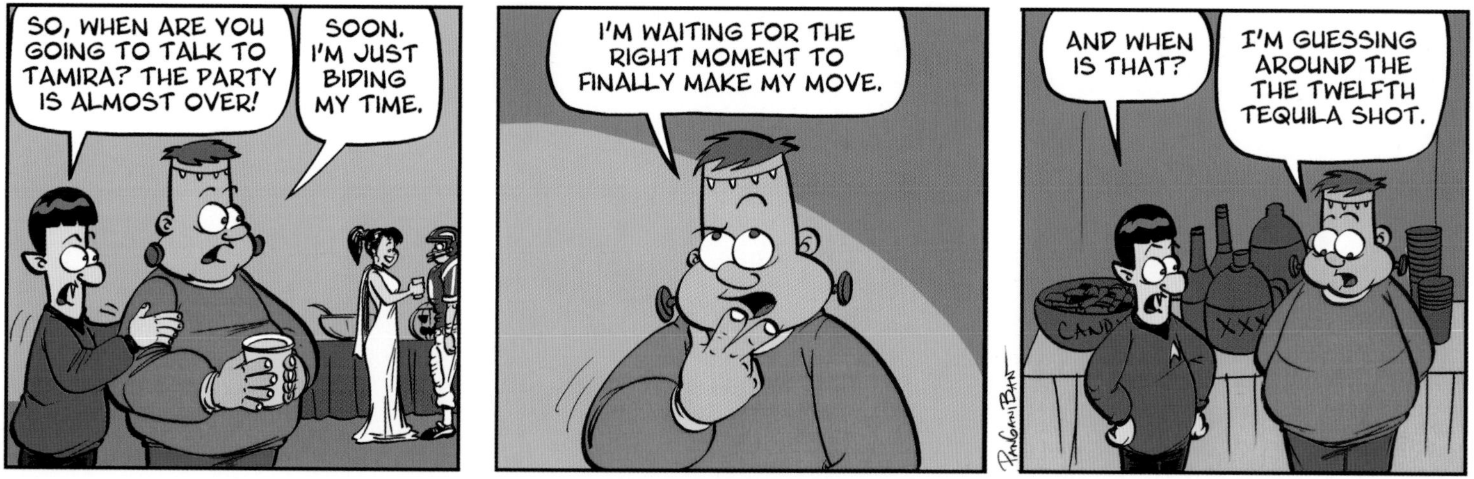
SO, WHEN ARE YOU GOING TO TALK TO TAMIRA? THE PARTY IS ALMOST OVER!
SOON. I'M JUST BIDING MY TIME.
I'M WAITING FOR THE RIGHT MOMENT TO FINALLY MAKE MY MOVE.
AND WHEN IS THAT?
I'M GUESSING AROUND THE THE TWELFTH TEQUILA SHOT.
CANDY
XXX

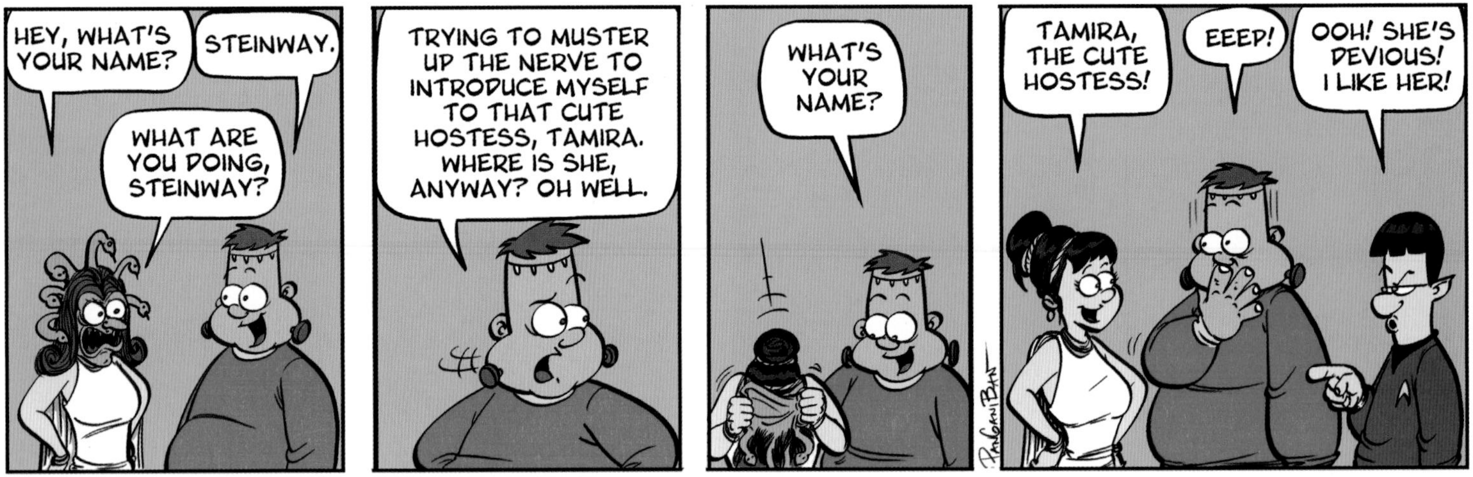
HEY, WHAT'S YOUR NAME?
STEINWAY.
WHAT ARE YOU DOING, STEINWAY?
TRYING TO MUSTER UP THE NERVE TO INTRODUCE MYSELF TO THAT CUTE HOSTESS, TAMIRA. WHERE IS SHE, ANYWAY? OH WELL.
WHAT'S YOUR NAME?
TAMIRA, THE CUTE HOSTESS!
EEEP!
OOH! SHE'S DEVIOUS! I LIKE HER!

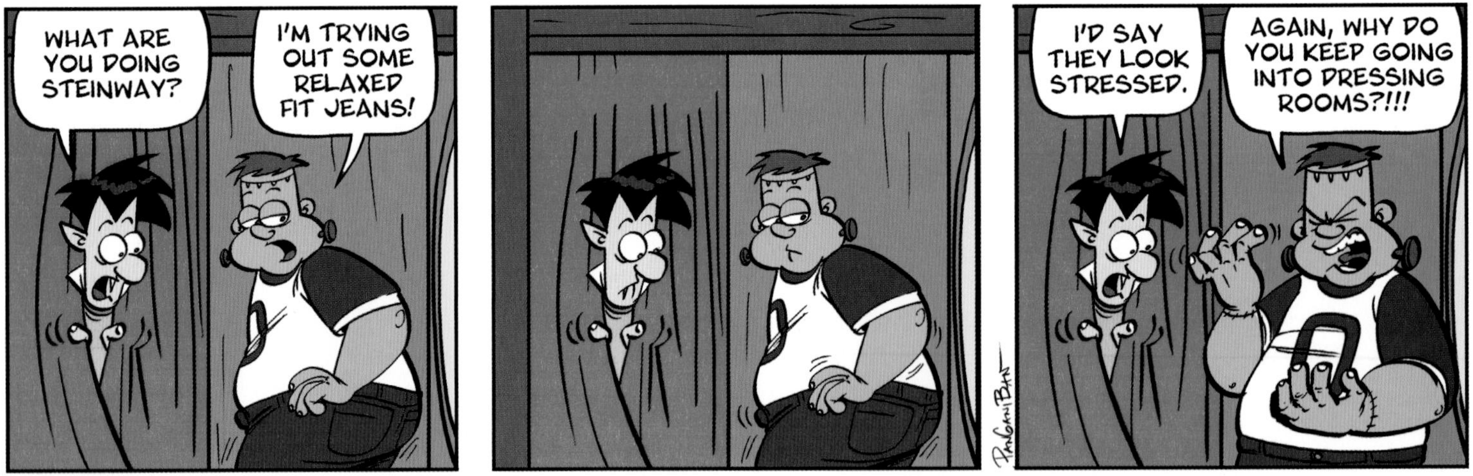
WHAT ARE YOU DOING STEINWAY?
I'M TRYING OUT SOME RELAXED FIT JEANS!
I'D SAY THEY LOOK STRESSED.
AGAIN, WHY DO YOU KEEP GOING INTO DRESSING ROOMS?!!!

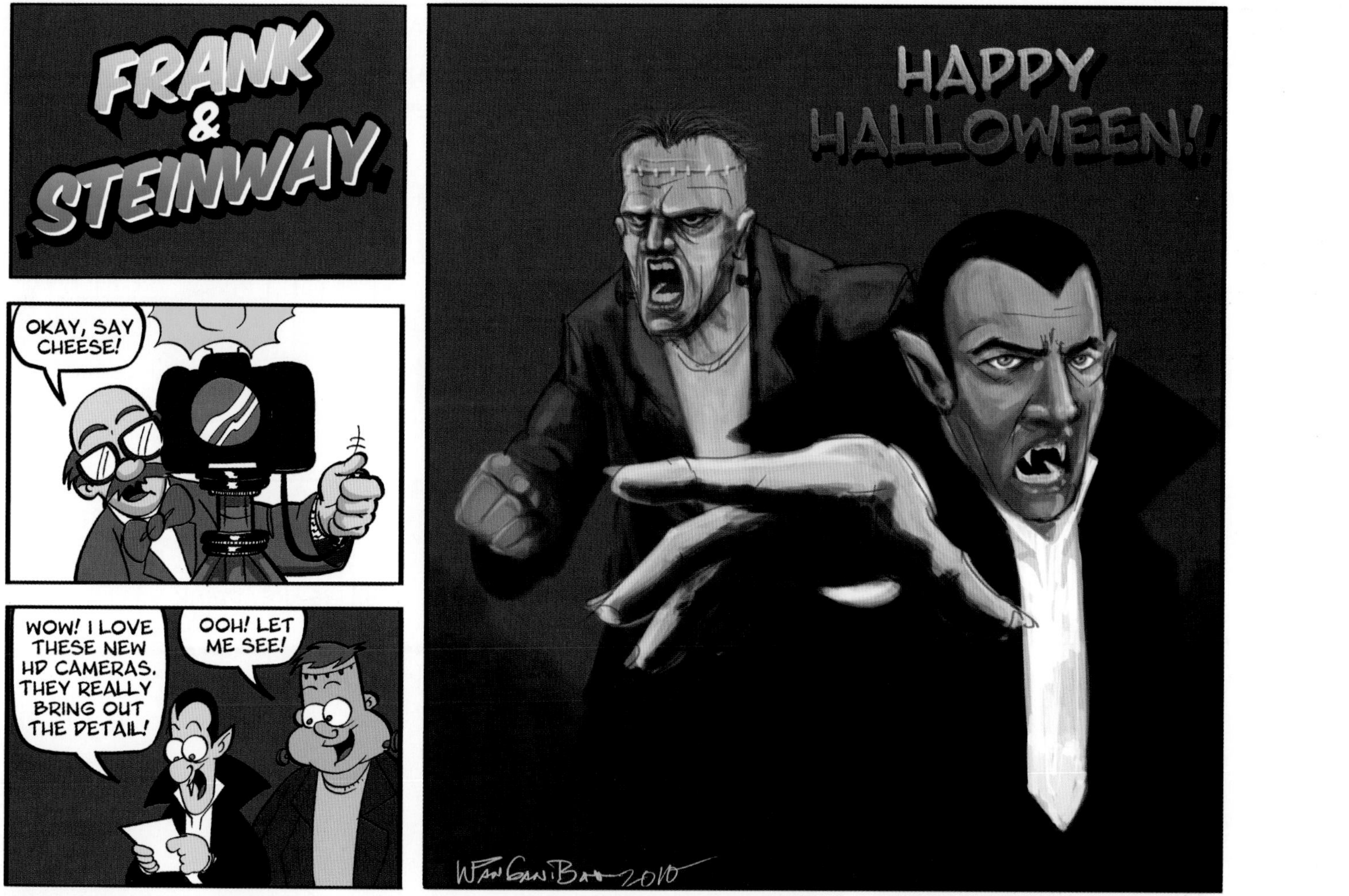
FRANK & STEINWAY
OKAY, SAY CHEESE!
WOW! I LOVE THESE NEW HD CAMERAS. THEY REALLY BRING OUT THE DETAIL!
OOH! LET ME SEE!
HAPPY HALLOWEEN!!

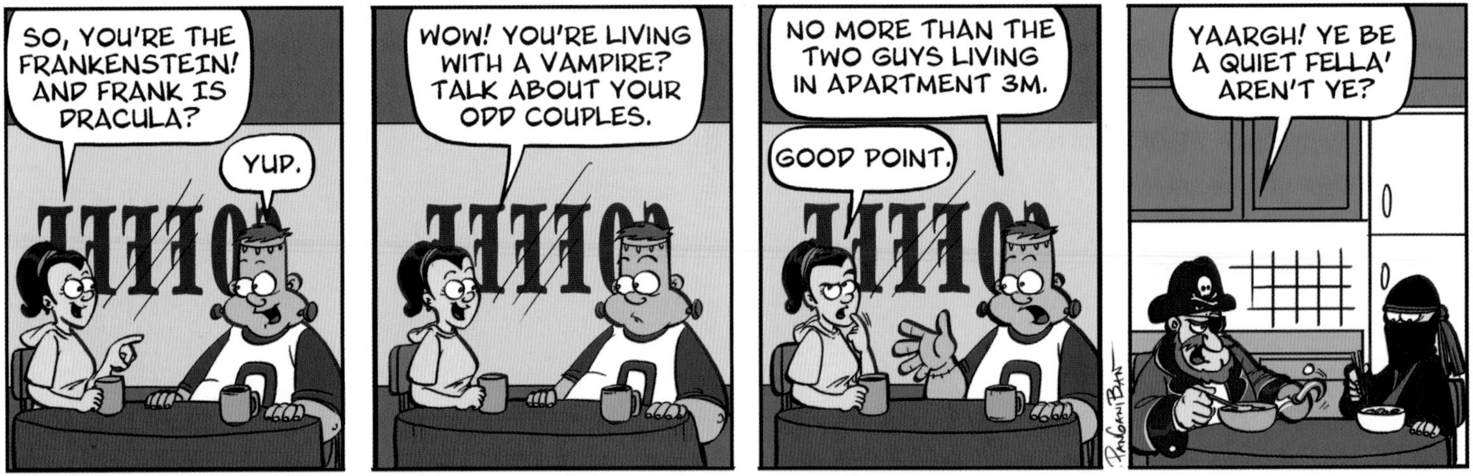
SO, YOU'RE THE FRANKENSTEIN! AND FRANK IS DRACULA?
YUP.
WOW! YOU'RE LIVING WITH A VAMPIRE? TALK ABOUT YOUR ODD COUPLES.
NO MORE THAN THE TWO GUYS LIVING IN APARTMENT 3M.
GOOD POINT.
YAARGH! YE BE A QUIET FELLA' AREN'T YE?

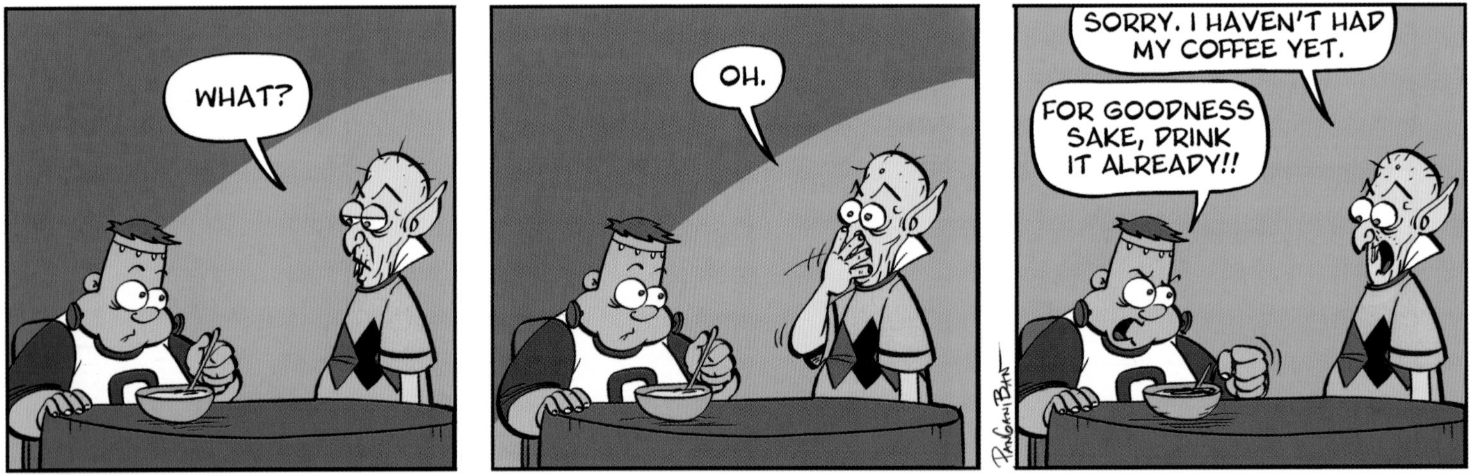
WHAT?
OH.
SORRY. I HAVEN'T HAD MY COFFEE YET.
FOR GOODNESS SAKE, DRINK IT ALREADY!!

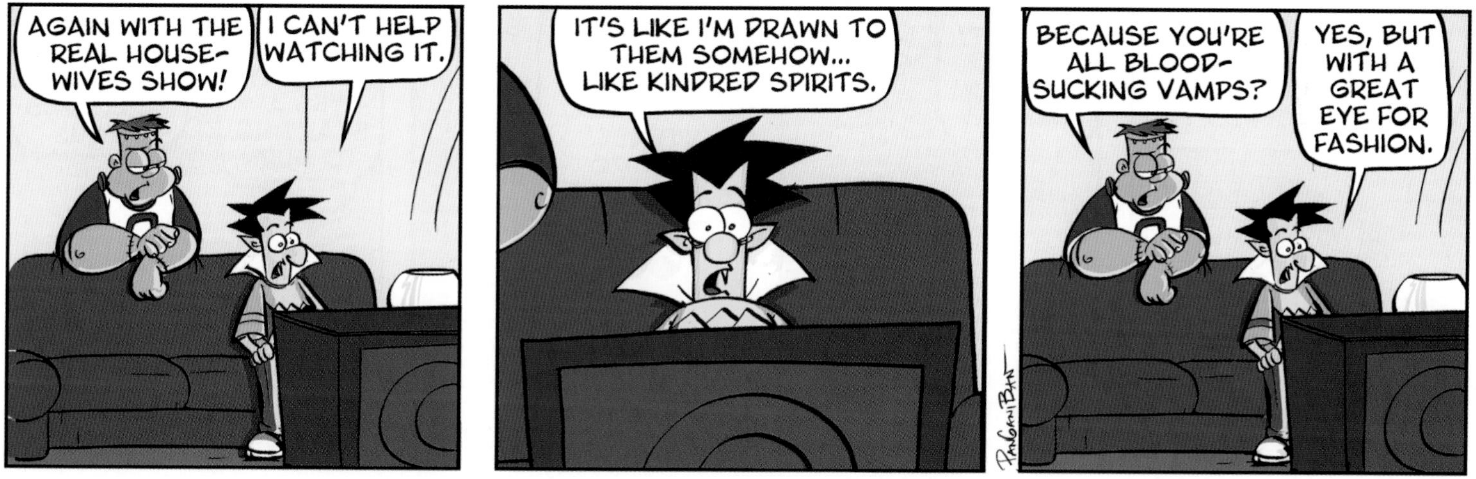
AGAIN WITH THE REAL HOUSE-WIVES SHOW!
I CAN'T HELP WATCHING IT.
IT'S LIKE I'M DRAWN TO THEM SOMEHOW... LIKE KINDRED SPIRITS.
BECAUSE YOU'RE ALL BLOOD-SUCKING VAMPS?
YES, BUT WITH A GREAT EYE FOR FASHION.

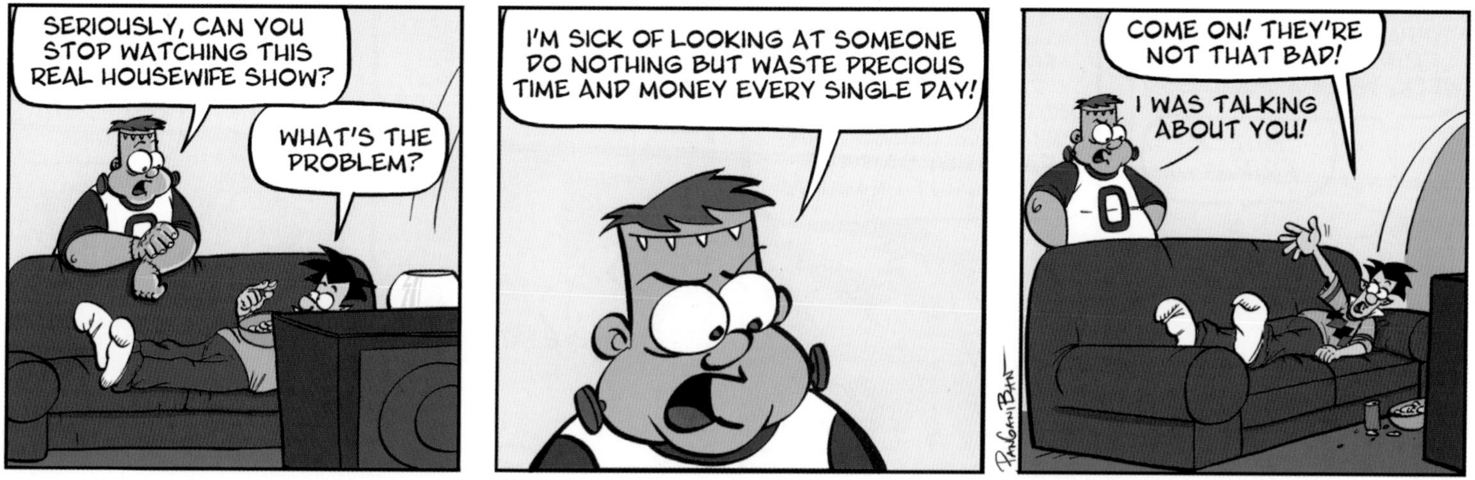
SERIOUSLY, CAN YOU STOP WATCHING THIS REAL HOUSEWIFE SHOW?
WHAT'S THE PROBLEM?
I'M SICK OF LOOKING AT SOMEONE DO NOTHING BUT WASTE PRECIOUS TIME AND MONEY EVERY SINGLE DAY!
COME ON! THEY'RE NOT THAT BAD!
I WAS TALKING ABOUT YOU!

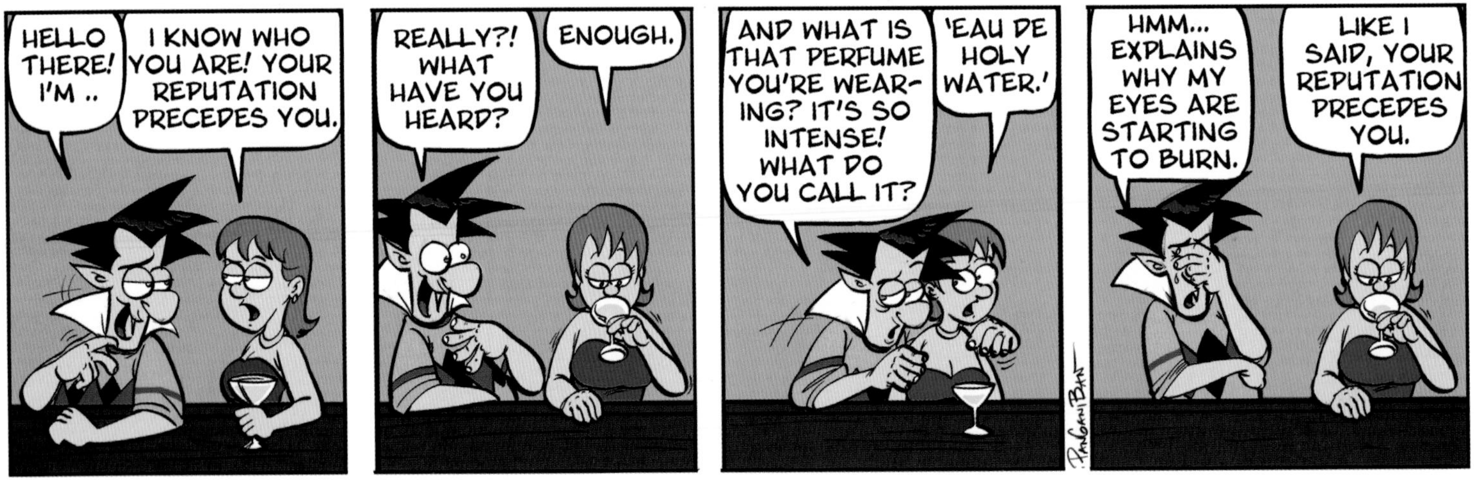
HELLO THERE! I'M ..
I KNOW WHO YOU ARE! YOUR REPUTATION PRECEDES YOU.
REALLY?! WHAT HAVE YOU HEARD?
ENOUGH.
AND WHAT IS THAT PERFUME YOU'RE WEAR-ING? IT'S SO INTENSE! WHAT DO YOU CALL IT?
'EAU DE HOLY WATER.'
HMM... EXPLAINS WHY MY EYES ARE STARTING TO BURN.
LIKE I SAID, YOUR REPUTATION PRECEDES YOU.

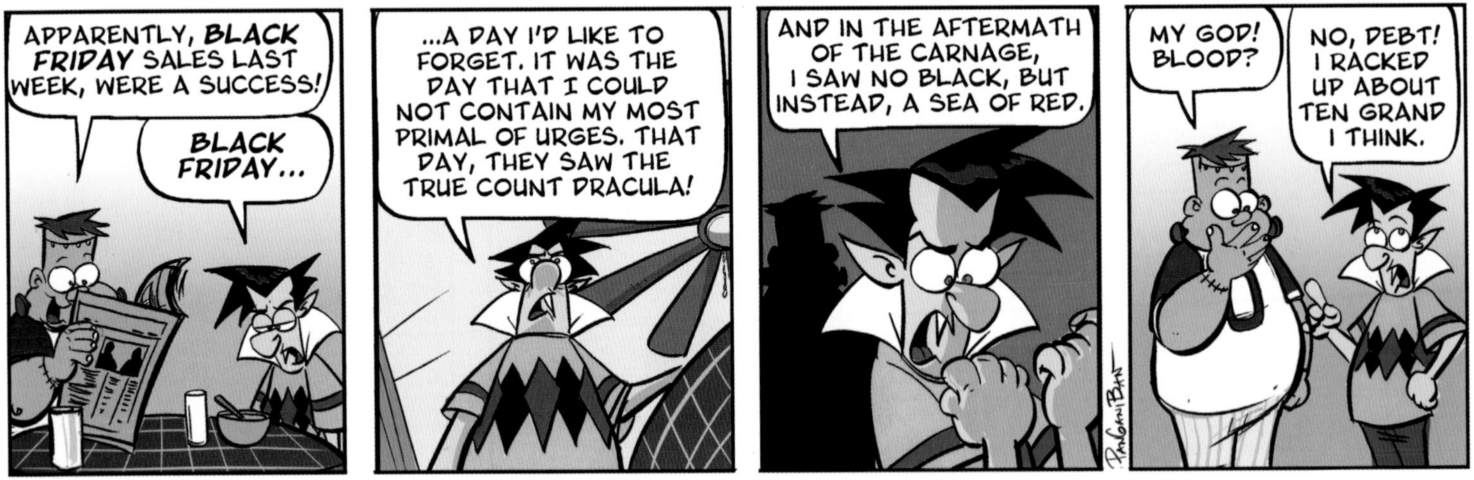
APPARENTLY, BLACK FRIDAY SALES LAST WEEK, WERE A SUCCESS!
BLACK FRIDAY...
...A DAY I'D LIKE TO FORGET. IT WAS THE DAY THAT I COULD NOT CONTAIN MY MOST PRIMAL OF URGES. THAT DAY, THEY SAW THE TRUE COUNT DRACULA!
AND IN THE AFTERMATH OF THE CARNAGE, I SAW NO BLACK, BUT INSTEAD, A SEA OF RED.
MY GOD! BLOOD?
NO, DEBT! I RACKED UP ABOUT TEN GRAND I THINK.

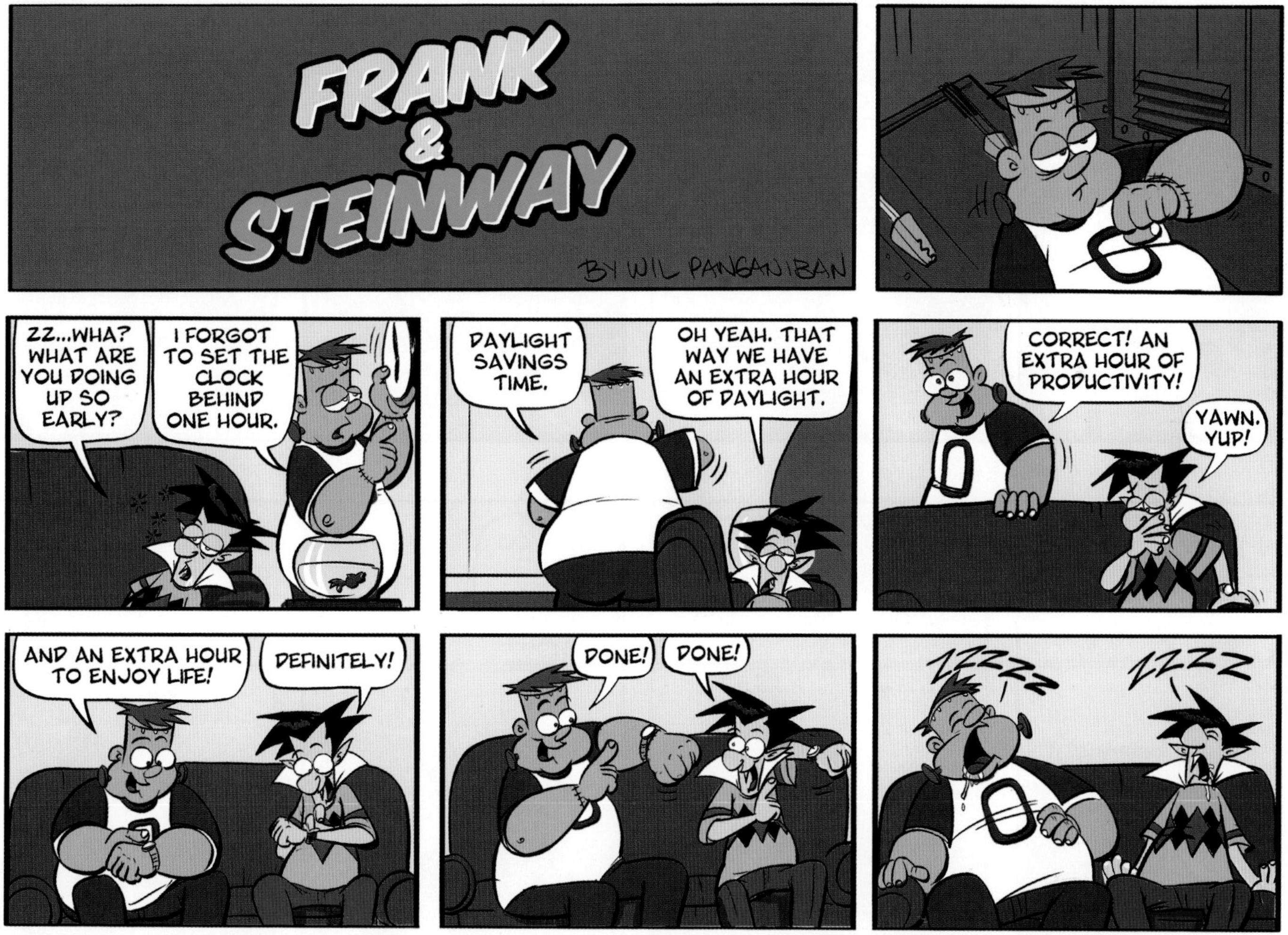
FRANK & STEINWAY
BY WIL PANGANIBAN
ZZ...WHA? WHAT ARE YOU DOING UP SO EARLY?
I FORGOT TO SET THE CLOCK BEHIND ONE HOUR.
DAYLIGHT SAVINGS TIME.
OH YEAH. THAT WAY WE HAVE AN EXTRA HOUR OF DAYLIGHT.
CORRECT! AN EXTRA HOUR OF PRODUCTIVITY!
YAWN. YUP!
AND AN EXTRA HOUR TO ENJOY LIFE!
DEFINITELY!
DONE!
DONE!
ZZZZZZZ
ZZZZ

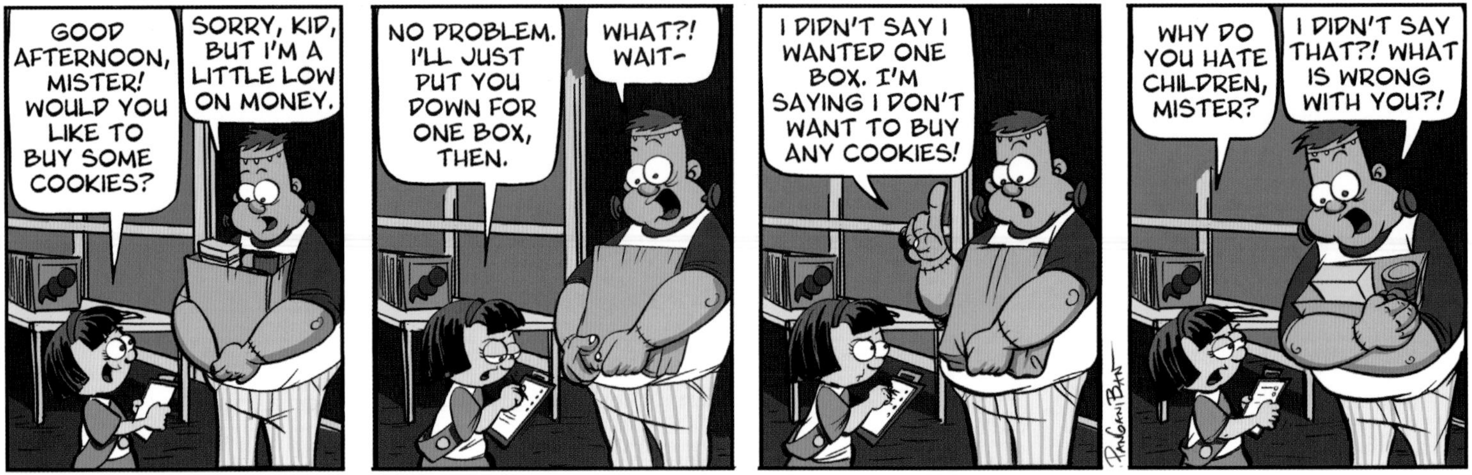
GOOD AFTERNOON, MISTER! WOULD YOU LIKE TO BUY SOME COOKIES?
SORRY, KID, BUT I'M A LITTLE LOW ON MONEY.
NO PROBLEM. I'LL JUST PUT YOU DOWN FOR ONE BOX, THEN.
WHAT?! WAIT-
I DIDN'T SAY I WANTED ONE BOX. I'M SAYING I DON'T WANT TO BUY ANY COOKIES!
WHY DO YOU HATE CHILDREN, MISTER?
I DIDN'T SAY THAT?! WHAT IS WRONG WITH YOU?!

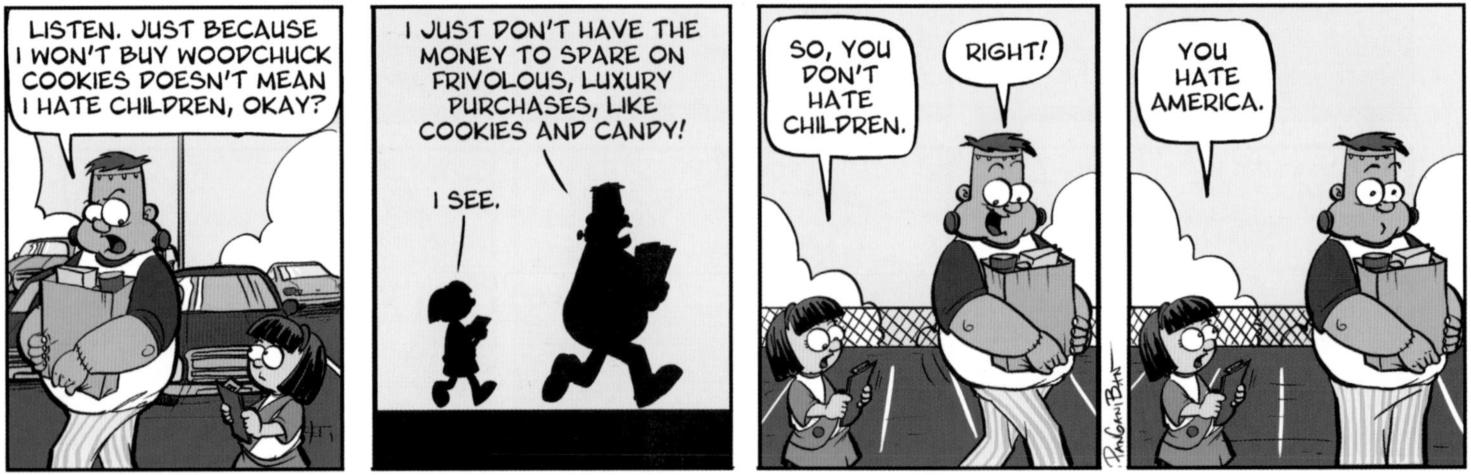
LISTEN. JUST BECAUSE I WON'T BUY WOODCHUCK COOKIES DOESN'T MEAN I HATE CHILDREN, OKAY?
I JUST DON'T HAVE THE MONEY TO SPARE ON FRIVOLOUS, LUXURY PURCHASES, LIKE COOKIES AND CANDY!
I SEE.
SO, YOU DON'T HATE CHILDREN.
RIGHT!
YOU HATE AMERICA.

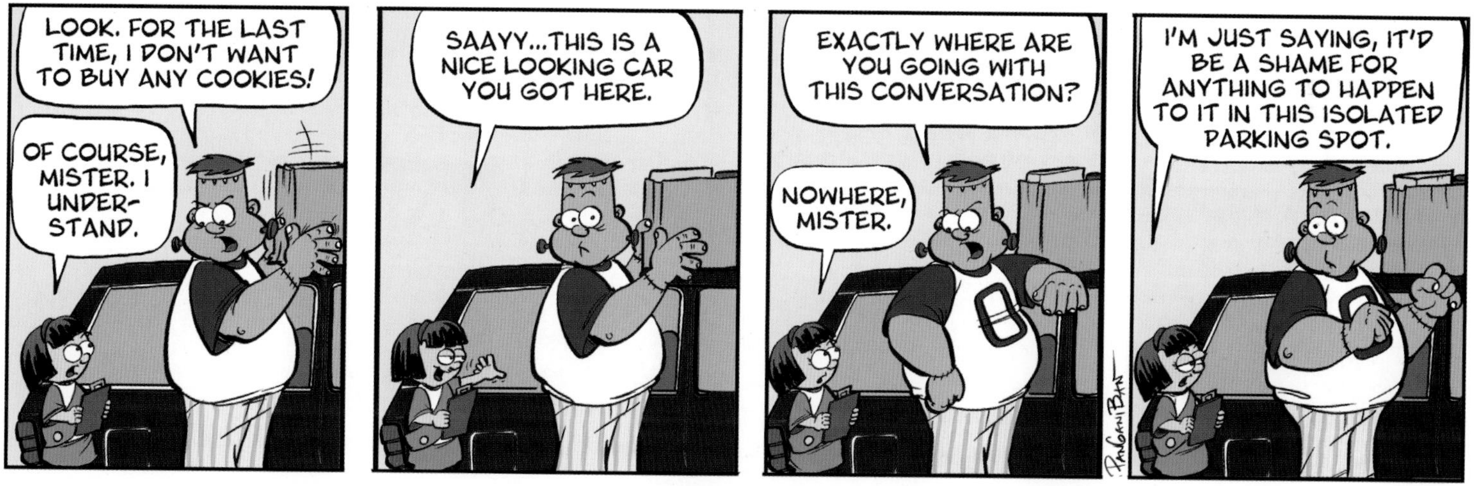
LOOK. FOR THE LAST TIME, I DON'T WANT TO BUY ANY COOKIES!
OF COURSE, MISTER. I UNDER-STAND.
SAAYY...THIS IS A NICE LOOKING CAR YOU GOT HERE.
EXACTLY WHERE ARE YOU GOING WITH THIS CONVERSATION?
NOWHERE, MISTER.
I'M JUST SAYING, IT'D BE A SHAME FOR ANYTHING TO HAPPEN TO IT IN THIS ISOLATED PARKING SPOT.

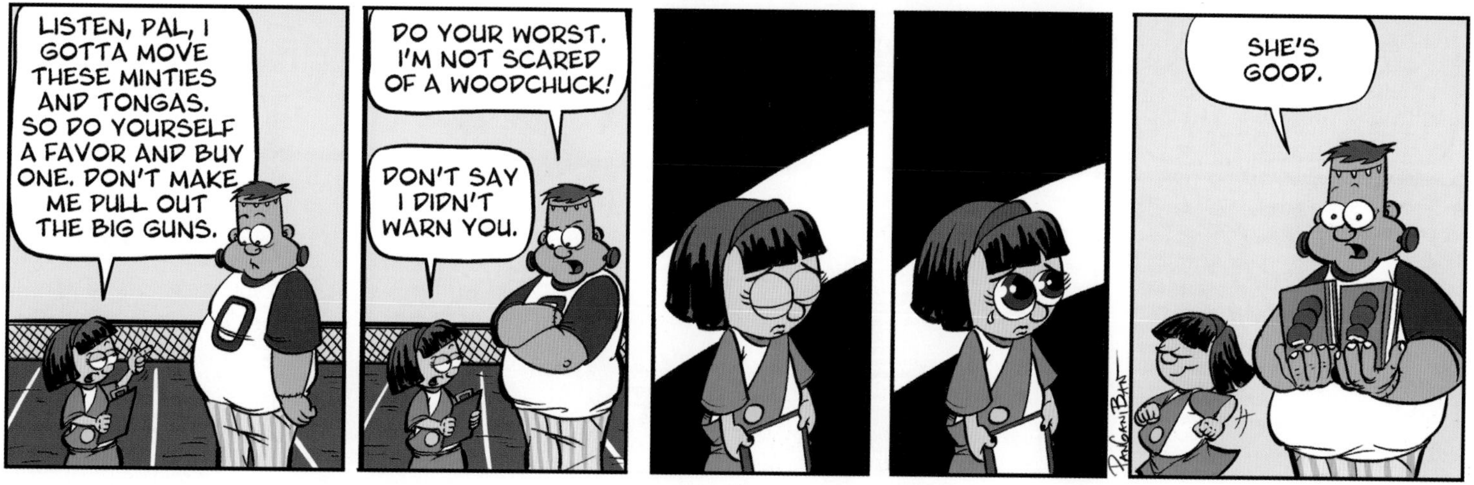
LISTEN, PAL, I GOTTA MOVE THESE MINTIES AND TONGAS. SO DO YOURSELF A FAVOR AND BUY ONE. DON'T MAKE ME PULL OUT THE BIG GUNS.
DO YOUR WORST. I'M NOT SCARED OF A WOODCHUCK!
DON'T SAY I DIDN'T WARN YOU.
SHE'S GOOD.

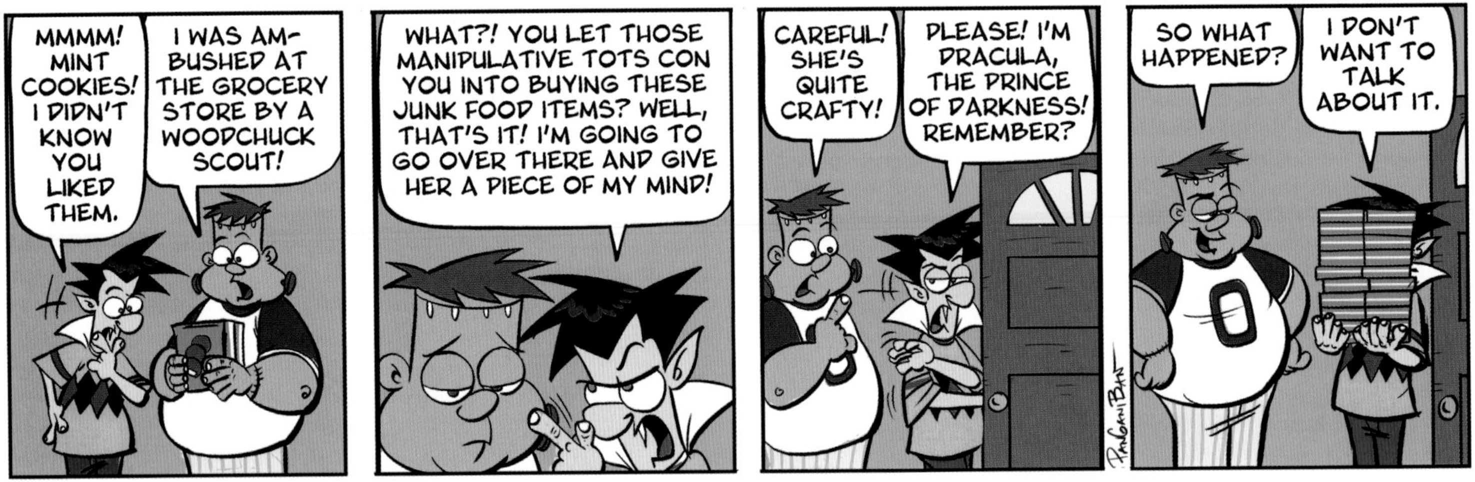
MMMM! MINT COOKIES! I DIDN'T KNOW YOU LIKED THEM.
I WAS AMBUSHED AT THE GROCERY STORE BY A WOODCHUCK SCOUT!
WHAT?! YOU LET THOSE MANIPULATIVE TOTS CON YOU INTO BUYING THESE JUNK FOOD ITEMS? WELL, THAT'S IT! I'M GOING TO GO OVER THERE AND GIVE HER A PIECE OF MY MIND!
CAREFUL! SHE'S QUITE CRAFTY!
PLEASE! I'M DRACULA, THE PRINCE OF DARKNESS! REMEMBER?
SO WHAT HAPPENED?
I DON'T WANT TO TALK ABOUT IT.

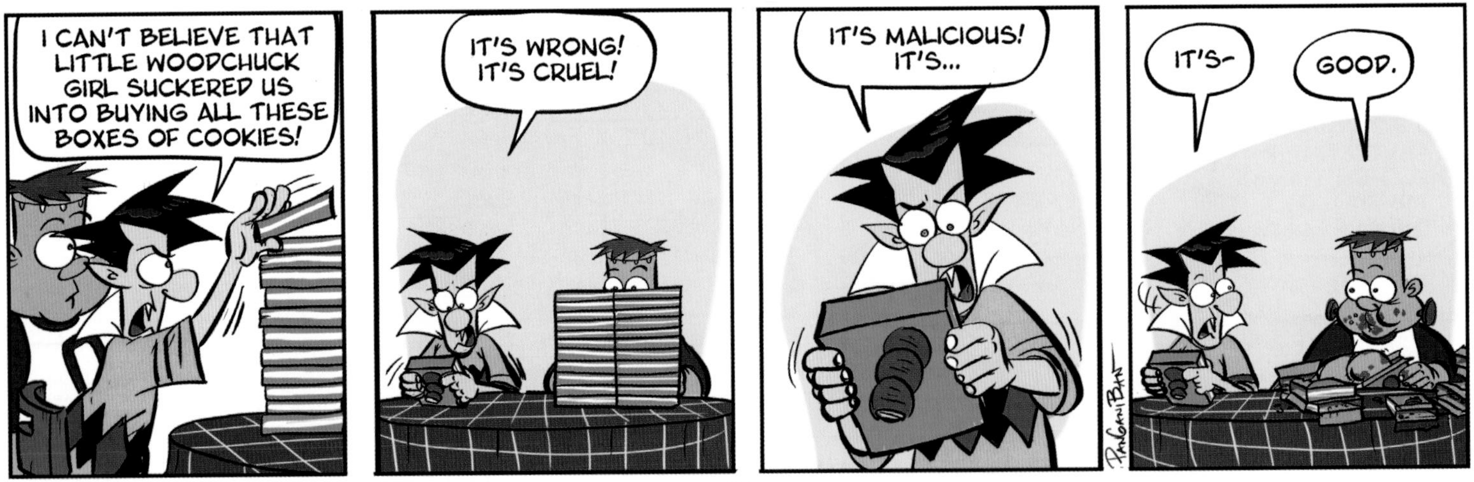
I CAN'T BELIEVE THAT LITTLE WOODCHUCK GIRL SUCKERED US INTO BUYING ALL THESE BOXES OF COOKIES!
IT'S WRONG! IT'S CRUEL!
IT'S MALICIOUS! IT'S...
IT'S-
GOOD.

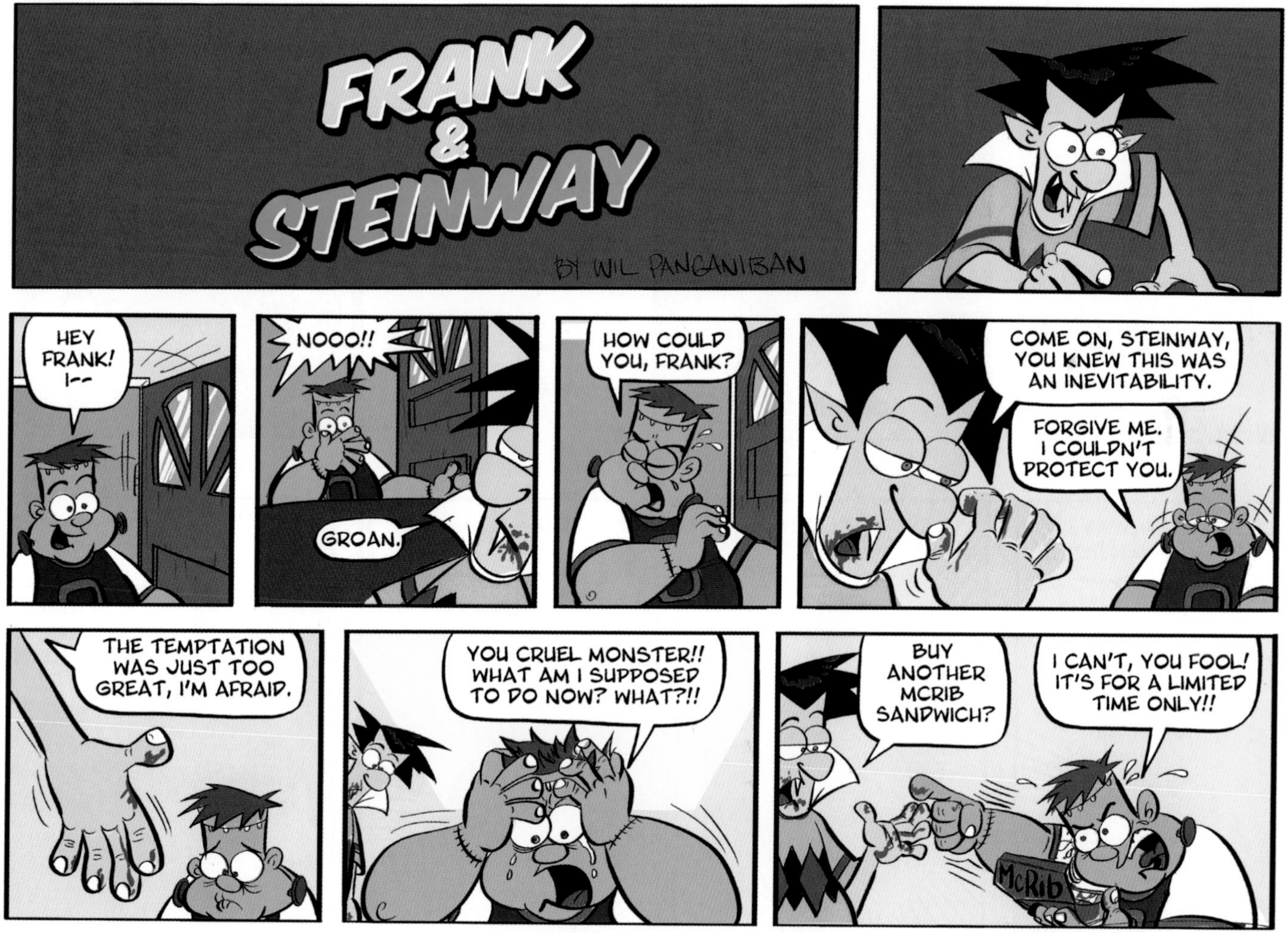
FRANK & STEINWAY
BY WIL PANGANIBAN
HEY FRANK! I--
NOOO!!
GROAN.
HOW COULD YOU, FRANK?
COME ON, STEINWAY, YOU KNEW THIS WAS AN INEVITABILITY.
FORGIVE ME. I COULDN'T PROTECT YOU.
THE TEMPTATION WAS JUST TOO GREAT, I'M AFRAID.
YOU CRUEL MONSTER!! WHAT AM I SUPPOSED TO DO NOW? WHAT?!!
BUY ANOTHER MCRIB SANDWICH?
I CAN'T, YOU FOOL! IT'S FOR A LIMITED TIME ONLY!!
McRib

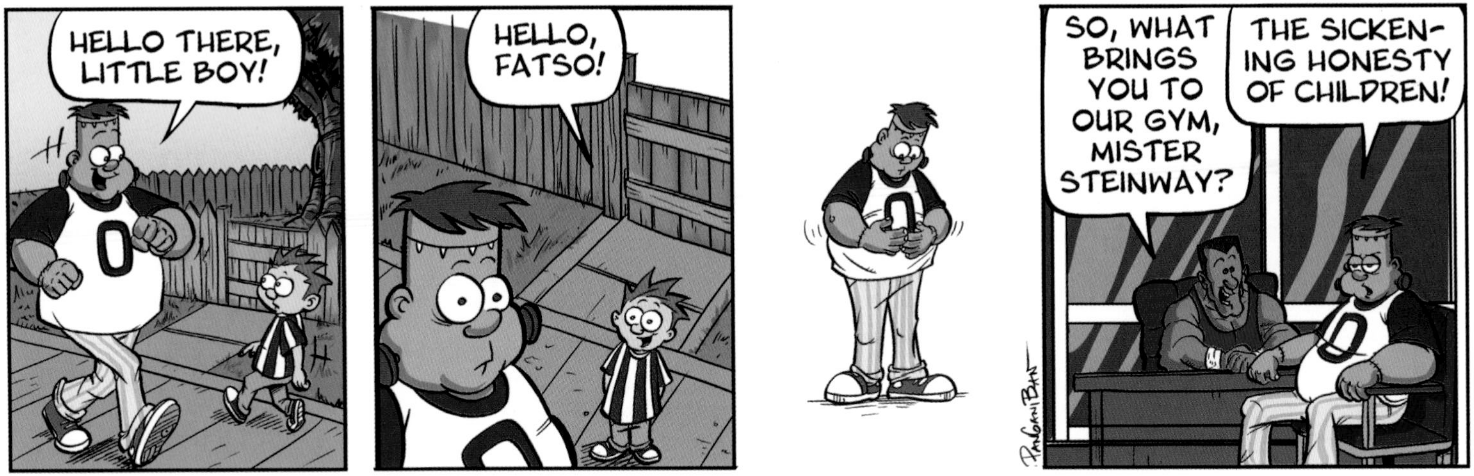
HELLO THERE, LITTLE BOY!
HELLO, FATSO!
SO, WHAT BRINGS YOU TO OUR GYM, MISTER STEINWAY?
THE SICKEN-ING HONESTY OF CHILDREN!

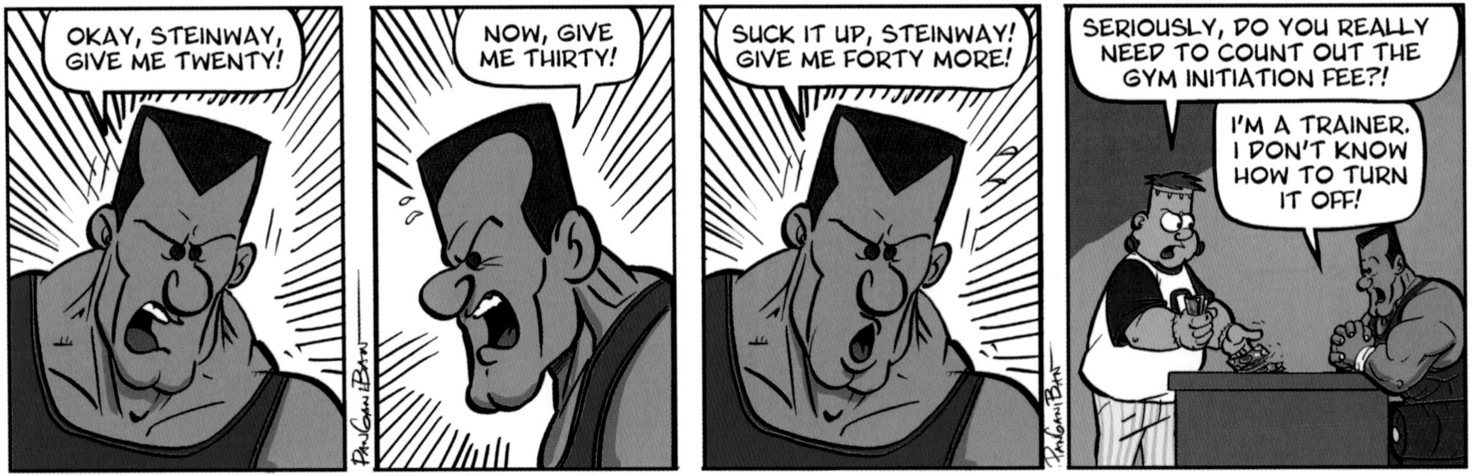
OKAY, STEINWAY, GIVE ME TWENTY!
NOW, GIVE ME THIRTY!
SUCK IT UP, STEINWAY! GIVE ME FORTY MORE!
SERIOUSLY, DO YOU REALLY NEED TO COUNT OUT THE GYM INITIATION FEE?!
I'M A TRAINER. I DON'T KNOW HOW TO TURN IT OFF!

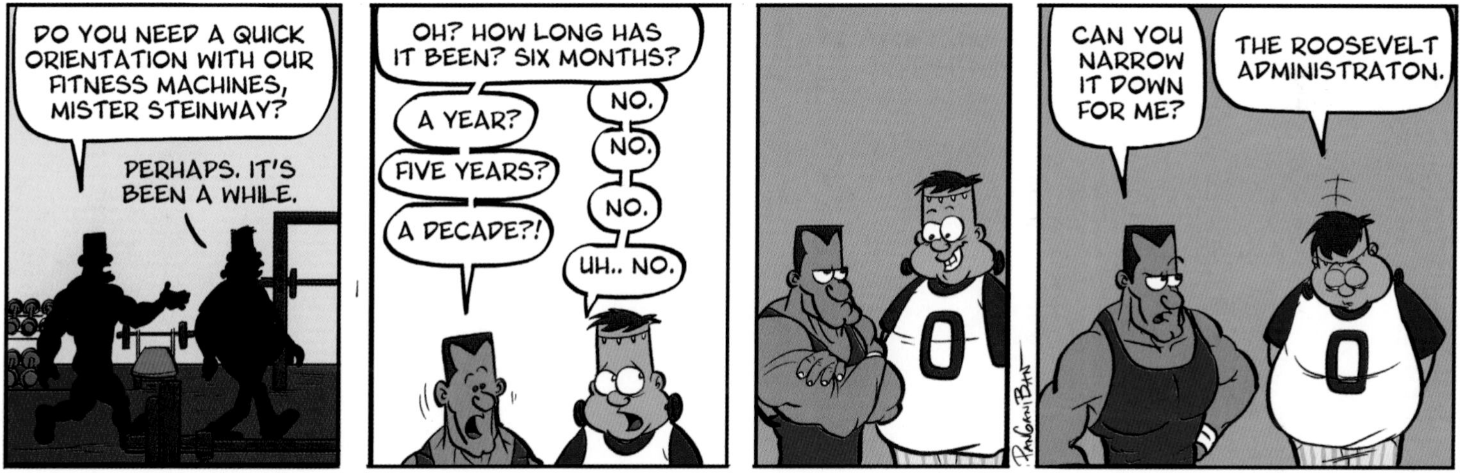
DO YOU NEED A QUICK ORIENTATION WITH OUR FITNESS MACHINES, MISTER STEINWAY?
PERHAPS. IT'S BEEN A WHILE.
OH? HOW LONG HAS IT BEEN? SIX MONTHS?
NO.
A YEAR?
NO.
FIVE YEARS?
NO.
A DECADE?!
UH.. NO.
CAN YOU NARROW IT DOWN FOR ME?
THE ROOSEVELT ADMINISTRATON.

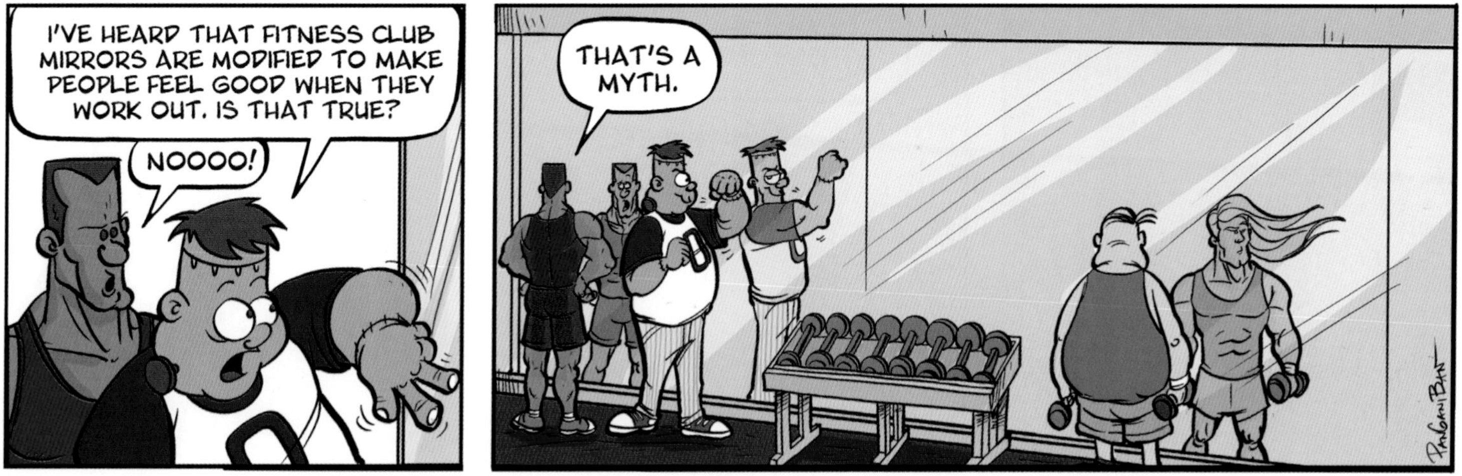
I'VE HEARD THAT FITNESS CLUB MIRRORS ARE MODIFIED TO MAKE PEOPLE FEEL GOOD WHEN THEY WORK OUT. IS THAT TRUE?
NOOOO!
THAT'S A MYTH.

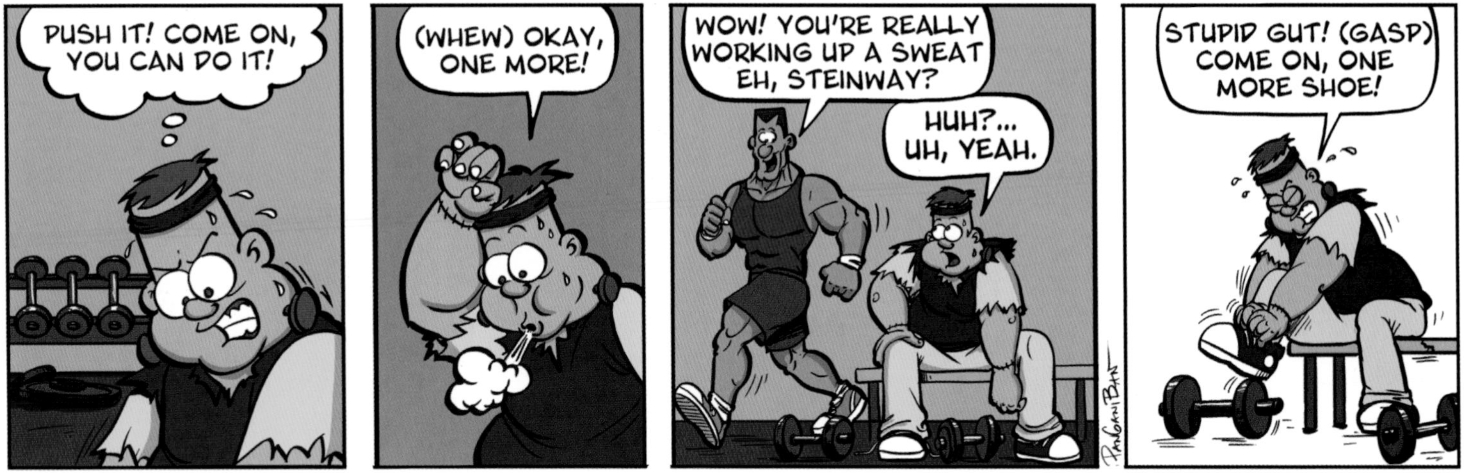
PUSH IT! COME ON, YOU CAN DO IT!
(WHEW) OKAY, ONE MORE!
WOW! YOU'RE REALLY WORKING UP A SWEAT EH, STEINWAY?
HUH?... UH, YEAH.
STUPID GUT! (GASP) COME ON, ONE MORE SHOE!

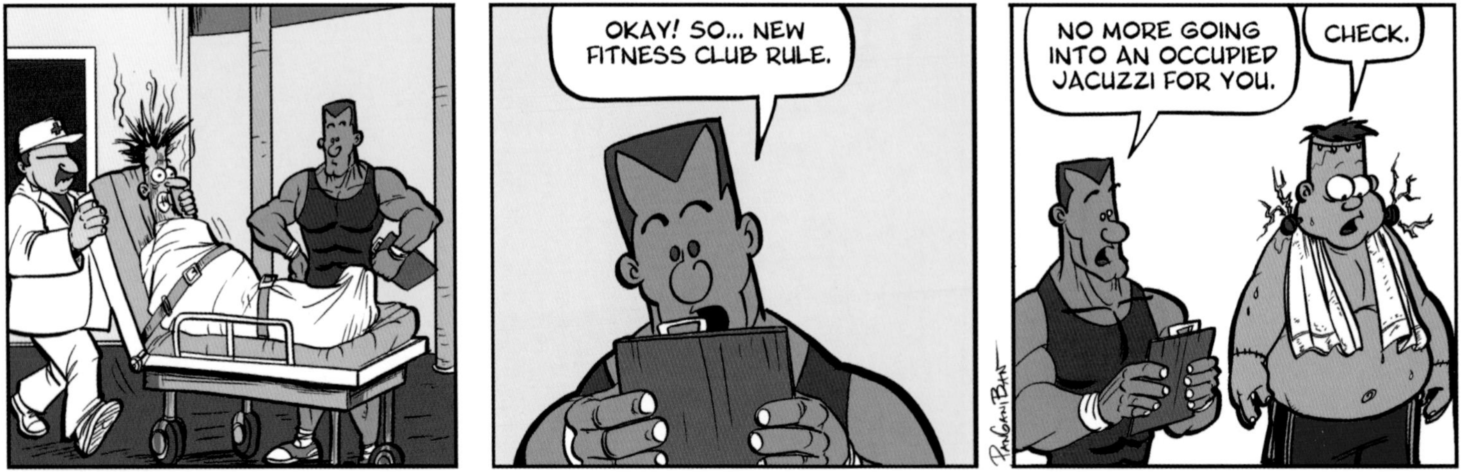
OKAY! SO... NEW FITNESS CLUB RULE.
NO MORE GOING INTO AN OCCUPIED JACUZZI FOR YOU.
CHECK.

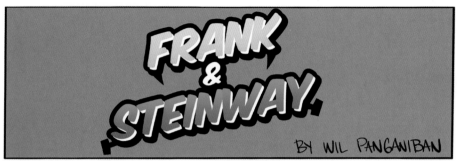

FRANK & STEINWAY.

BY WIL PANGANIBAN

MMMMM...

MAY I TAKE YOUR ORDERS, GENTLEMEN?

YES, YOU MAY!

I'D LIKE A LARGE PLATE OF SPAGHETTI, PLEASE.

AND FOR YOU, SIR?

I'D LIKE TO ORDER THE 26 OUNCE PORTERHOUSE STEAK, VERY BLOODY PLEASE!

BUT HOLD THE SAUCE, HOLD THE SEASONINGS, AND HOLD THE SIDES.

IN FACT, WHY DON'T YOU GO AHEAD AND JUST HOLD THE STEAK TOO.

PLATE O' BLOOD COMING RIGHT UP.

AND A STRAW PLEASE.

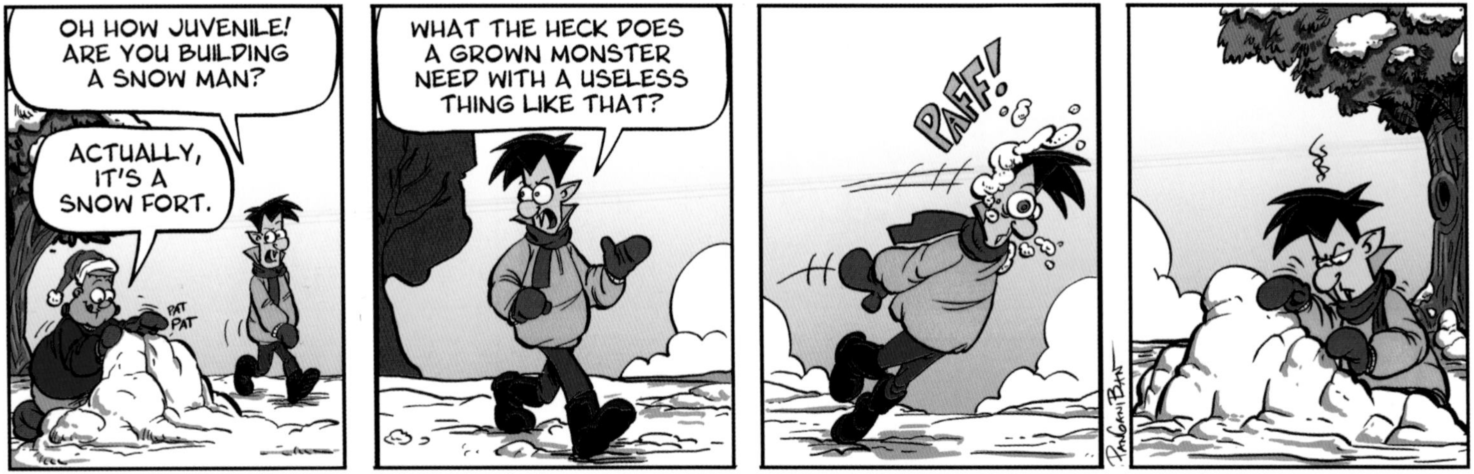
OH HOW JUVENILE! ARE YOU BUILDING A SNOW MAN?
ACTUALLY, IT'S A SNOW FORT.
PAT PAT
WHAT THE HECK DOES A GROWN MONSTER NEED WITH A USELESS THING LIKE THAT?
PAFF!

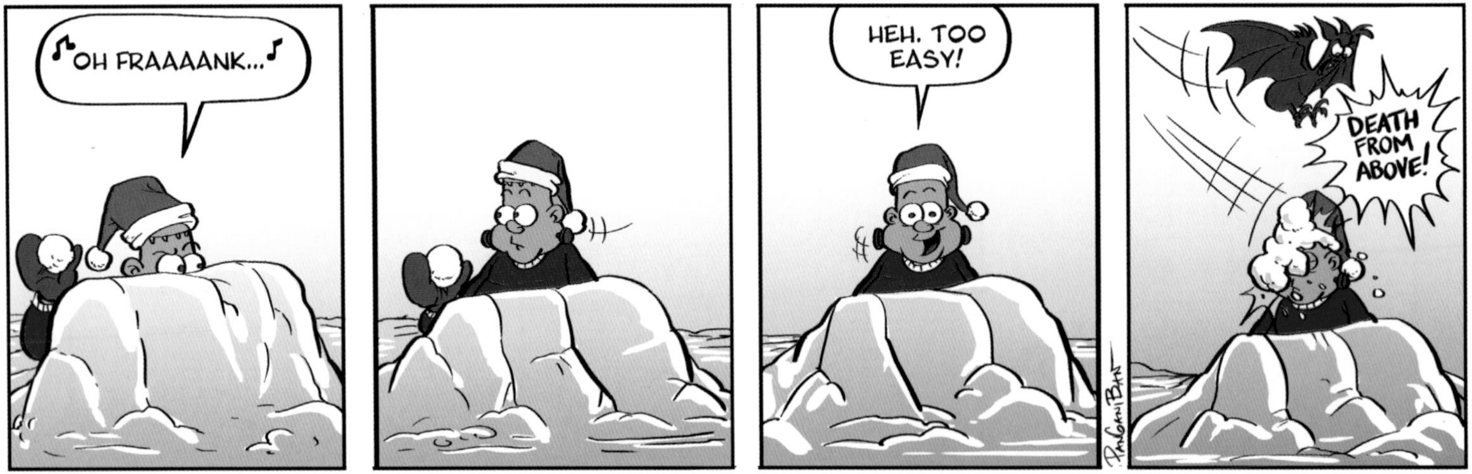
OH FRAAAANK...
HEH. TOO EASY!
DEATH FROM ABOVE!

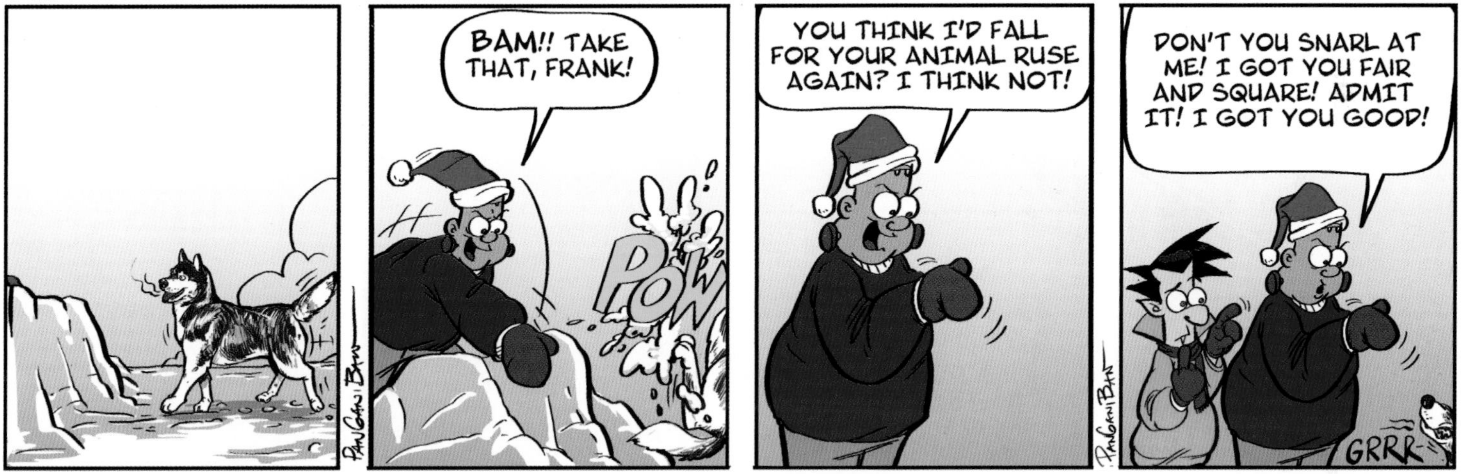
BAM!! TAKE THAT, FRANK!
POW
YOU THINK I'D FALL FOR YOUR ANIMAL RUSE AGAIN? I THINK NOT!
DON'T YOU SNARL AT ME! I GOT YOU FAIR AND SQUARE! ADMIT IT! I GOT YOU GOOD!
GRRR

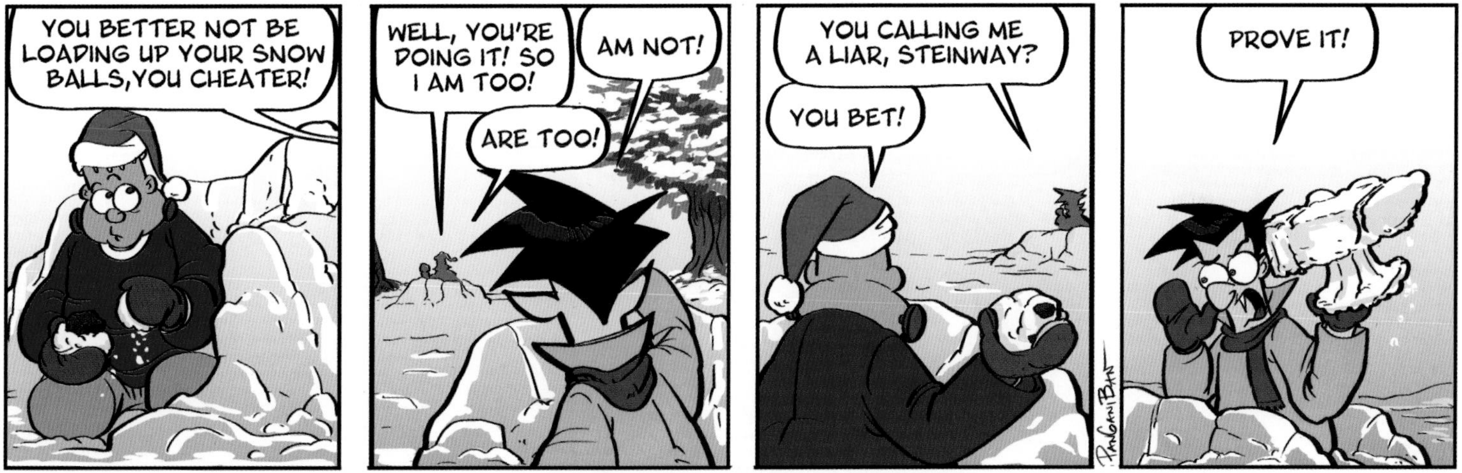
YOU BETTER NOT BE LOADING UP YOUR SNOW BALLS,YOU CHEATER!
WELL, YOU'RE DOING IT! SO I AM TOO!
AM NOT!
ARE TOO!
YOU CALLING ME A LIAR, STEINWAY?
YOU BET!
PROVE IT!

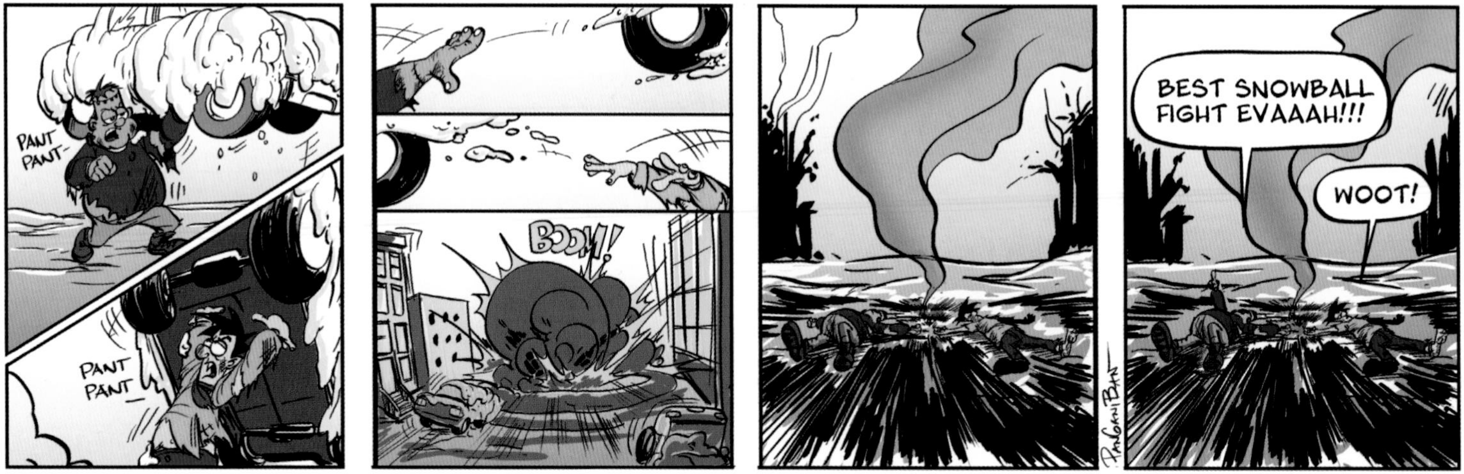
PANT
PANT
PANT
PANT
BOOM!
BEST SNOWBALL FIGHT EVAAAH!!!
WOOT!

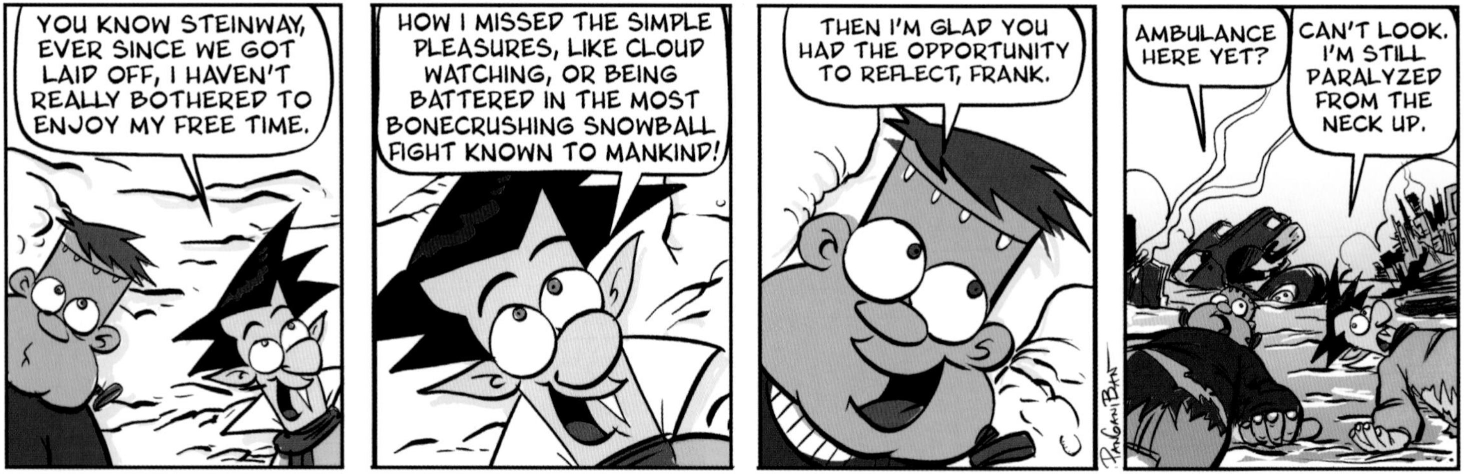
YOU KNOW STEINWAY, EVER SINCE WE GOT LAID OFF, I HAVEN'T REALLY BOTHERED TO ENJOY MY FREE TIME.
HOW I MISSED THE SIMPLE PLEASURES, LIKE CLOUD WATCHING, OR BEING BATTERED IN THE MOST BONECRUSHING SNOWBALL FIGHT KNOWN TO MANKIND!
THEN I'M GLAD YOU HAD THE OPPORTUNITY TO REFLECT, FRANK.
AMBULANCE HERE YET?
CAN'T LOOK. I'M STILL PARALYZED FROM THE NECK UP.

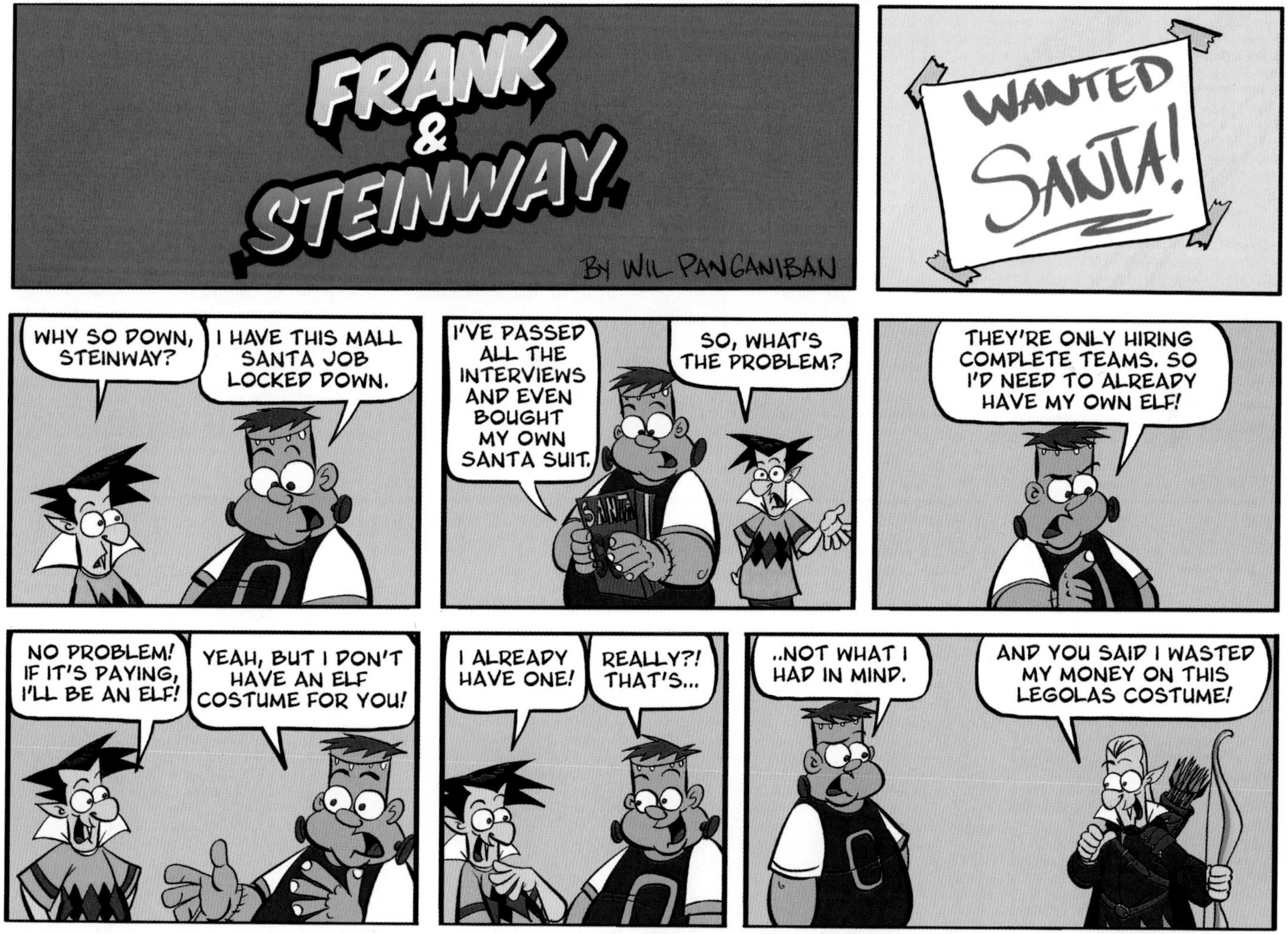
FRANK & STEINWAY
BY WIL PANGANIBAN
WANTED SANTA!
WHY SO DOWN, STEINWAY?
I HAVE THIS MALL SANTA JOB LOCKED DOWN.
I'VE PASSED ALL THE INTERVIEWS AND EVEN BOUGHT MY OWN SANTA SUIT.
SO, WHAT'S THE PROBLEM?
THEY'RE ONLY HIRING COMPLETE TEAMS. SO I'D NEED TO ALREADY HAVE MY OWN ELF!
NO PROBLEM! IF IT'S PAYING, I'LL BE AN ELF!
YEAH, BUT I DON'T HAVE AN ELF COSTUME FOR YOU!
I ALREADY HAVE ONE!
REALLY?! THAT'S...
..NOT WHAT I HAD IN MIND.
AND YOU SAID I WASTED MY MONEY ON THIS LEGOLAS COSTUME!

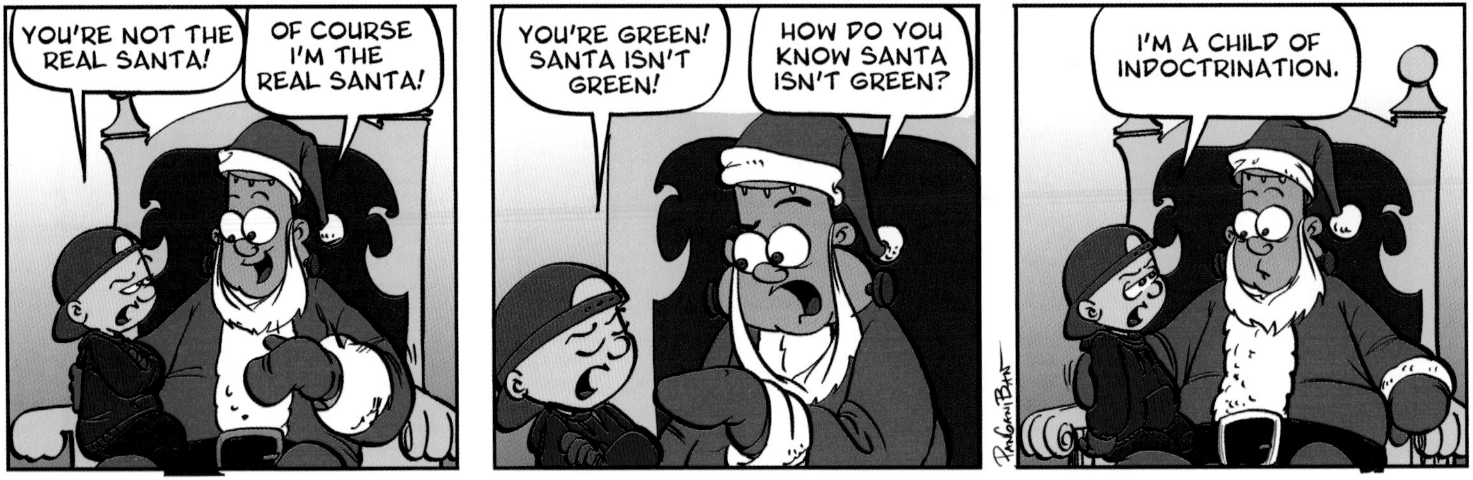
YOU'RE NOT THE REAL SANTA!
OF COURSE I'M THE REAL SANTA!
YOU'RE GREEN! SANTA ISN'T GREEN!
HOW DO YOU KNOW SANTA ISN'T GREEN?
I'M A CHILD OF INDOCTRINATION.

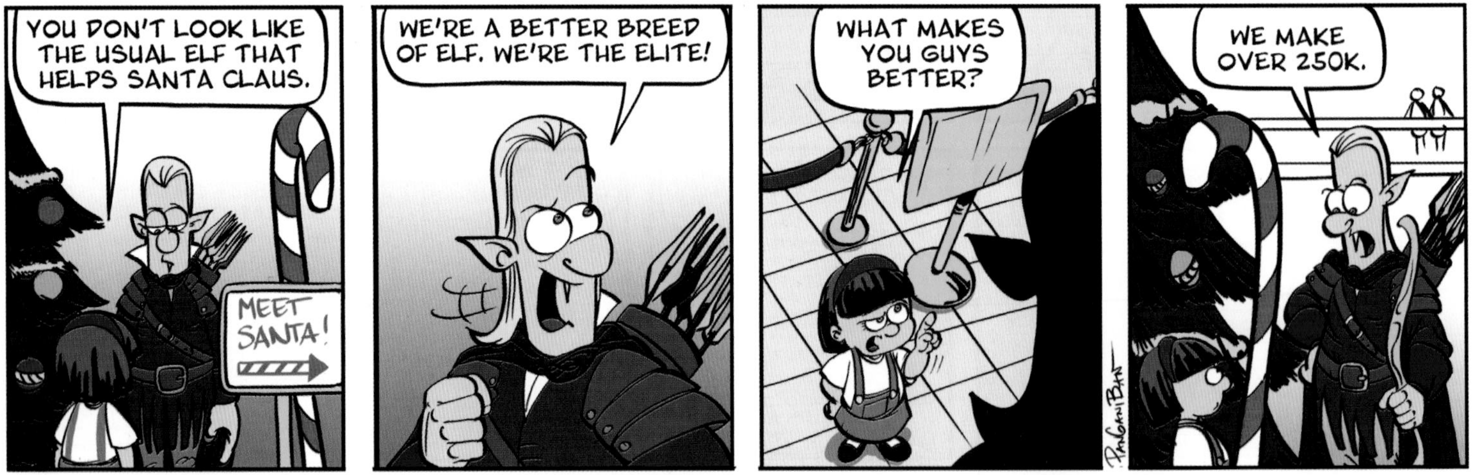
YOU DON'T LOOK LIKE THE USUAL ELF THAT HELPS SANTA CLAUS.
MEET SANTA!
WE'RE A BETTER BREED OF ELF. WE'RE THE ELITE!
WHAT MAKES YOU GUYS BETTER?
WE MAKE OVER 250K.

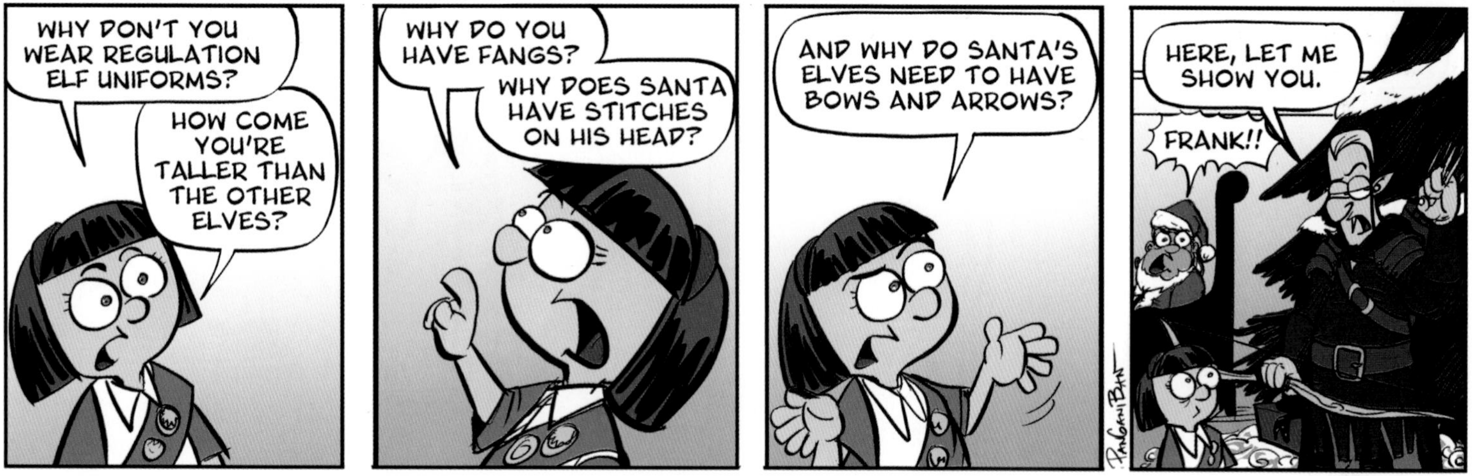
WHY DON'T YOU WEAR REGULATION ELF UNIFORMS?
HOW COME YOU'RE TALLER THAN THE OTHER ELVES?
WHY DO YOU HAVE FANGS?
WHY DOES SANTA HAVE STITCHES ON HIS HEAD?
AND WHY DO SANTA'S ELVES NEED TO HAVE BOWS AND ARROWS?
HERE, LET ME SHOW YOU.
FRANK!!

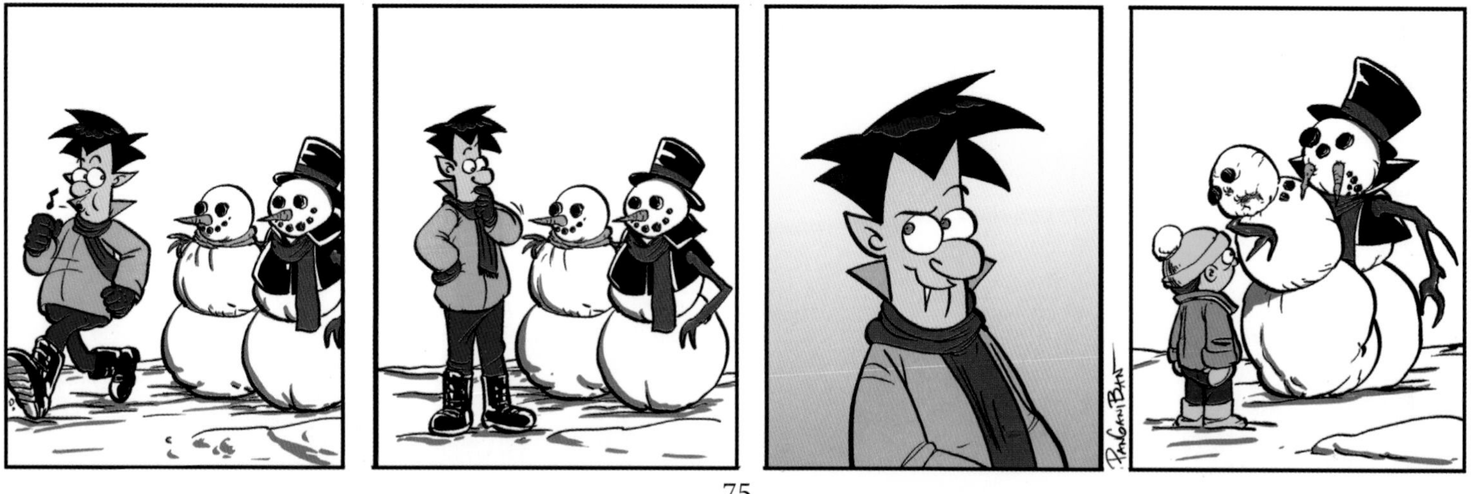

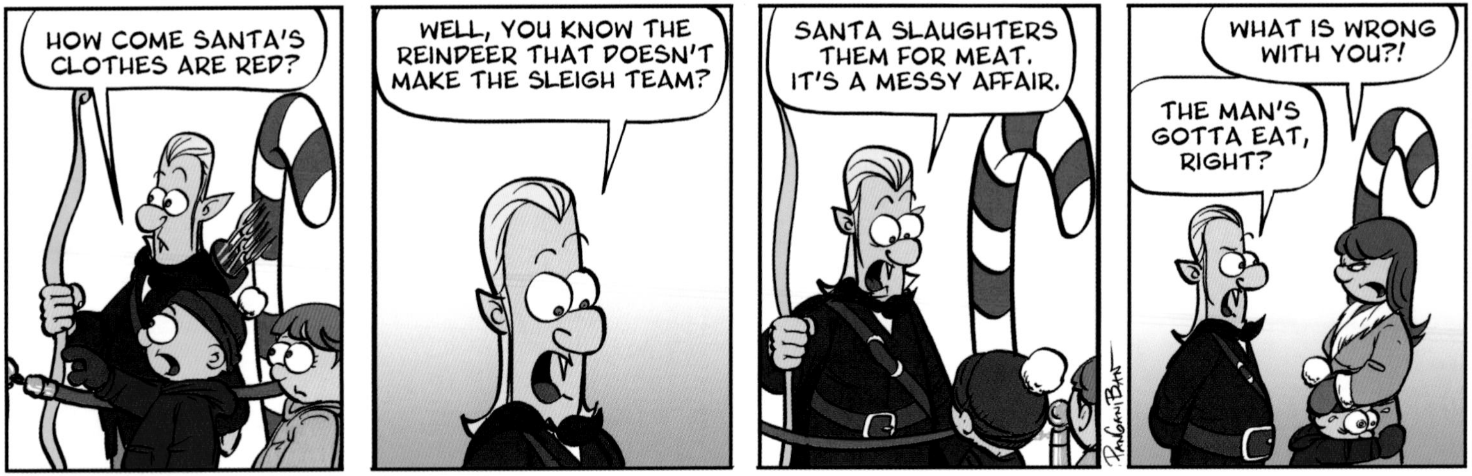
HOW COME SANTA'S CLOTHES ARE RED?
WELL, YOU KNOW THE REINDEER THAT DOESN'T MAKE THE SLEIGH TEAM?
SANTA SLAUGHTERS THEM FOR MEAT. IT'S A MESSY AFFAIR.
THE MAN'S GOTTA EAT, RIGHT?
WHAT IS WRONG WITH YOU?!

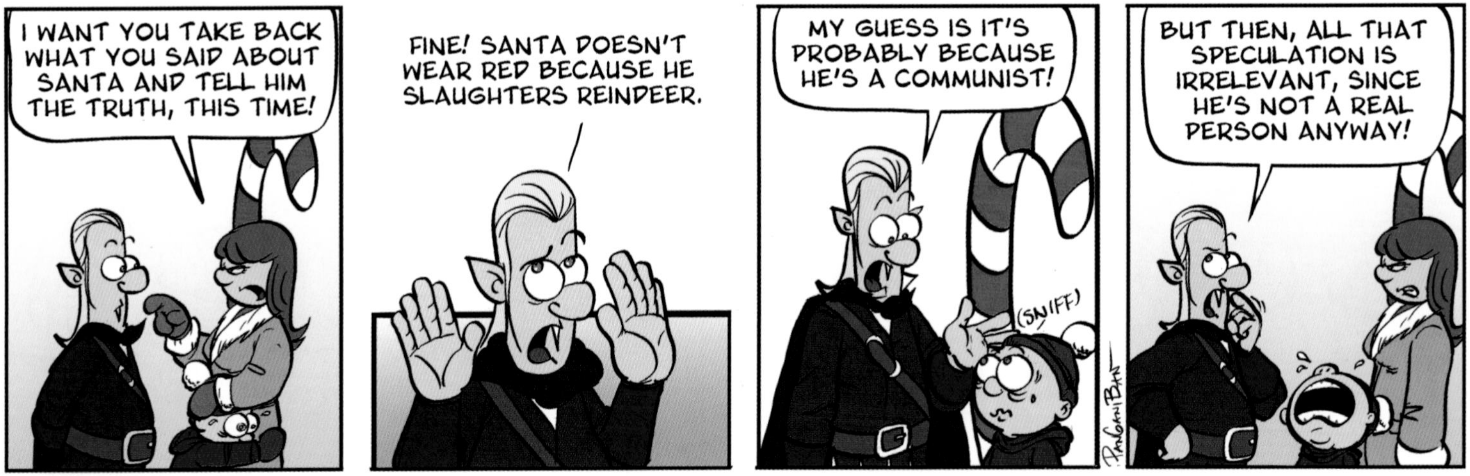
I WANT YOU TAKE BACK WHAT YOU SAID ABOUT SANTA AND TELL HIM THE TRUTH, THIS TIME!
FINE! SANTA DOESN'T WEAR RED BECAUSE HE SLAUGHTERS REINDEER.
MY GUESS IS IT'S PROBABLY BECAUSE HE'S A COMMUNIST!
(SNIFF)
BUT THEN, ALL THAT SPECULATION IS IRRELEVANT, SINCE HE'S NOT A REAL PERSON ANYWAY!

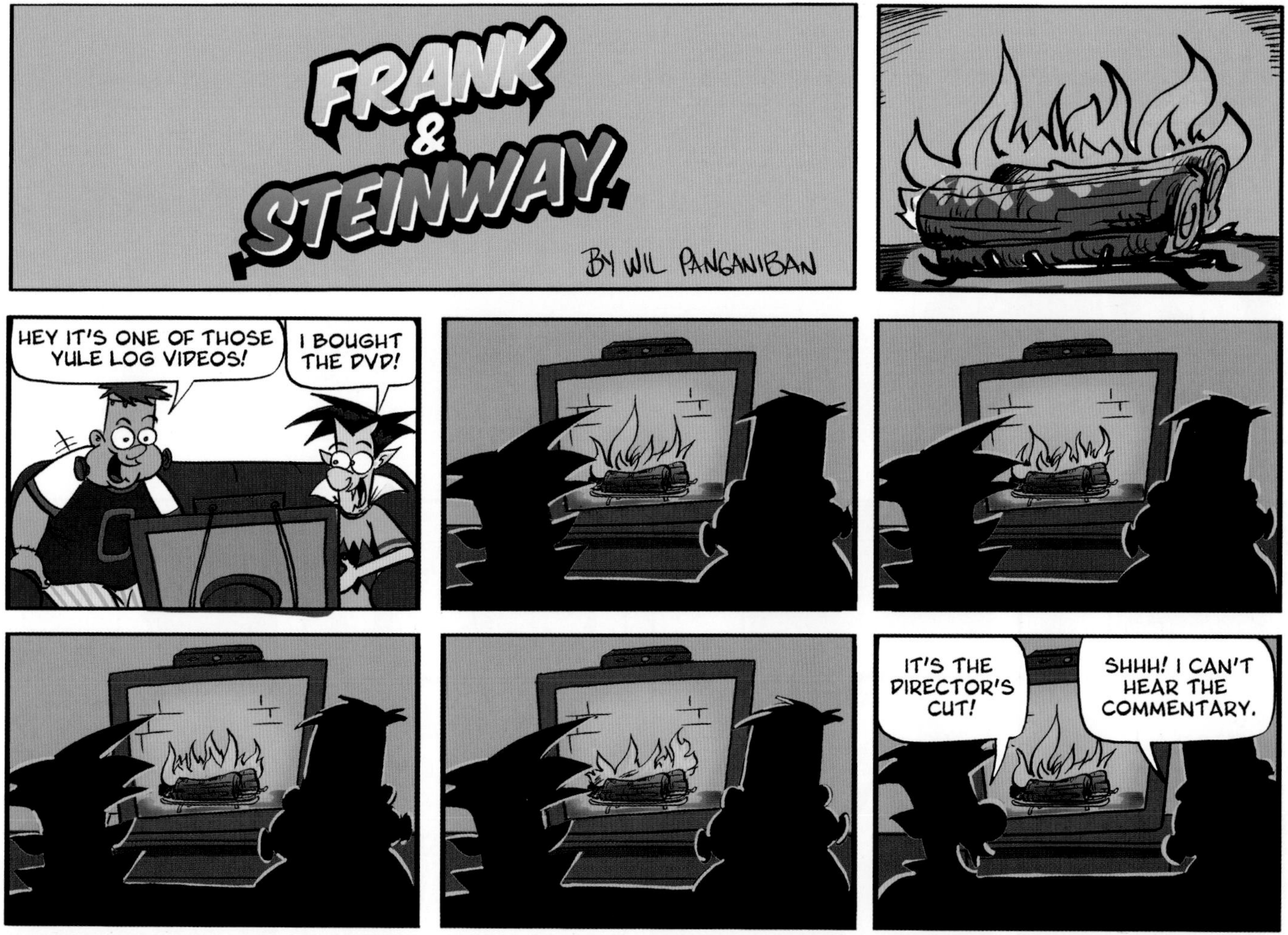
FRANK & STEINWAY
BY WIL PANGANIBAN
HEY IT'S ONE OF THOSE YULE LOG VIDEOS!
I BOUGHT THE DVD!
IT'S THE DIRECTOR'S CUT!
SHHH! I CAN'T HEAR THE COMMENTARY.

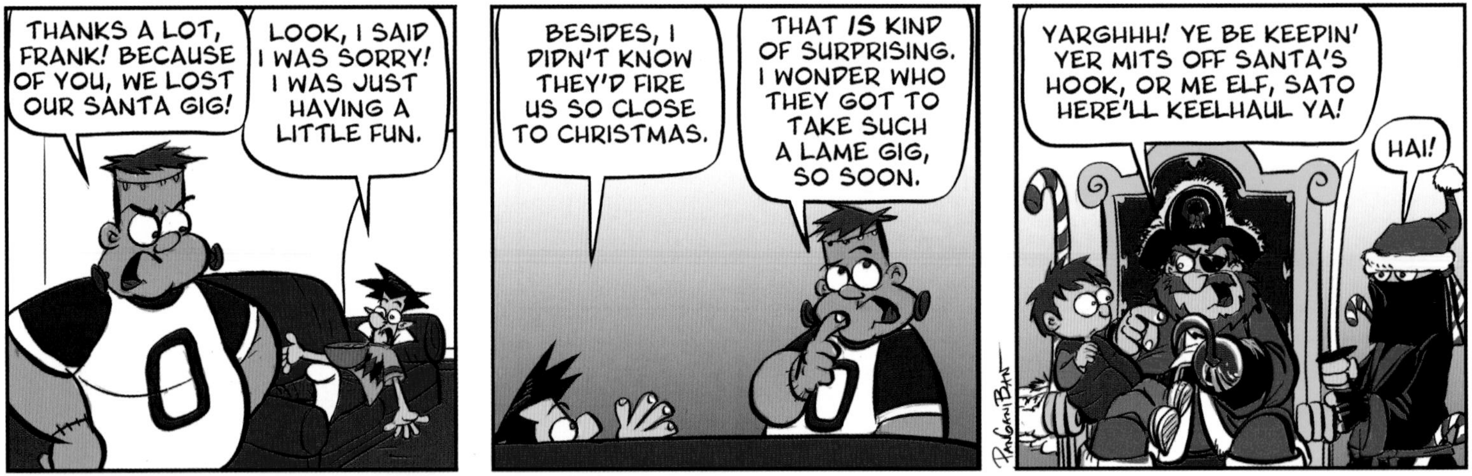
THANKS A LOT, FRANK! BECAUSE OF YOU, WE LOST OUR SANTA GIG!
LOOK, I SAID I WAS SORRY! I WAS JUST HAVING A LITTLE FUN.
BESIDES, I DIDN'T KNOW THEY'D FIRE US SO CLOSE TO CHRISTMAS.
THAT IS KIND OF SURPRISING. I WONDER WHO THEY GOT TO TAKE SUCH A LAME GIG, SO SOON.
YARGHHH! YE BE KEEPIN' YER MITS OFF SANTA'S HOOK, OR ME ELF, SATO HERE'LL KEELHAUL YA!
HAI!

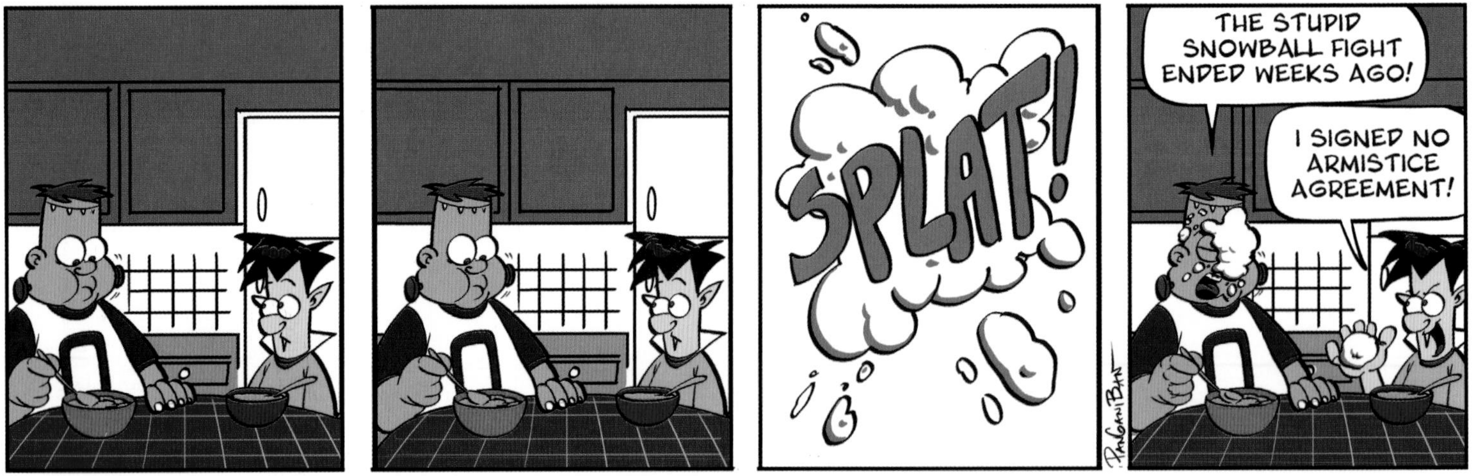
SPLAT!
THE STUPID SNOWBALL FIGHT ENDED WEEKS AGO!
I SIGNED NO ARMISTICE AGREEMENT!

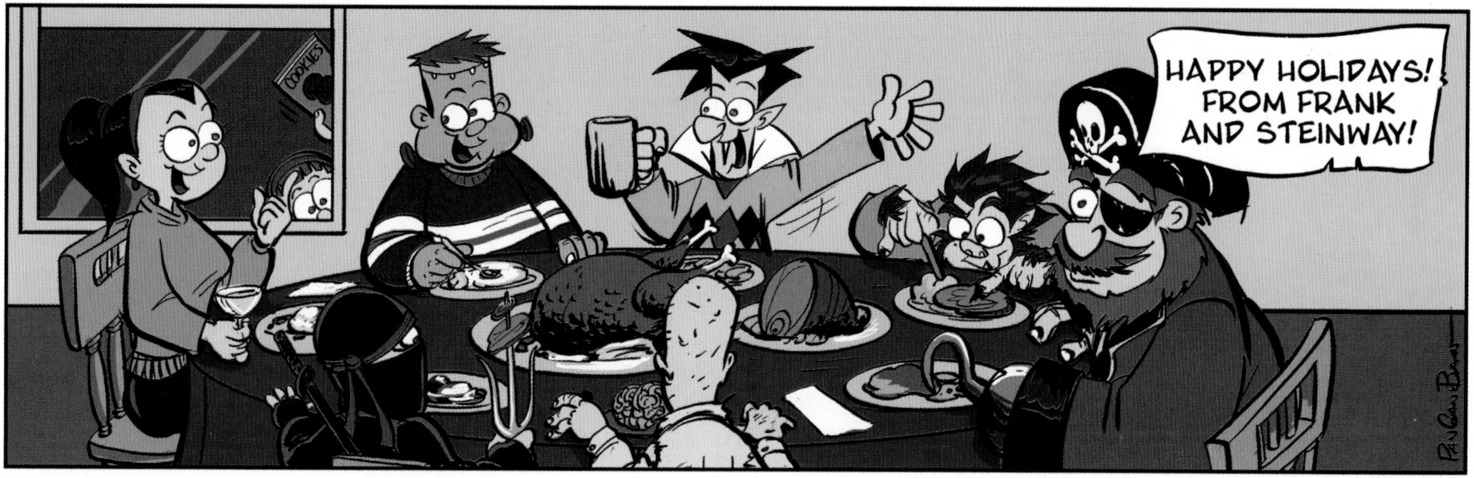
COOKIES
HAPPY HOLIDAYS! FROM FRANK AND STEINWAY!

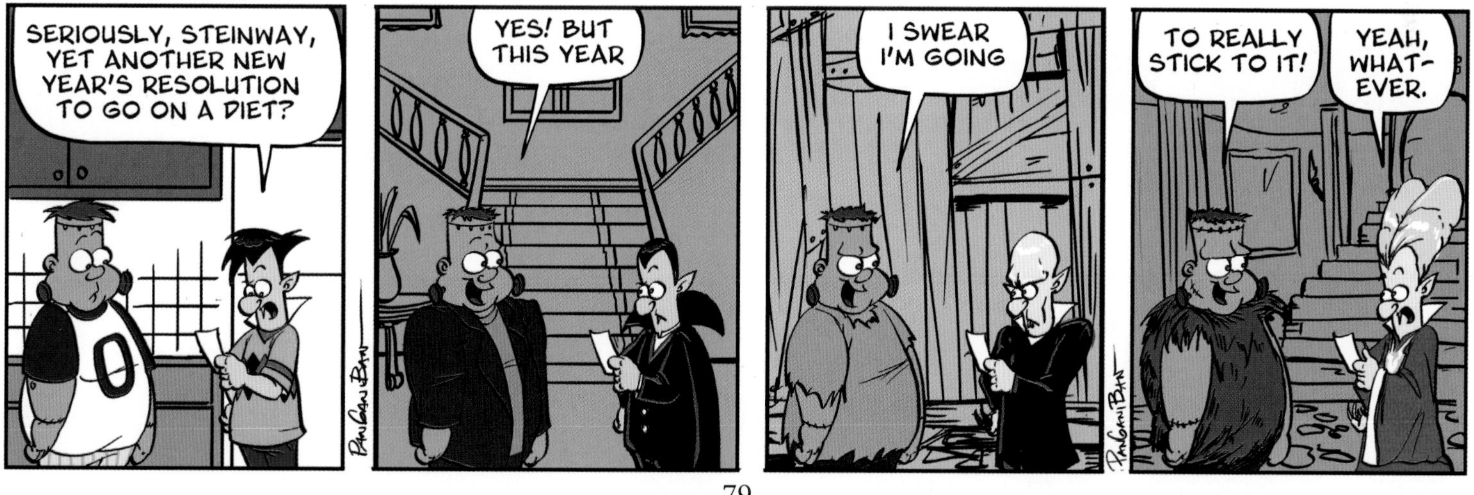
SERIOUSLY, STEINWAY, YET ANOTHER NEW YEAR'S RESOLUTION TO GO ON A DIET?
YES! BUT THIS YEAR
I SWEAR I'M GOING
TO REALLY STICK TO IT!
YEAH, WHAT-EVER.

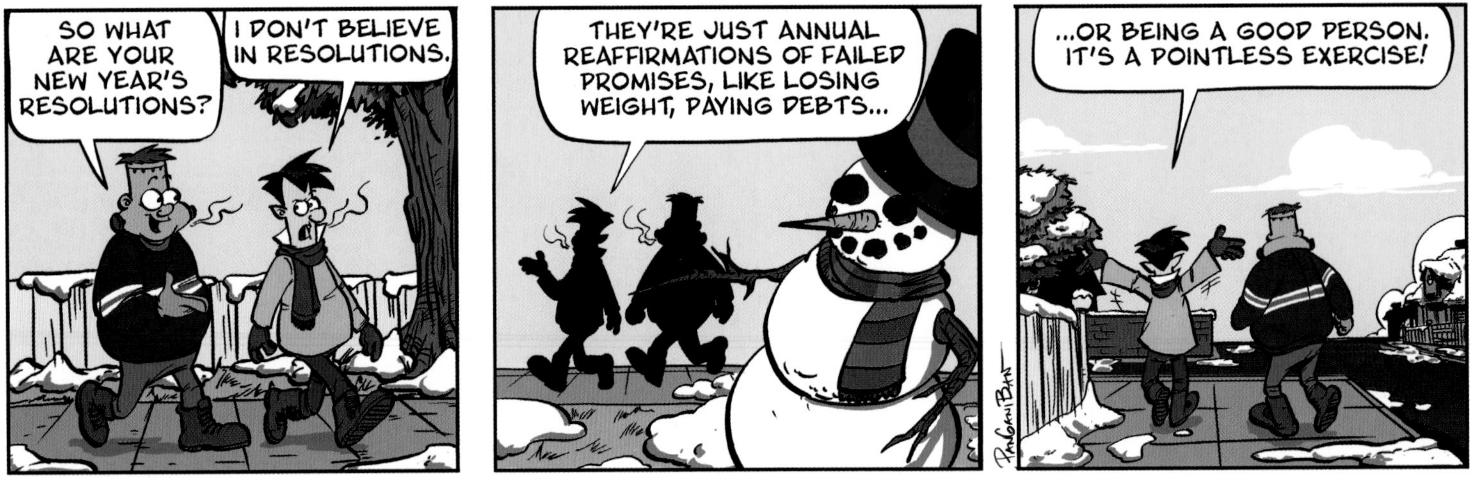
SO WHAT ARE YOUR NEW YEAR'S RESOLUTIONS?
I DON'T BELIEVE IN RESOLUTIONS.
THEY'RE JUST ANNUAL REAFFIRMATIONS OF FAILED PROMISES, LIKE LOSING WEIGHT, PAYING DEBTS...
...OR BEING A GOOD PERSON. IT'S A POINTLESS EXERCISE!

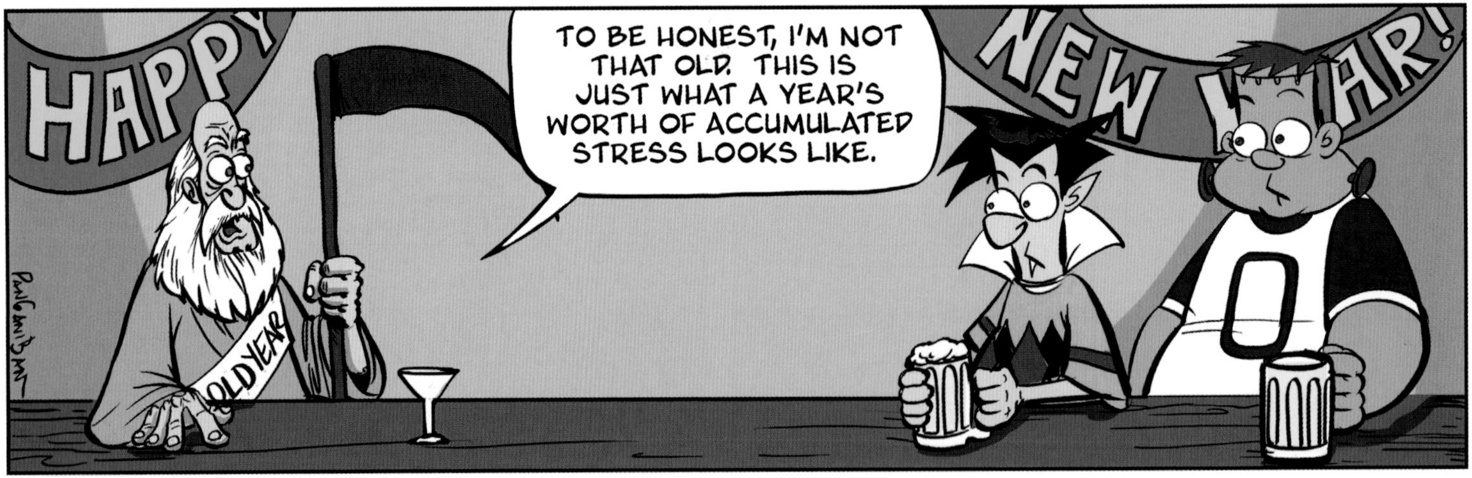
HAPPY
TO BE HONEST, I'M NOT THAT OLD. THIS IS JUST WHAT A YEAR'S WORTH OF ACCUMULATED STRESS LOOKS LIKE.
OLD YEAR

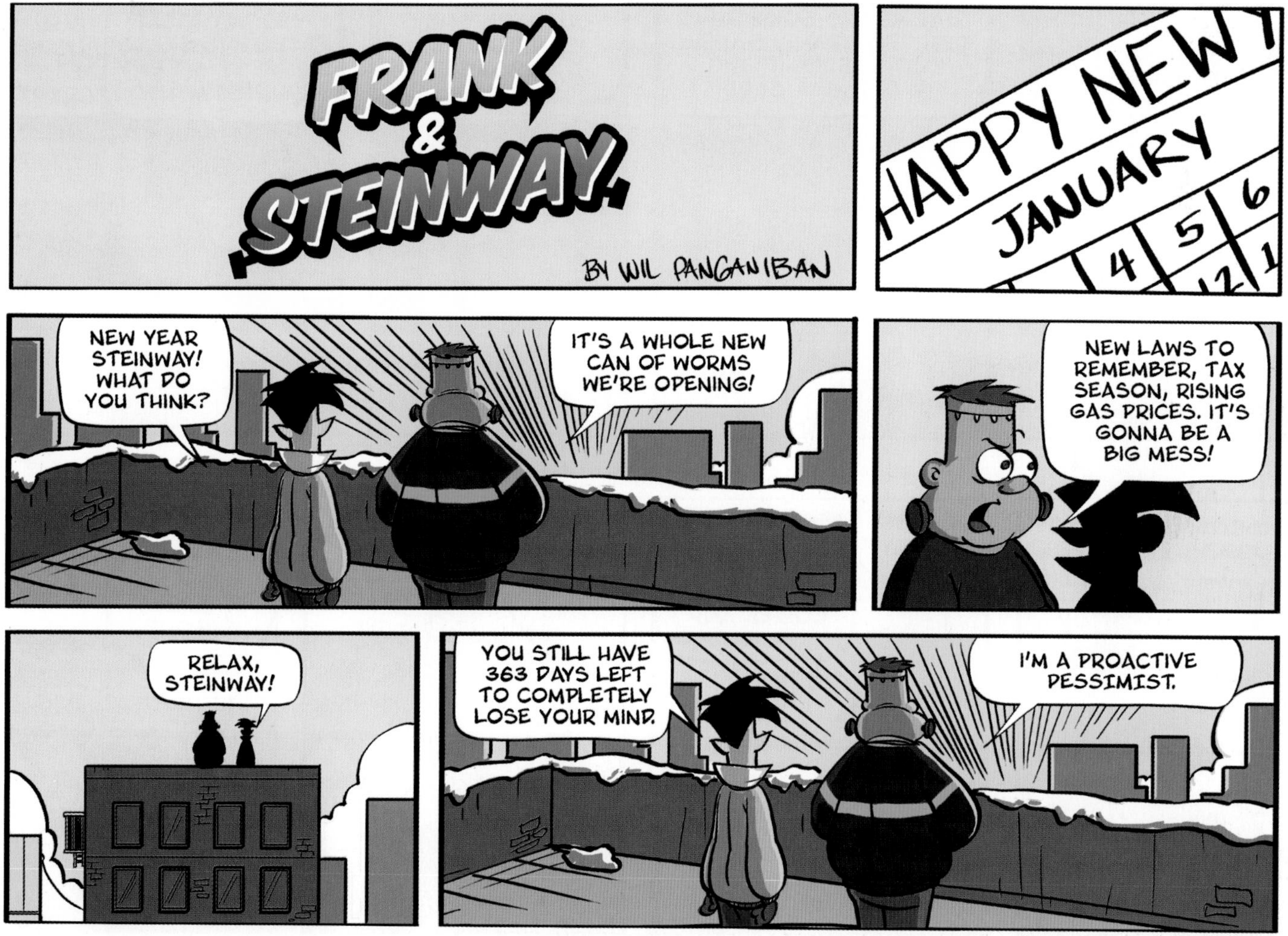
FRANK & STEINWAY
BY WIL PANGANIBAN
HAPPY NEW
JANUARY
4 5 6
12 1
NEW YEAR STEINWAY! WHAT DO YOU THINK?
IT'S A WHOLE NEW CAN OF WORMS WE'RE OPENING!
NEW LAWS TO REMEMBER, TAX SEASON, RISING GAS PRICES. IT'S GONNA BE A BIG MESS!
RELAX, STEINWAY!
YOU STILL HAVE 363 DAYS LEFT TO COMPLETELY LOSE YOUR MIND.
I'M A PROACTIVE PESSIMIST.

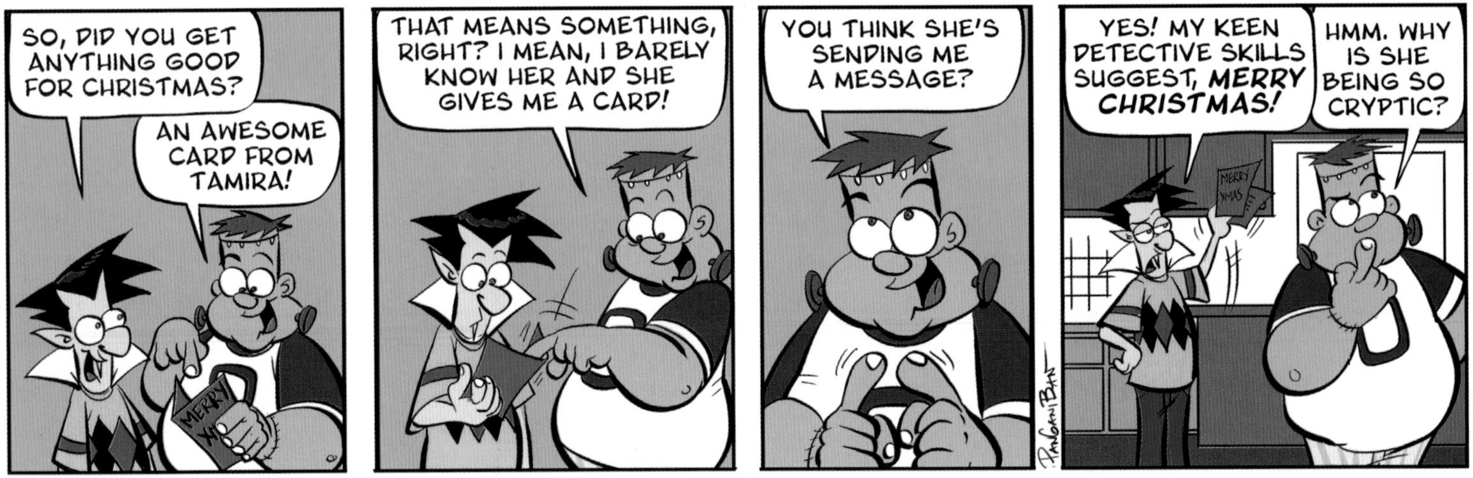
SO, DID YOU GET ANYTHING GOOD FOR CHRISTMAS?
AN AWESOME CARD FROM TAMIRA!
THAT MEANS SOMETHING, RIGHT? I MEAN, I BARELY KNOW HER AND SHE GIVES ME A CARD!
YOU THINK SHE'S SENDING ME A MESSAGE?
YES! MY KEEN DETECTIVE SKILLS SUGGEST, **MERRY CHRISTMAS!**
HMM. WHY IS SHE BEING SO CRYPTIC?
MERRY XMAS

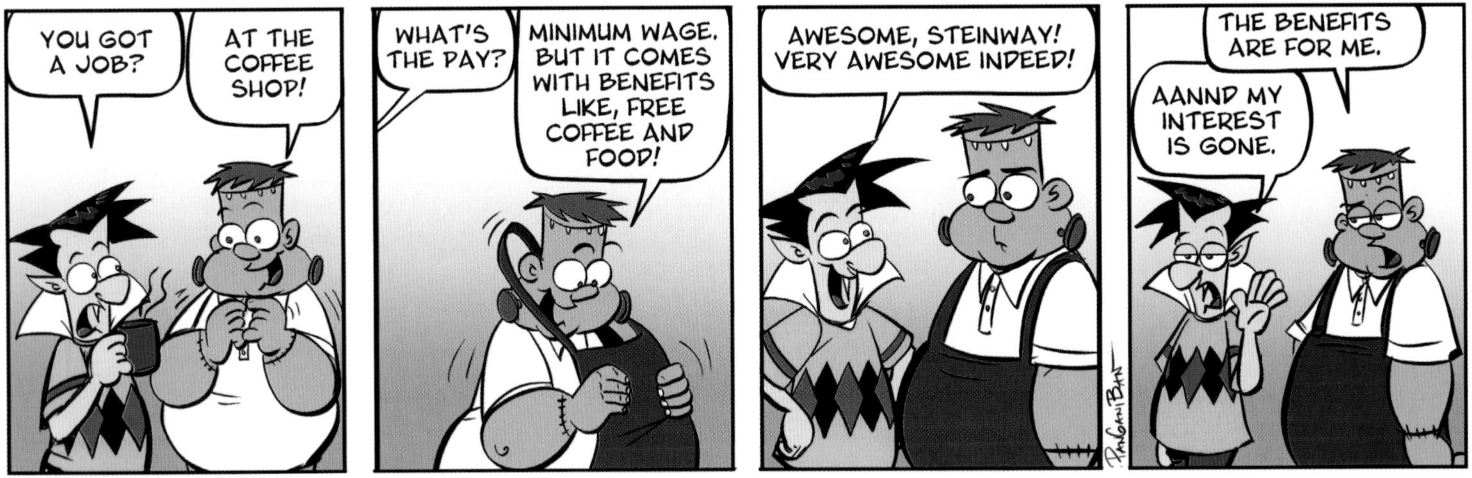
YOU GOT A JOB?
AT THE COFFEE SHOP!
WHAT'S THE PAY?
MINIMUM WAGE. BUT IT COMES WITH BENEFITS LIKE, FREE COFFEE AND FOOD!
AWESOME, STEINWAY! VERY AWESOME INDEED!
THE BENEFITS ARE FOR ME.
AANND MY INTEREST IS GONE.

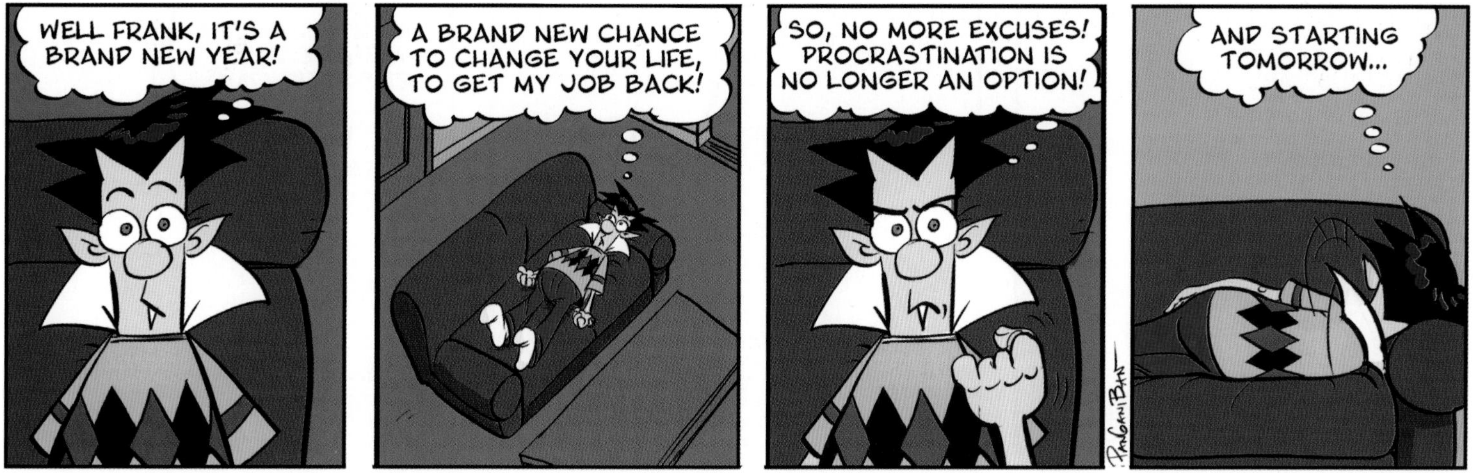
WELL FRANK, IT'S A BRAND NEW YEAR!
A BRAND NEW CHANCE TO CHANGE YOUR LIFE, TO GET MY JOB BACK!
SO, NO MORE EXCUSES! PROCRASTINATION IS NO LONGER AN OPTION!
AND STARTING TOMORROW...
PANGANIBAN

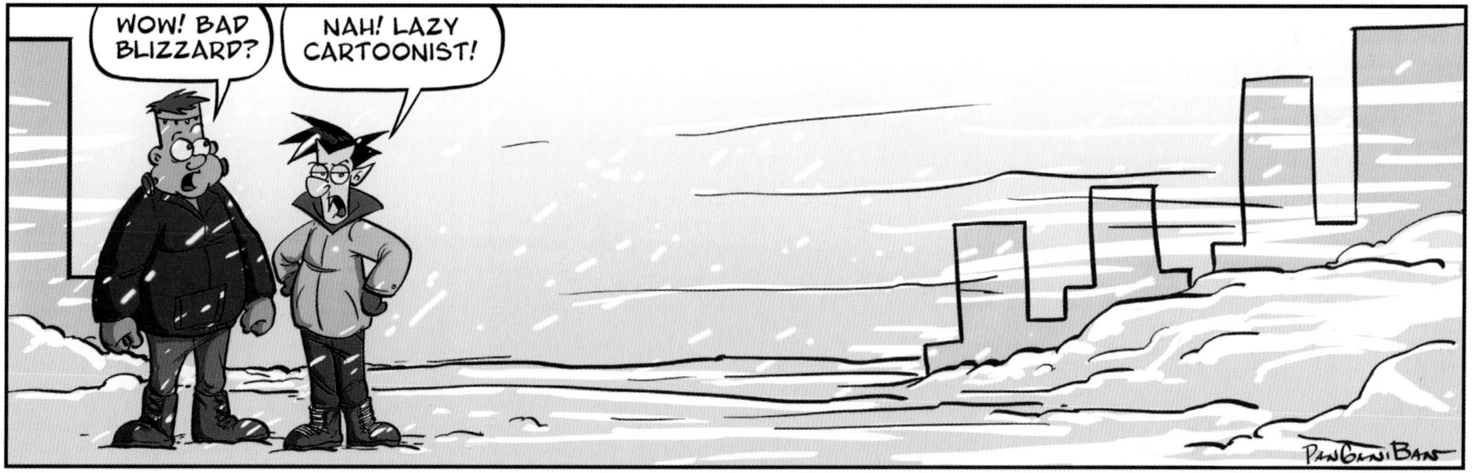
WOW! BAD BLIZZARD?
NAH! LAZY CARTOONIST!
PANGANIBAN

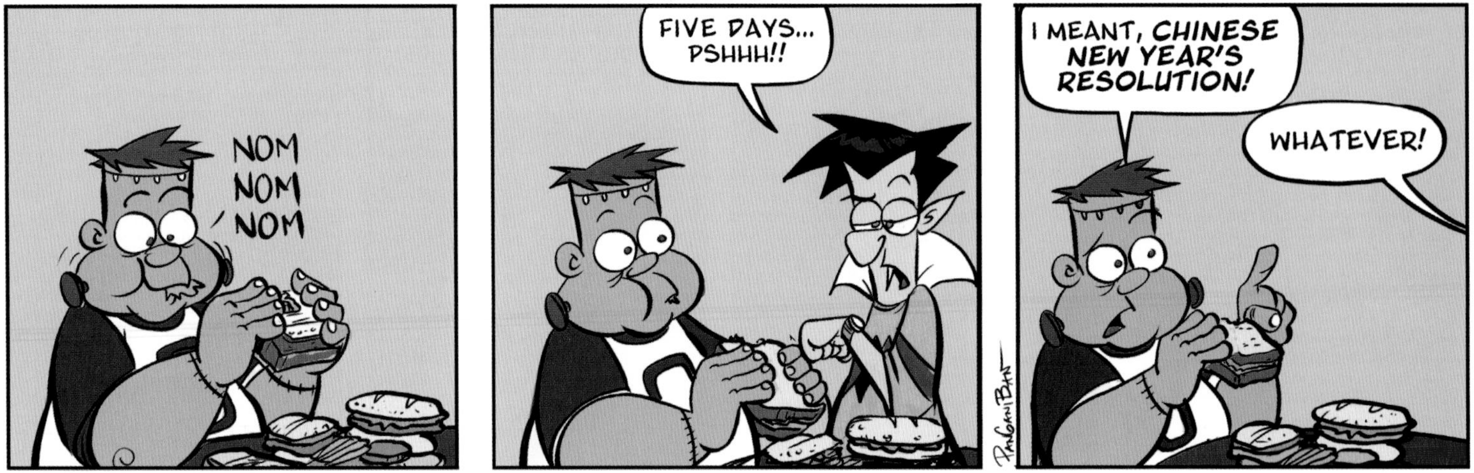
NOM
NOM
NOM
FIVE DAYS... PSHHH!!
I MEANT, CHINESE NEW YEAR'S RESOLUTION!
WHATEVER!

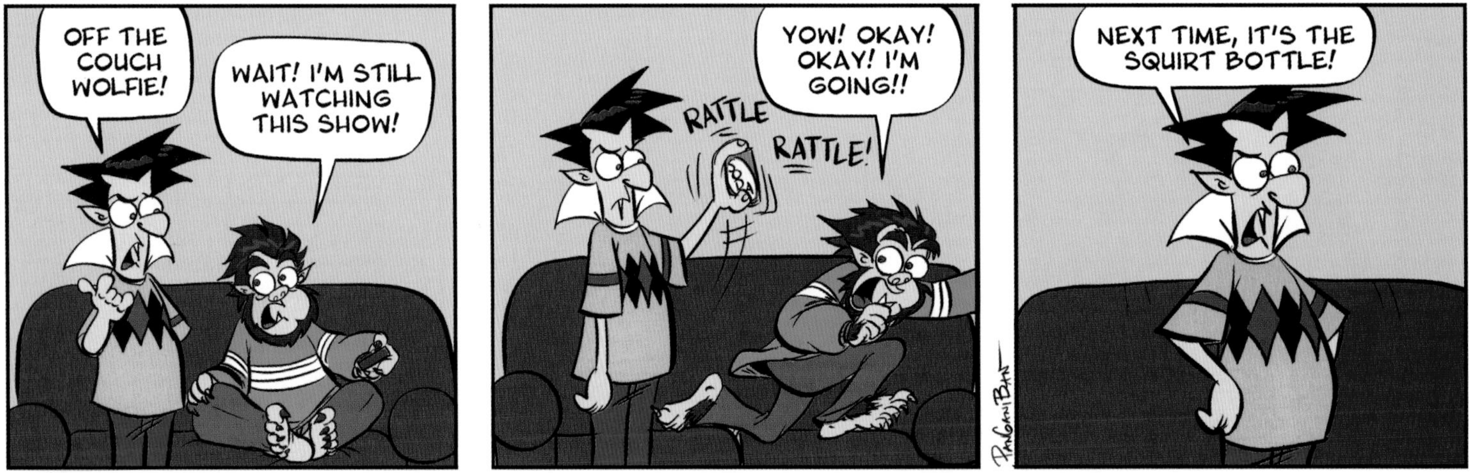
OFF THE COUCH WOLFIE!
WAIT! I'M STILL WATCHING THIS SHOW!
RATTLE
RATTLE!
YOW! OKAY! OKAY! I'M GOING!!
NEXT TIME, IT'S THE SQUIRT BOTTLE!

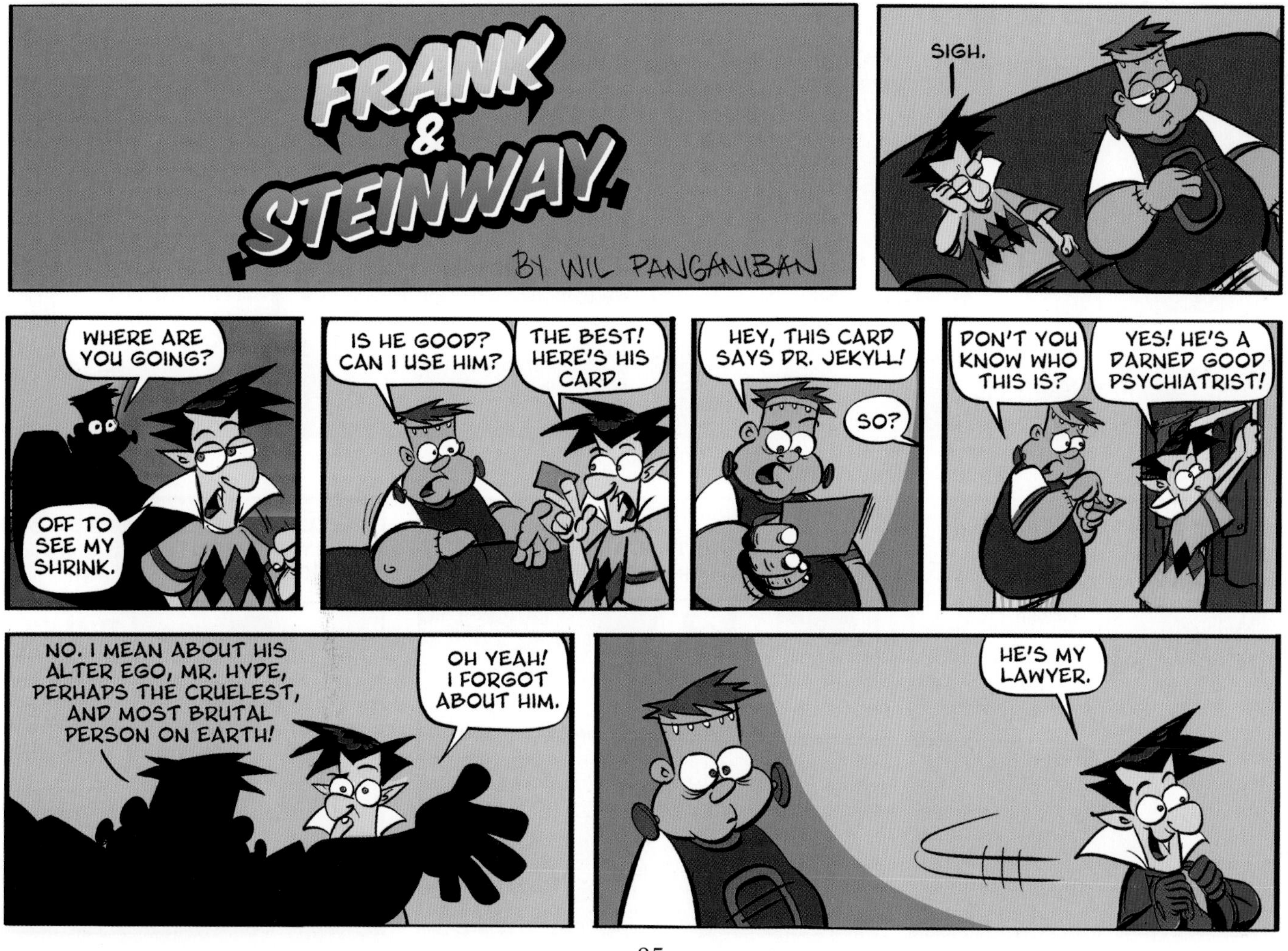
FRANK & STEINWAY
BY WIL PANGANIBAN
SIGH.
WHERE ARE YOU GOING?
OFF TO SEE MY SHRINK.
IS HE GOOD? CAN I USE HIM?
THE BEST! HERE'S HIS CARD.
HEY, THIS CARD SAYS DR. JEKYLL!
SO?
DON'T YOU KNOW WHO THIS IS?
YES! HE'S A DARNED GOOD PSYCHIATRIST!
NO. I MEAN ABOUT HIS ALTER EGO, MR. HYDE, PERHAPS THE CRUELEST, AND MOST BRUTAL PERSON ON EARTH!
OH YEAH! I FORGOT ABOUT HIM.
HE'S MY LAWYER.

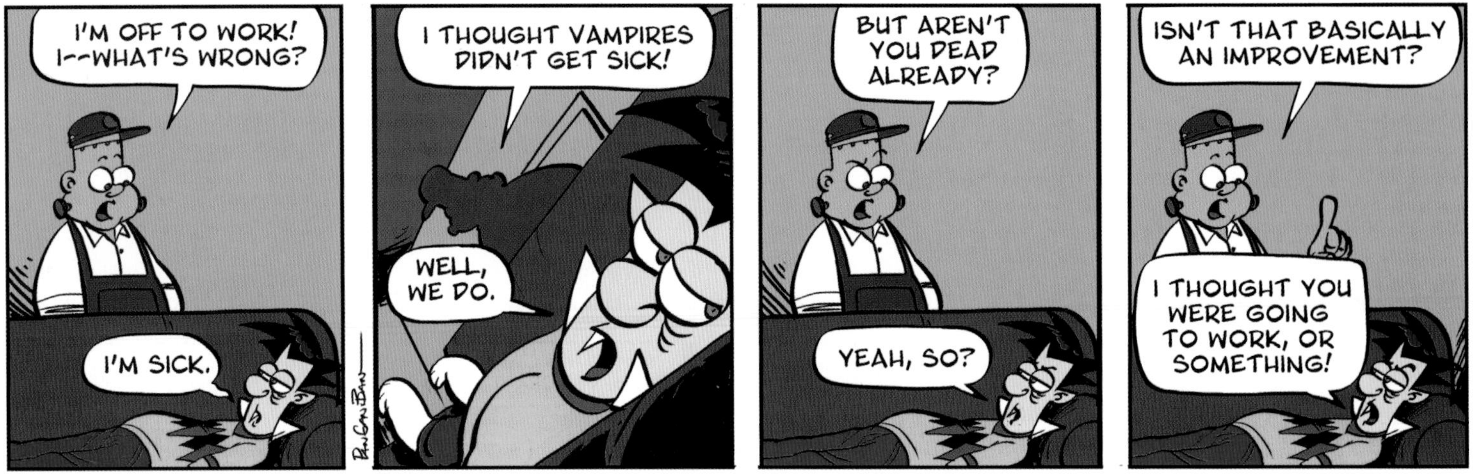
I'M OFF TO WORK! I--WHAT'S WRONG?
I'M SICK.
I THOUGHT VAMPIRES DIDN'T GET SICK!
WELL, WE DO.
BUT AREN'T YOU DEAD ALREADY?
YEAH, SO?
ISN'T THAT BASICALLY AN IMPROVEMENT?
I THOUGHT YOU WERE GOING TO WORK, OR SOMETHING!

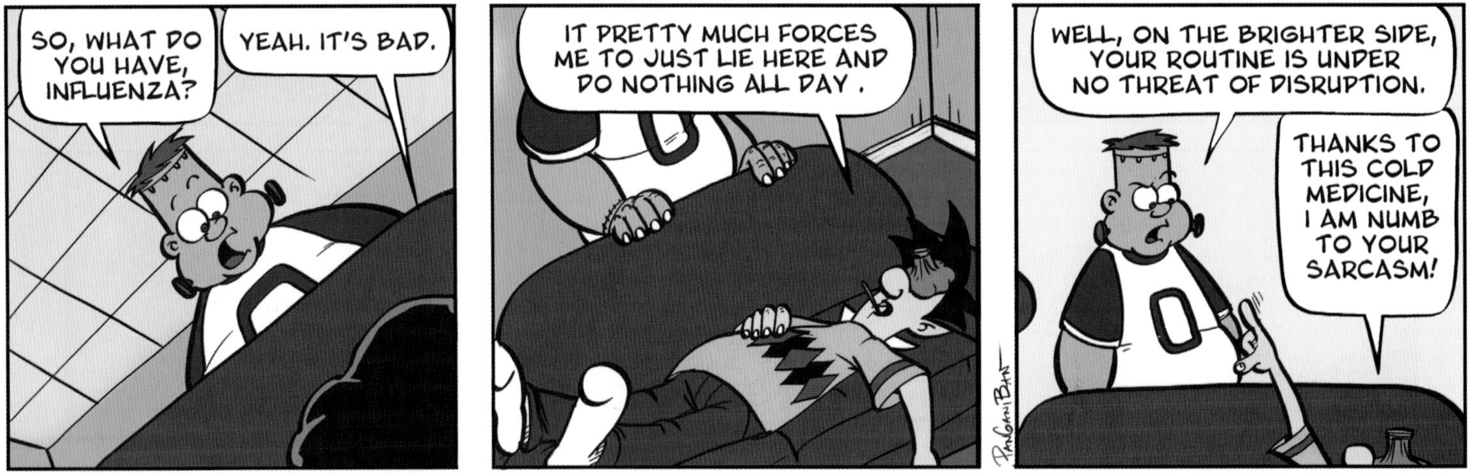
SO, WHAT DO YOU HAVE, INFLUENZA?
YEAH. IT'S BAD.
IT PRETTY MUCH FORCES ME TO JUST LIE HERE AND DO NOTHING ALL DAY .
WELL, ON THE BRIGHTER SIDE, YOUR ROUTINE IS UNDER NO THREAT OF DISRUPTION.
THANKS TO THIS COLD MEDICINE, I AM NUMB TO YOUR SARCASM!

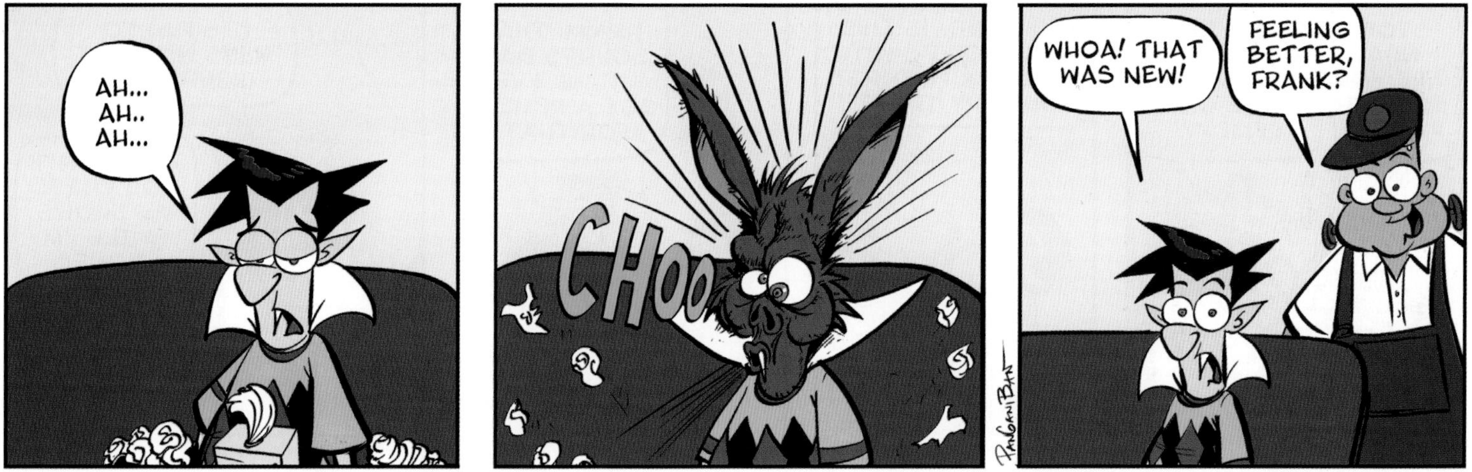
AH... AH.. AH...
CHOO
WHOA! THAT WAS NEW!
FEELING BETTER, FRANK?

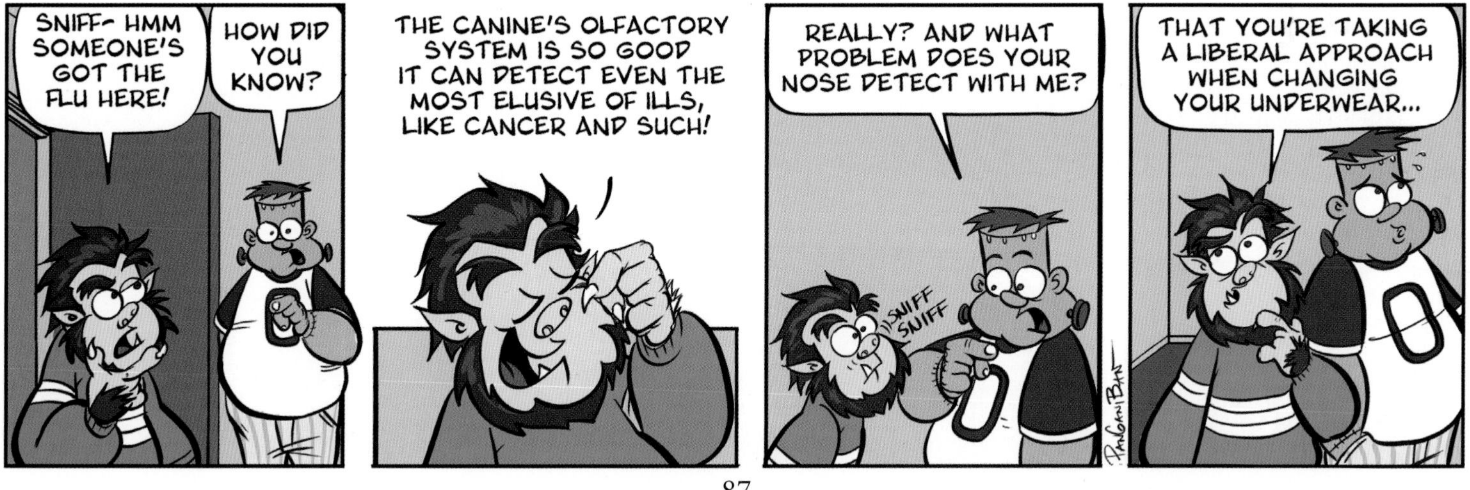
SNIFF- HMM SOMEONE'S GOT THE FLU HERE!
HOW DID YOU KNOW?
THE CANINE'S OLFACTORY SYSTEM IS SO GOOD IT CAN DETECT EVEN THE MOST ELUSIVE OF ILLS, LIKE CANCER AND SUCH!
REALLY? AND WHAT PROBLEM DOES YOUR NOSE DETECT WITH ME?
SNIFF SNIFF
THAT YOU'RE TAKING A LIBERAL APPROACH WHEN CHANGING YOUR UNDERWEAR...

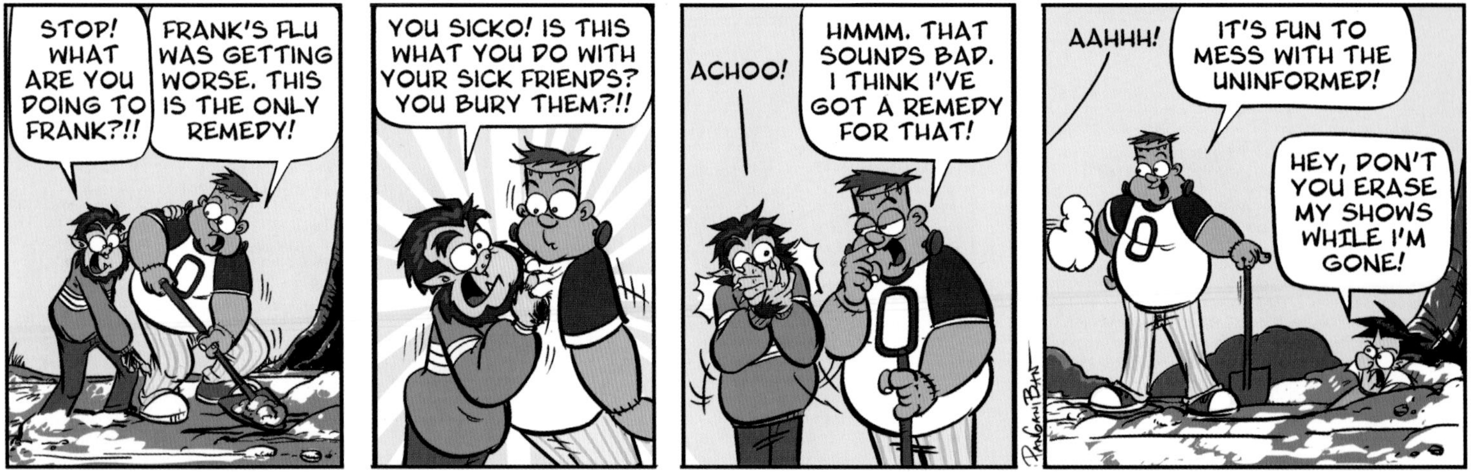
STOP! WHAT ARE YOU DOING TO FRANK?!!
FRANK'S FLU WAS GETTING WORSE. THIS IS THE ONLY REMEDY!
YOU SICKO! IS THIS WHAT YOU DO WITH YOUR SICK FRIENDS? YOU BURY THEM?!!
ACHOO!
HMMM. THAT SOUNDS BAD. I THINK I'VE GOT A REMEDY FOR THAT!
AAHHH!
IT'S FUN TO MESS WITH THE UNINFORMED!
HEY, DON'T YOU ERASE MY SHOWS WHILE I'M GONE!

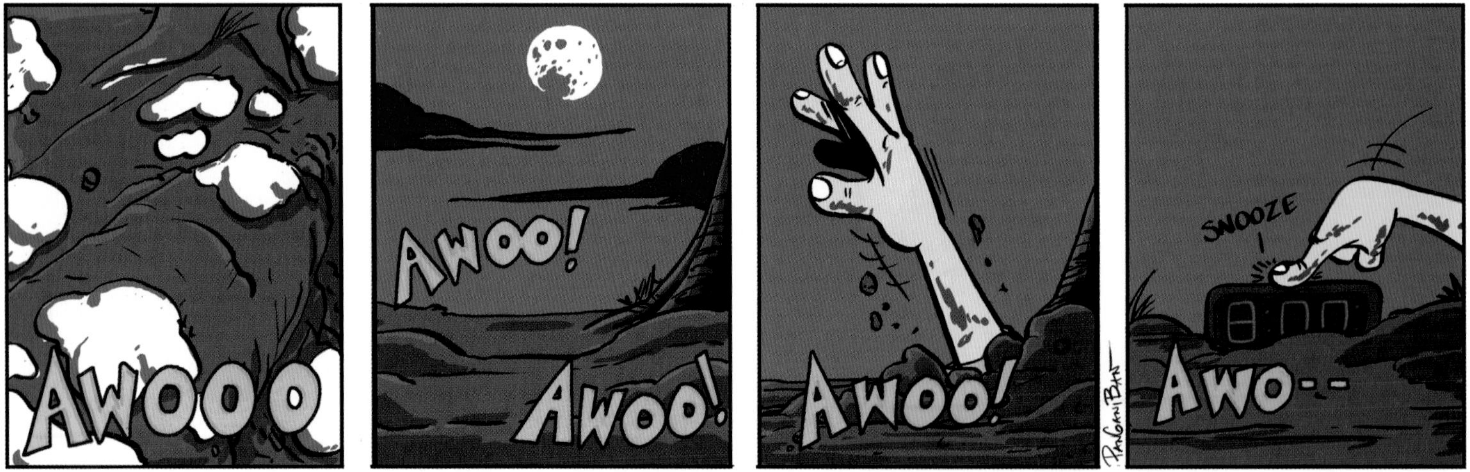
AWOOO
AWOO!
AWOO!
AWOO!
SNOOZE
AWO--

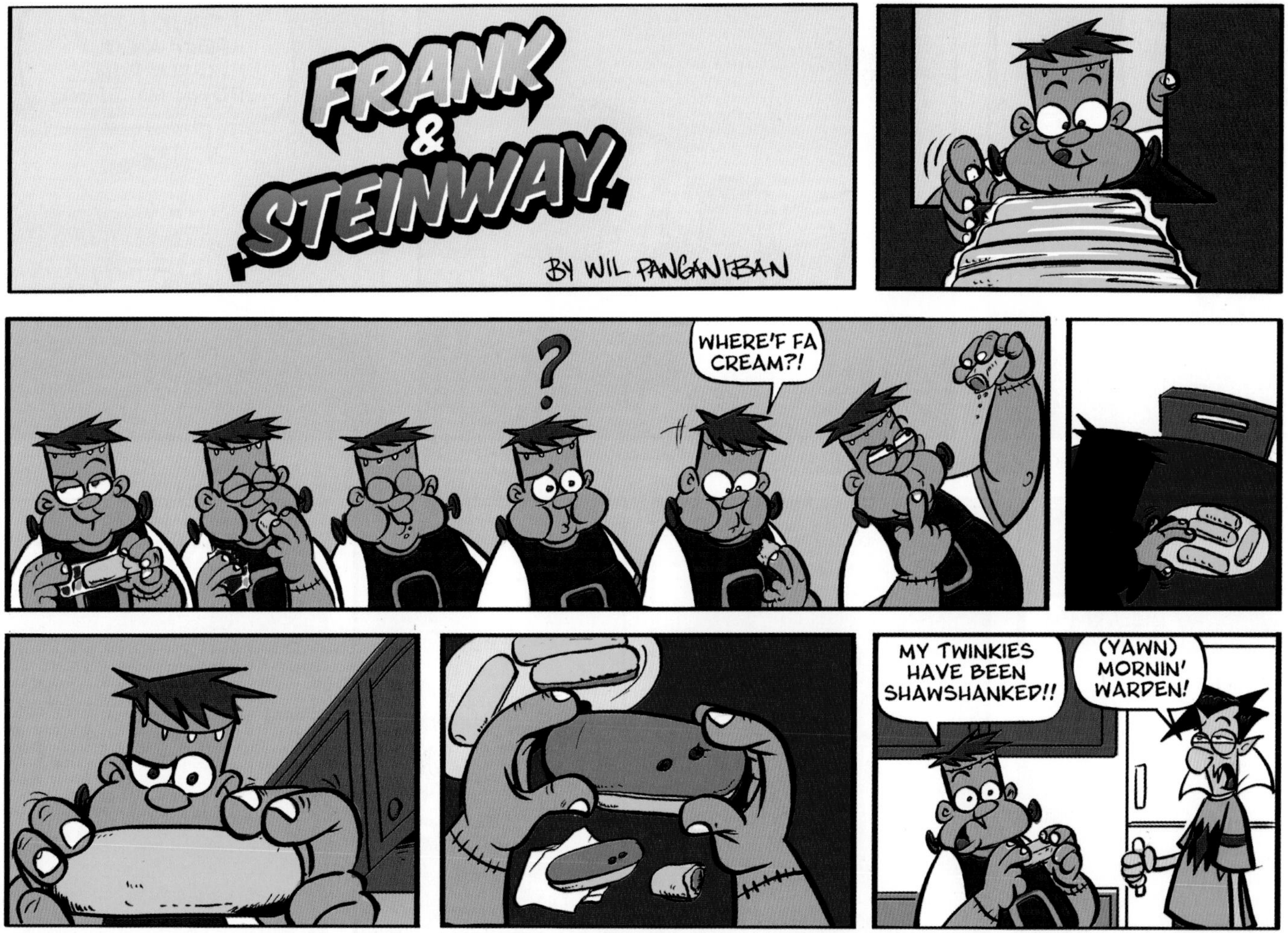
FRANK & STEINWAY
BY WIL PANGANIBAN
?
WHERE'F FA CREAM?!
MY TWINKIES HAVE BEEN SHAWSHANKED!!
(YAWN) MORNIN' WARDEN!

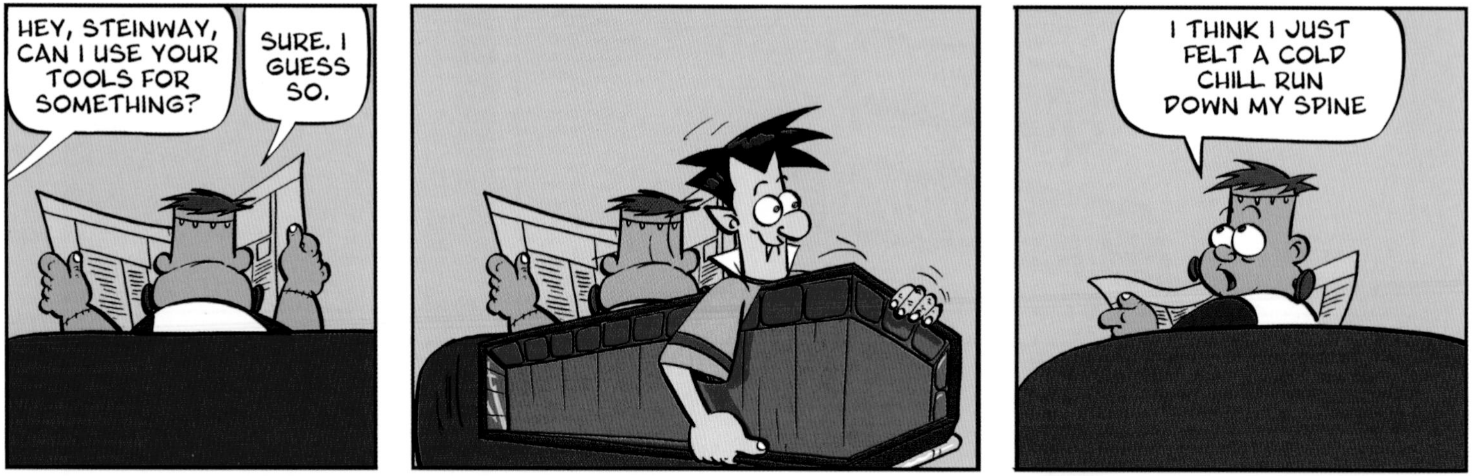
HEY, STEINWAY, CAN I USE YOUR TOOLS FOR SOMETHING?
SURE. I GUESS SO.
I THINK I JUST FELT A COLD CHILL RUN DOWN MY SPINE

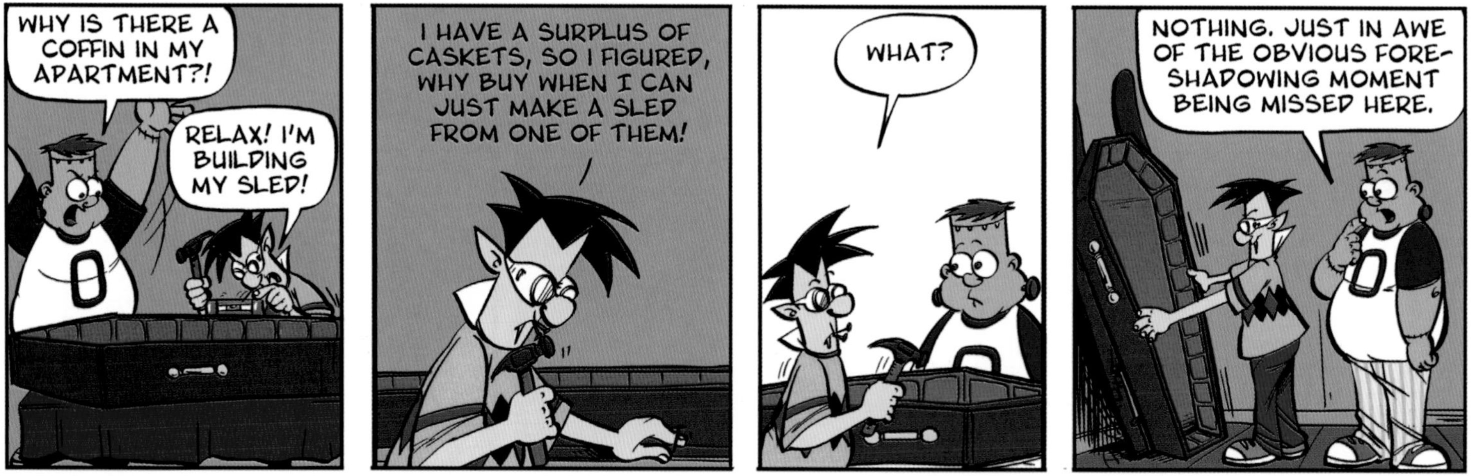
WHY IS THERE A COFFIN IN MY APARTMENT?!
RELAX! I'M BUILDING MY SLED!
I HAVE A SURPLUS OF CASKETS, SO I FIGURED, WHY BUY WHEN I CAN JUST MAKE A SLED FROM ONE OF THEM!
WHAT?
NOTHING. JUST IN AWE OF THE OBVIOUS FORE-SHADOWING MOMENT BEING MISSED HERE.

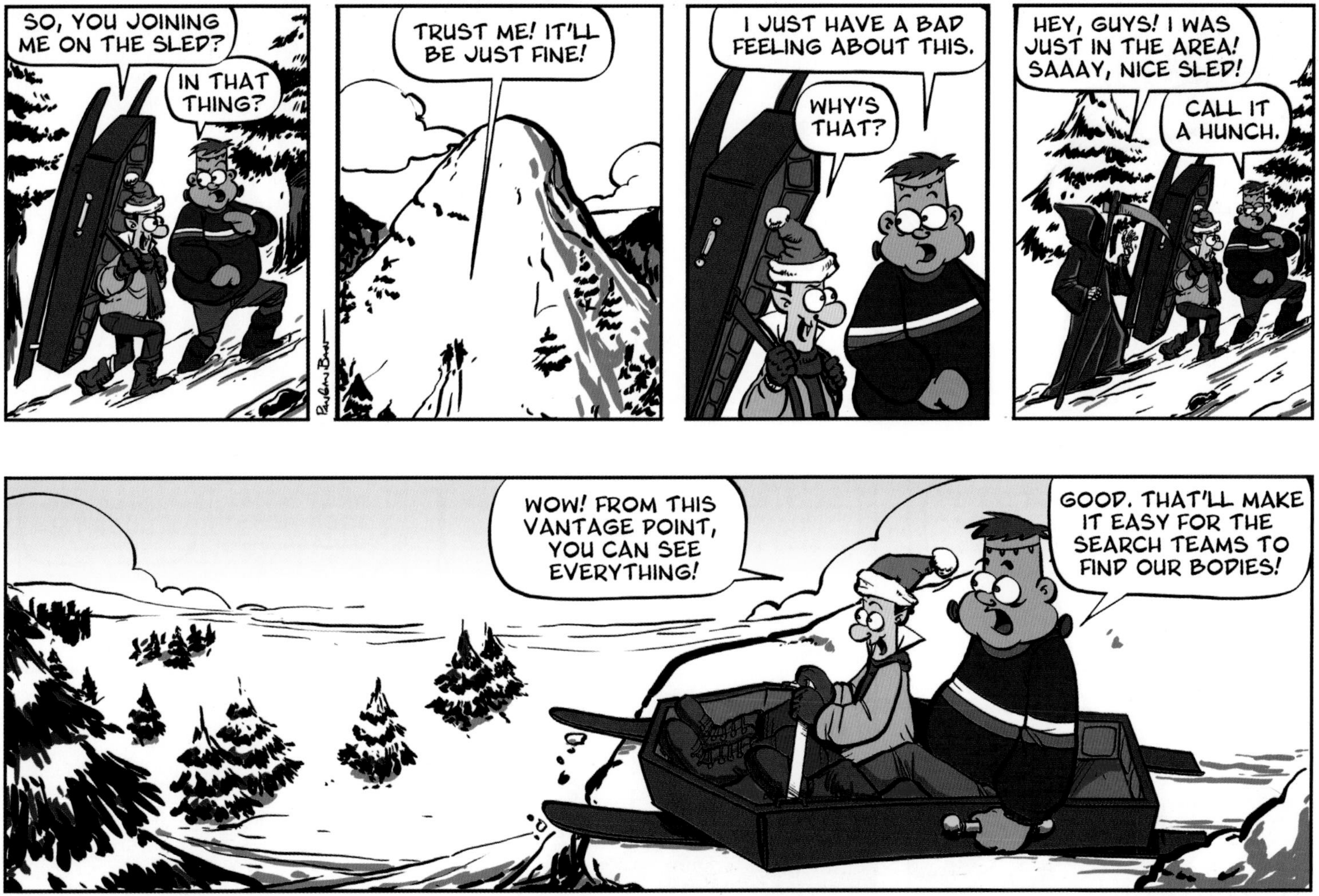
SO, YOU JOINING ME ON THE SLED?
IN THAT THING?
TRUST ME! IT'LL BE JUST FINE!
I JUST HAVE A BAD FEELING ABOUT THIS.
WHY'S THAT?
HEY, GUYS! I WAS JUST IN THE AREA! SAAAY, NICE SLED!
CALL IT A HUNCH.
WOW! FROM THIS VANTAGE POINT, YOU CAN SEE EVERYTHING!
GOOD. THAT'LL MAKE IT EASY FOR THE SEARCH TEAMS TO FIND OUR BODIES!

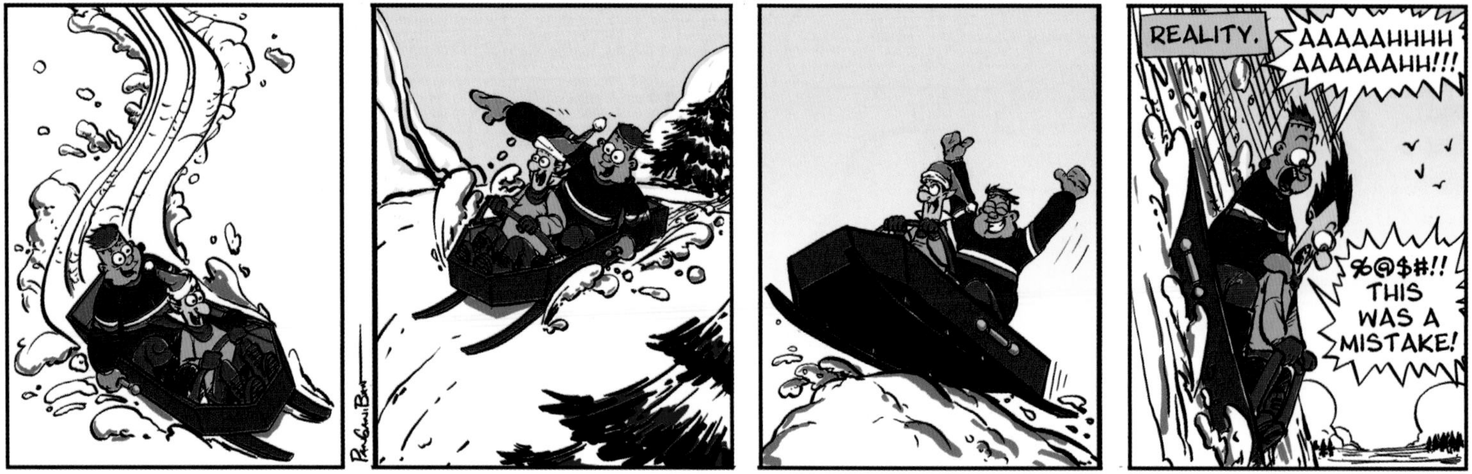
REALITY.
AAAAAHHHH AAAAAAHH!!!
%@$#!! THIS WAS A MISTAKE!

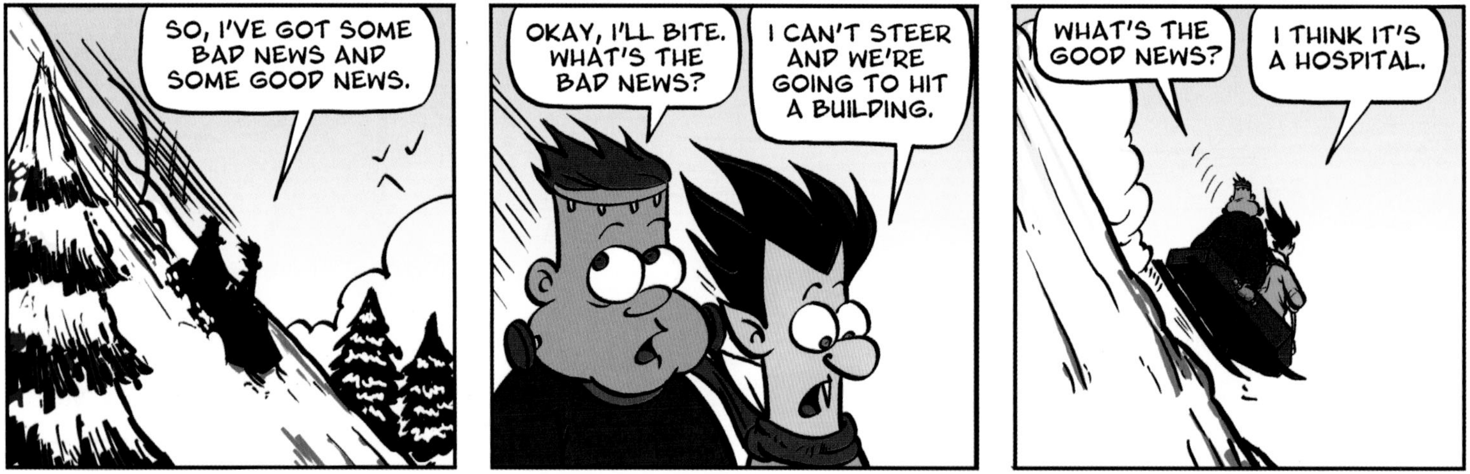
SO, I'VE GOT SOME BAD NEWS AND SOME GOOD NEWS.
OKAY, I'LL BITE. WHAT'S THE BAD NEWS?
I CAN'T STEER AND WE'RE GOING TO HIT A BUILDING.
WHAT'S THE GOOD NEWS?
I THINK IT'S A HOSPITAL.

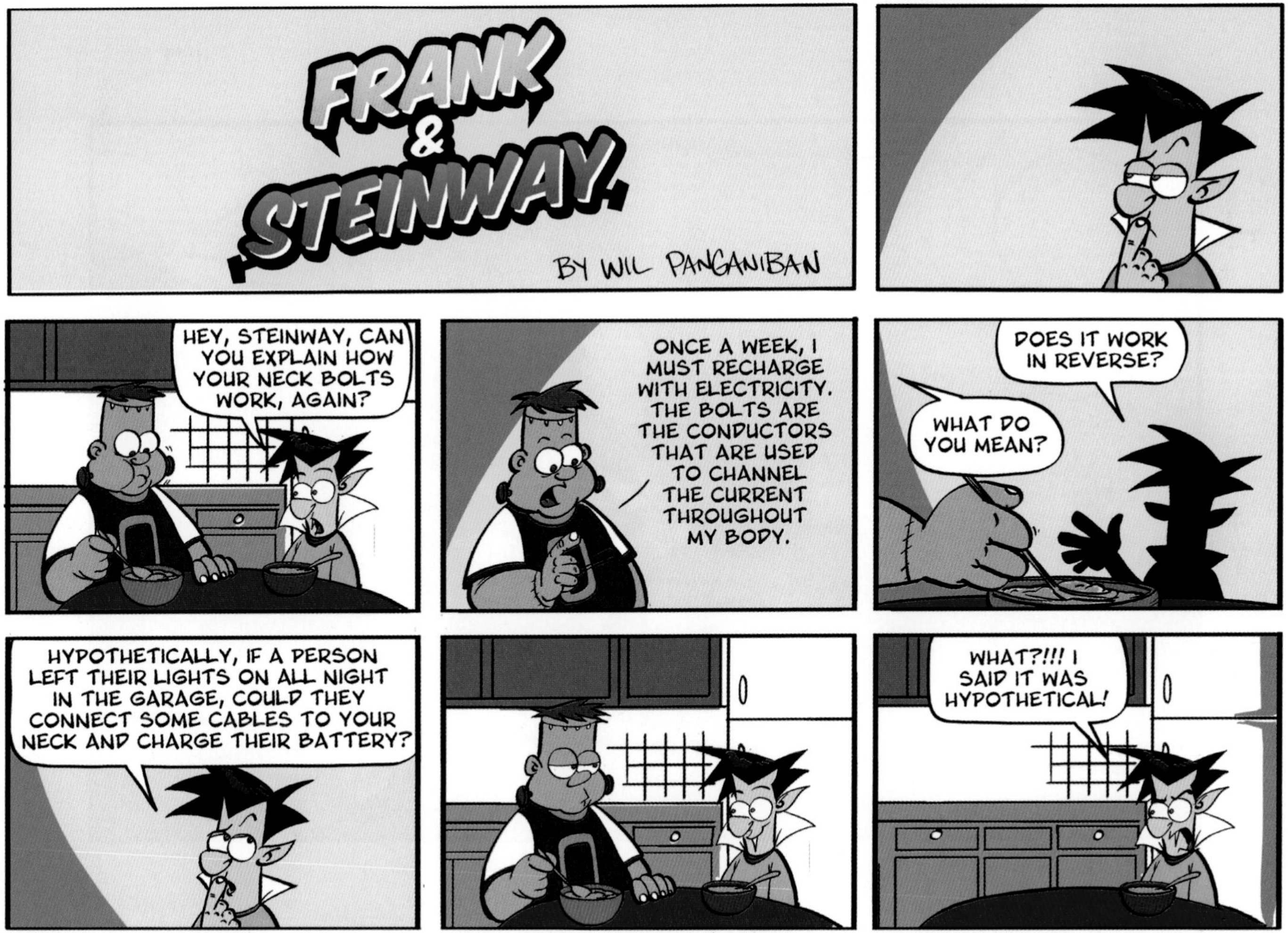
FRANK & STEINWAY
BY WIL PANGANIBAN
HEY, STEINWAY, CAN YOU EXPLAIN HOW YOUR NECK BOLTS WORK, AGAIN?
ONCE A WEEK, I MUST RECHARGE WITH ELECTRICITY. THE BOLTS ARE THE CONDUCTORS THAT ARE USED TO CHANNEL THE CURRENT THROUGHOUT MY BODY.
DOES IT WORK IN REVERSE?
WHAT DO YOU MEAN?
HYPOTHETICALLY, IF A PERSON LEFT THEIR LIGHTS ON ALL NIGHT IN THE GARAGE, COULD THEY CONNECT SOME CABLES TO YOUR NECK AND CHARGE THEIR BATTERY?
WHAT?!!! I SAID IT WAS HYPOTHETICAL!

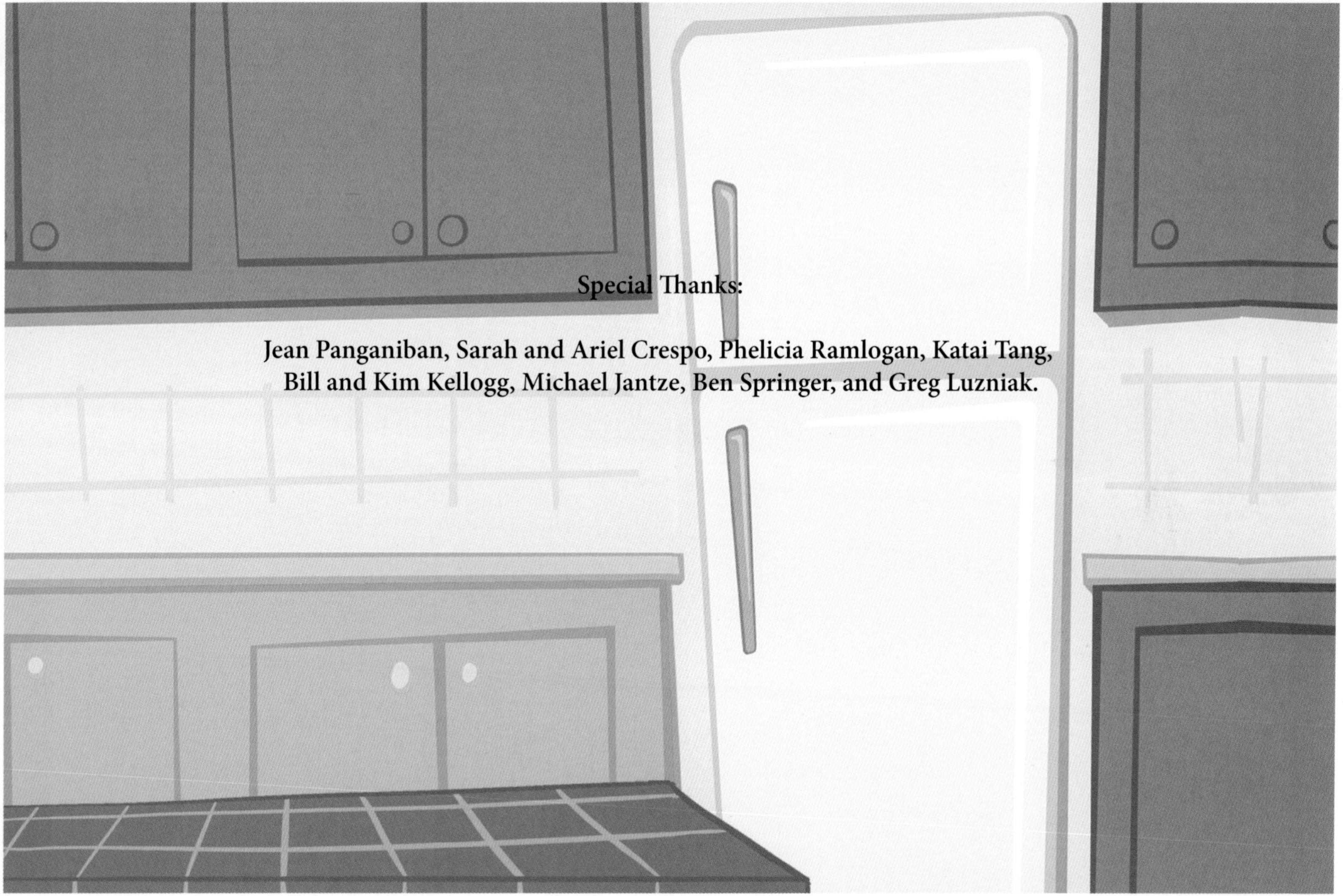

Special Thanks:

Jean Panganiban, Sarah and Ariel Crespo, Phelicia Ramlogan, Katai Tang, Bill and Kim Kellogg, Michael Jantze, Ben Springer, and Greg Luzniak.